# The Power and the Brewery
## *The Story of a House and its People*

*They say the prayers differently there ... They say,*
*"For thine is the kingdom, the power and the brewery."*

A friend of the Rev. John Light on hearing that
Light was to become vicar of Marlow.

*A view of Marlow bridge and All Saints' church, from a watercolour by Sophia Fenwick (née Wethered), 1882*

# The Power and the Brewery
## *The Story of a House and its People*

Anthony Wethered

Phillimore

2004

Published by
PHILLIMORE & CO. LTD,
Shopwyke Manor Barn, Chichester, West Sussex, England

ISBN 1 86077 319 2

Printed and bound in Great Britain by
CAMBRIDGE PRINTING

# *Contents*

*Dedication*

To Diana

# List of Illustrations

# *Acknowledgements*

The making of this book has been largely a family affair, with as many as ten cousins of varying degrees of separation contributing to it in various ways. For the use of family letters and papers I am grateful to Robert and William Fearnley-Whittingstall, to Tom Godfrey-Faussett, to Jean May-Golding, and to the late Robin Copeland, Ursula Wethered, Bridget Power and and Jack Trefusis. John Power provided me with useful information about the brewery; and Jo Macdonald, who owns the drawings and watercolours of our late (great x 2) Aunt Sophie, has kindly allowed me to reproduce some of them here.

Thanks are due to Professor Ian Beckett for advice on military matters, to Mrs M.I.L. de Lee for access to the Sandhurst Collection, and to Barrie Lea for his skilful adaptation of the William Francis map. Mark Paterson, former headmaster of Woodcote House, was my source of information on James Pears, an instructor at the Royal Military College. Valuable insights into the architecture of Remnantz were given me by architectural historian Richard Garnier. Nicholas Redman, former archivist for Whitbread, allowed me unlimited access to the Wethered brewery archive and even fed me on many occasions.

My consultant on local history has been, and continues to be, Miss S.M. 'Bill' Purser, who has given freely of her time and expertise over many years to the great benefit of the book. I am grateful to my brother Julian for information on Tenerife, and to my daughter-in-law Colleen Wethered, who read the book both in draft and in proof with an English teacher's eye and made many useful suggestions.

I must also acknowledge two unexpected windfalls. A letter written in a moment of anxiety to Thomas Wethered by his intended bride in 1788 had come into the hands of Mrs Eileen Younghusband of South Glamorgan, who was kind enough to pass it on to me. And I have enjoyed an e-mail correspondence with Mr Keith Sherwood, of Cambridge, whose historical researches tangentially touched mine, to the benefit of both parties.

Dr Kate Tiller, a leading authority on local history, kindly agreed to contribute a foreword. I am grateful for her generous words about the book.

My wife Diana has brought her love of history to bear on every phase of the book's development, accompanying me to libraries, record offices and wherever else our researches have taken us, from Ince in Cheshire to Woolwich in Kent. Without her help and encouragement the book might still be at the planning stage. Early in our marriage Diana was instructed by my formidable great-aunt Esbell to acquaint herself with the Wethered annals because, she was told, it was the wives who had to do that. Wherever you are now, Aunt Esbell, you can be proud of her.

# The Author

Anthony Wethered has spent most of his working life appraising or editing other people's books. A degree in English from Oxford led to jobs in two London publishing houses before he joined the London office of *The Reader's Digest* in 1955. Six years later he moved to the company's headquarters in Chappaqua, New York, taking with him his wife Diana and their two sons and a daughter. He retired in 1983 as managing editor of *The Reader's Digest* book club. Returning to England, he continued to work for the *Digest* as a freelance while taking an interest in environmental causes. As chairman of the Marlow Society he led a hard-fought and ultimately successful campaign to prevent the Wethered brewery site being developed as a shopping mall – today it is an attractive housing development in keeping with the original buildings. He and his wife live at Remnantz, the family home for 180 years.

# Foreword

*by Dr Kate Tiller*

Reader Emeritus in Local History, University of Oxford

*The Power and the Brewery* is a skilful and affectionate, fluent and astute piece of story telling, which I have read with great pleasure and profit. It is rooted in the history of a family, the Wethereds, and a house, Remnantz, whilst at the same time illuminating a striking range of wider historical themes through both public and private perspectives.

The Wethered fortunes stemmed from their malting and then brewing business (closed only in 1987), which for a long time made them the largest employers in the riverside market town of Marlow. Their influence on the town, and its on them, obviously made for a dynamic interaction, sometimes benign and sometimes contentious, but always powerful as the local version of the Lord's Prayer adopted for the book's title suggests. Researching and writing their story has made a significant contribution to the history of Marlow and added to the studies of 'company towns'. Equally, this is a rich picture of business and industry – malting, brewing, iron founding – and of the commercial and personal preoccupations with property, inheritance, and social status experienced by a prosperous middle-class family in the heyday of 19th-century self-confidence.

Other Wethered involvements were politics, county and Westminster, and religion, with fiercely held Evangelicalism alert for perceived 'ritualist' threats. The central importance of personal faith is vividly clear from the life stories and diaries of members of the family who, in the 18th and 19th centuries, were very often faced with early death, through accident, childbirth, and illnesses including TB. Military history also figures large, for Remnantz was the first, pre-Sandhurst home of Britain's army college. Its sometimes uncertain development and staffing during this key period (1802-12) of the Napoleonic Wars are revealing indeed. Later Wethered military connections include Owen Peel Wethered, founding influence and subsequent stalwart of the Bucks Volunteers, whilst many members of the extended family served, and wrote letters from, imperial outposts and wartime fronts.

As the author rightly states, this is not 'a family tree with bits of information dangling from it like a Christmas tree'. True, there are intriguing connections, with Jane Austen, Disraeli, or the American president's widow sending a pioneering morse message to her friend, Mrs Wethered, in 1844. There is also a sympathetic, but admirably clear-sighted family study which gives us access to an array of unpublished evidence, at the same time adding valuable understanding on many other fronts. I hope many readers will enjoy and appreciate it as much as I have.

# *Introduction*

Why do people write family histories?

Back in the 1950s the popular writer Eric Linklater published a highly entertaining novel called *Position at Noon*. The book's narrator, owner of a small and rather shady antiques business, sees himself as one of life's losers. After some research he finds that the explanation lies with his male ancestors. One of these, it transpires, was the very 'person from Porlock' whose visit distracted Coleridge from the writing of *Kubla Kahn*; another spent years labouring over a history of the Roman empire, only to find on emerging from his seclusion that Gibbon had beaten him to it. And so on: in one way or another, all turned out to have fallen short.

My reasons for writing are not self-vindicating since I blame no one but myself for my own miscalculations. (Any errors in this book are also mine.) Nor is this a family history in the usual sense. While it attempts to tell the story of the Wethereds of Marlow, it is also about the town itself, about the brewery that made our name here, and about Remnantz, the family home, which for the first decade of the 19th century was home to the cadets of the Royal Military College. What it is not is a family tree with bits of information dangling from it like Christmas tree ornaments that happened to come to hand.

Originally we were from Hertfordshire, and the pedigree that I have used is from the three-volume history of that county by John Edwin Cussans, published 1879-81. It is very complete and has saved me a lot of painstaking work. Cussans traces us back to the 15th century, although there is a question mark in the seventeenth where there is only 'strong probability' of linkage between two generations. My story really begins in the 18th century, with the arrival of the family in Marlow. That is when people cease to be just names and dates, and take on personalities and motivations – in other words, become interesting. To a large extent it is they and their various pursuits that have shaped the book, moving the story forward from one episode to the next rather than by strict chronology.

One thing that Linklater's book points up is a tendency of men – and Wethered men in particular, I suspect – to take cognisance only of the male line, forgetting that an equal proportion of our genes are introduced via our mothers and grandmothers. In truth it appears to be the Wethered women, rather than the men, who have the more enduring and traceable characteristics: broadly speaking, they are deeply caring, rise magnificently to any occasion, and manage their husbands for their husbands' own good. Examples can be shown right down to the present day. I myself plead guilty to this masculine bias, although it is difficult to see how the book could have been written another way. At least I believe I have given the Wethered ladies their due.

Obviously, any undertaking of this sort must depend on the information available, and in this I have been lucky in several ways. We are a family of pack rats; we hate to throw anything away (My father collected those tiny gold safety pins once used by the laundry, and was found, after his death, to have made a chain of them twenty feet long.) Thus letters and other papers going back many years have somehow survived and have yielded a rich harvest.

Then, the early days of my research happened to coincide with a decision of the local solicitors, Messrs Cripps & Shone, to clear out their cellars. Every few weeks, it seemed, there would be a telephone call: 'We have found another tin box with your family's name on it. Would you like to have it?' Well, of course I would. It helped that we had lived in Marlow for more than two and a half centuries, and at Remnantz for about a hundred and sixty years.

Some Wethered papers were lent by family members, others arrived almost out of the blue. One of the most prized letters of all, written in 1788 to Thomas Wethered by his future bride, came unsolicited through the kindness of a family connection who actually had to seek me out.

Because I do not think of them as history I have not included my parents in this book, although both are now dead and I revere their memories. It was my mother's choice to bring the family to Remnantz; she loved the house and fought off an attempt by the War Department to requisition it for wartime use in 1939.

'Remnantz loves a party', she used to say, and my wife Diana and I have found that to be true.

Coupled with the question of why we write family histories is another: Why do we leave it so late? A distantly related cousin from Nampa, Idaho, recalls getting into his car and driving many miles to interview an aunt in another state, only to be met on arrival by the hearse bringing her body for burial. I missed similar opportunities. The sad fact is that family histories are seen as retirement projects. It's not just that we pensioners have more time on our hands, but as the future grows shorter we tend to dwell more in the past. And even if we no longer believe, as our ancestors did, that we shall meet our loved ones again in the hereafter, we shall nevertheless be gathered to our forefathers in a figurative sense, and it would be rather nice to know who they are.

Thanks to a well-preserved brewery archive, among other sources, Thomas Wethered, whom we think of as the founder of the family fortunes, can be brought quite sharply into focus. His meticulousness with the brewing process, his care for his family, his interest in education – these, along with a natural generosity of spirit, are plain from the evidence and contribute to our understanding of the man. His granddaughter Sophia speaks clearly to us through her letters to her mother from India, and her brothers Tom and Owen (OPW, as we know him, to distinguish him from his father Owen) – big men in Marlow in their day – are similarly well documented in different ways. It is this Victorian generation, born about the time of the queen's accession, that comes through most visibly as members of a close-knit family, and I find them thoroughly endearing.

A history of any sort is bound to have missing pieces. Letters are destroyed, records go astray. People whose place is in the front row fade into the background, and inevitably distortions occur. One can well understand the urge of historical novelists to fill in the gaps. But in our case, I believe, the material exists to form a coherent and interesting story that can be told against the background of its times. I hope I have done it justice.

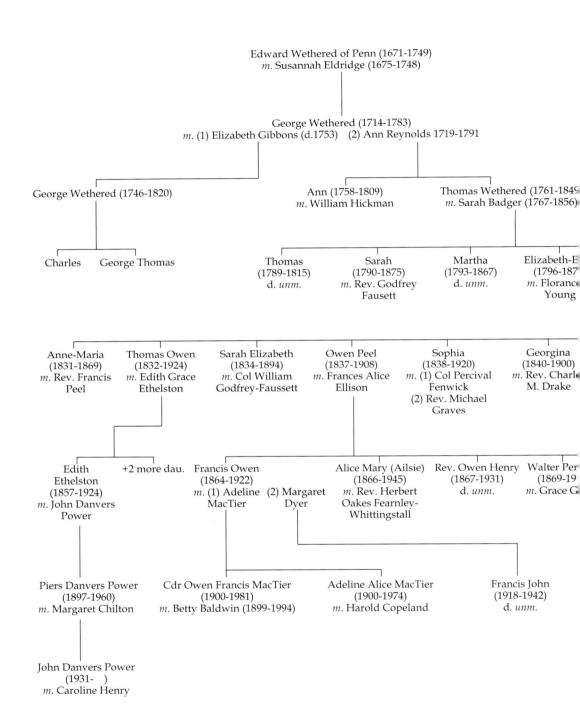

Edward Wethered of Penn (1671-1749)
*m.* Susannah Eldridge (1675-1748)

George Wethered (1714-1783)
*m.* (1) Elizabeth Gibbons (d.1753)   (2) Ann Reynolds 1719-1791

George Wethered (1746-1820)

Ann (1758-1809)
*m.* William Hickman

Thomas Wethered (1761-1849)
*m.* Sarah Badger (1767-1856)

Charles   George Thomas

Thomas
(1789-1815)
*d. unm.*

Sarah
(1790-1875)
*m.* Rev. Godfrey
Fausett

Martha
(1793-1867)
*d. unm.*

Elizabeth-E
(1796-187
*m.* Florance
Young

Anne-Maria
(1831-1869)
*m.* Rev. Francis
Peel

Thomas Owen
(1832-1924)
*m.* Edith Grace
Ethelston

Sarah Elizabeth
(1834-1894)
*m.* Col William
Godfrey-Faussett

Owen Peel
(1837-1908)
*m.* Frances Alice
Ellison

Sophia
(1838-1920)
*m.* (1) Col Percival
Fenwick
(2) Rev. Michael
Graves

Georgina
(1840-1900)
*m.* Rev. Charl
M. Drake

Edith
Ethelston
(1857-1924)
*m.* John Danvers
Power

+2 more dau.

Francis Owen
(1864-1922)
*m.* (1) Adeline
MacTier

(2) Margaret
Dyer

Alice Mary (Ailsie)
(1866-1945)
*m.* Rev. Herbert
Oakes Fearnley-
Whittingstall

Rev. Owen Henry
(1867-1931)
*d. unm.*

Walter Per
(1869-19
*m.* Grace G

Piers Danvers Power
(1897-1960)
*m.* Margaret Chilton

Cdr Owen Francis MacTier
(1900-1981)
*m.* Betty Baldwin (1899-1994)

Adeline Alice MacTier
(1900-1974)
*m.* Harold Copeland

Francis John
(1918-1942)
*d. unm.*

John Danvers Power
(1931-   )
*m.* Caroline Henry

# Selective Pedigree
## of the Wethereds of Marlow

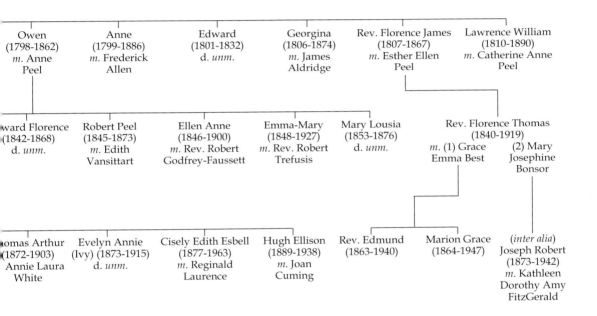

Owen
(1798-1862)
*m.* Anne
Peel

Anne
(1799-1886)
*m.* Frederick
Allen

Edward
(1801-1832)
d. *unm.*

Georgina
(1806-1874)
*m.* James
Aldridge

Rev. Florence James
(1807-1867)
*m.* Esther Ellen
Peel

Lawrence William
(1810-1890)
*m.* Catherine Anne
Peel

...ward Florence
(1842-1868)
d. *unm.*

Robert Peel
(1845-1873)
*m.* Edith
Vansittart

Ellen Anne
(1846-1900)
*m.* Rev. Robert
Godfrey-Faussett

Emma-Mary
(1848-1927)
*m.* Rev. Robert
Trefusis

Mary Lousia
(1853-1876)
d. *unm.*

Rev. Florence Thomas
(1840-1919)
*m.* (1) Grace
Emma Best

(2) Mary
Josephine
Bonsor

...omas Arthur
(1872-1903)
Annie Laura
White

Evelyn Annie
(Ivy) (1873-1915)
d. *unm.*

Cisely Edith Esbell
(1877-1963)
*m.* Reginald
Laurence

Hugh Ellison
(1889-1938)
*m.* Joan
Cuming

Rev. Edmund
(1863-1940)

Marion Grace
(1864-1947)

(*inter alia*)
Joseph Robert
(1873-1942)
*m.* Kathleen
Dorothy Amy
FitzGerald

# 1

# *The Golden Wedding*

Old Moore in his *Almanack* had predicted wind and rain, but as is wont to happen in the forecasting business, he got it wrong. The wet weather held off and the celebrations – the Family Jubilee they called it – went ahead under clear skies. In the meadow behind Remnantz a tent had been set up, where the brewery workers were given a festive lunch and no doubt drank the health of the founder and his wife of fifty years. Thomas and Sarah had wanted their household staff to enjoy a similar meal in the tent next day, but by then the threatened rain had arrived. So, as their daughter-in-law Anne noted in her diary, 'the different servants and attendants had tea and supper given them in the room over the Coach House & Stables'.

The summer of 1838 had been a time of celebration up and down the land. On 28 June the new young queen had been crowned at Westminster. In the towns and villages of Buckinghamshire, church bells rang out, cannons fired royal salutes, houses were festooned with flags, bands led parades through the streets, and there was much feasting of the poor. Certainly Marlow would have risen to the occasion, with the brewery distributing free beer as was its custom at times of public rejoicing. But a month had passed since then, and now it was the turn of the brewer himself to celebrate fifty years of marriage to his Sally.

At one point in the couple's courtship all those years ago it had looked as if the romance might founder. By some wonderful chance a letter has survived in which Sarah – Sarah Badger she was before her marriage – questioned whether Thomas's declared love for her was real.[1] It is dated 18 Feburary 1788, and postmarked Bicester, near the village of Fritwell in Oxfordshire where she was living with her widowed father. It is addressed to Mr Wethered, Brewer, Great Marlow, Bucks. There is no salutation; Sarah goes straight to the point:

> Chagrin'd at your long silence I had for this fortnight past determin'd not to answer your letter when I did receive one – but before I had half read it thro' *'Won by the pow'r of goodness irresistable'* my grateful heart quite forgave the disappointment and wish'd for nothing so much as the ability of thanking you as I ought for kindness unmerited.

The kindness has to do with Thomas's concern over Mr Badger's financial affairs, and it seems that some discussion about a dowry has taken place. Sarah too has been kept in ignorance by her father. She goes on:

> So far from being displeas'd at your solicitude to know my Father's intentions respecting his affairs I find it but natural to commend it, having the same desire to know, myself, but have not heard him say anything since you were here satisfactory enough to communicate by letter. I am afraid you have depended on my speaking decisively on this subject, but 'twill be but a few days … before we shall have the pleasure of seeing you at Fritwell, when I hope something will be determin'd on.

Arrangements had reached a fairly advanced stage, for Thomas had been furnishing their future home at his brewery in the High Street, with the advice of his sister Ann Hickman. Sarah writes that she 'intirely agree[s] with her respecting the sofa, that 'tis an unnecessary piece of furniture'. And she recommends that he 'buy nothing that you can with any convenience do without but what you must buy I think 'twou'd be more advisable to have good and substantial'.

It is noticeable that it is *his* convenience she talks about, avoiding saying *we*, for her doubts have not yet been set at rest. Next she comments on a recently published account of an 'amiable wife' who has been ill-treated by her husband, and asks, 'if such a woman as that has not pow'r to retain her husbands respect and attention, what must we of inferior charms expect? Yet (in this World),' she goes on, 'Rewards are not always measur'd by Deserts – that and a perfect knowledge *in whom I trust*, will be sufficient to justify my depending on more affectionate treatment.'

And there is a poignant final paragraph:

> This day three years – does my friend remember that day – was the first time I had the painful pleasure of hearing from himself he lov'd me. Fortune frown'd upon us – but now she's kind – and tell me Mr Wethered tell me true, have you never once repented of that day? In the hidden recesses of your heart does that reflection give that real and sincere happiness that is now indispensable to the plan of our whole lives? Sure I need not doubt it, sure I may trust to the *newest proofs* you have given me of your esteem – and if I may, none may be more blest, none more happy than
>
> Sarah Badger

So Sarah was a sweet young thing of 18 when this 23-year-old brewer first declared his love for her. Her reminder was written on the third anniversary of that day, which by chance fell in the February of a Leap Year. Five and a half months later they were married, on Thursday 31 July.

The wedding took place, not in Fritwell but in the tiny parish church of Shalden in Hampshire. Shalden was the home of Sarah's sister Martha who had herself been married only that May to a farmer named Thomas Smith. Perhaps it was felt that two daughters' weddings in as many months would be too much to ask of the 60-year-old Samuel Badger. *Jackson's Oxford Journal* carried an announcement of the marriage in its August issue.

A dowry of £200 had been promised, half to be paid that August and the other half by Christmas. But Samuel Badger, although a man of some standing (his daughters were listed as co-heirs and were entitled to their own coats of arms), could no longer be called a man of substance. It seems that his financial troubles were of quite recent occurrence, for he was still occupying, even if he did not own, the imposing Tudor manor house at Fritwell. After paying Thomas the first £100, some of it in goods such as linen and plate, he had difficulty in finding the rest. It came in dribs and drabs over the next two years and was still some £30 short when Samuel died in February 1791.

Sarah must soon have discovered that her earlier misgivings were no more than pre-wedding nerves, for Thomas appears to have been an excellent husband, just as she was a loving and most 'amiable' wife. On that July day in 1838, they could look back on a marriage as happy as it was long, though it had not been without its sorrows. Chief among these had been the sudden death of their eldest son Thomas at the age of only twenty-six.

The elder Thomas believed in trusting his children with responsibility as soon as he considered them ready for it, and this was certainly the case with young Tom. Some of the few letters of his that survive show him calmly taking charge of the household while his parents are away on a visit to London. In May 1812, when he was just 23, we find him writing to his mother that there has been a case of scarlet fever at his sister Anne's boarding school: 'I have written in answer [to a letter from the principal] to say that you are all in Town, & that in the present circumstances I do not think it necessary to remove Anne from her; but should she judge it *in the least* dangerous for her to remain at school, I will immediately send for her.' The same letter contains a message for his father about barrel hoops, showing that he had already been inducted into the family business.

That he was popular with his contemporaries in Marlow is obvious from references to musical evenings and other social events that he shared with them. 'Sarah & I went yesterday evening to Mr Pears,' he writes, again to his mother. 'We had a great deal of Music, as you may suppose, & did not get home (fie! for shame!) 'till two o'clock.'

The Rev. James Pears was a professor of history at the Royal Military College, then in its temporary quarters at Remnantz; his wife Mary had been much admired as a singer in her day. They lived at the lower end of the High Street, having at one time occupied the White House next to the brewery. Already by 1807 a close friendship had been formed between them and the Wethereds: Charles Wethered Pears was the name given to a son born to them that year, and they asked Tom's sister Sarah to be his godmother. Another son, born two years later, was named Thomas after young Tom.

Recalling those days many years later, the Pears' daughter Mary Ann remembered Tom as 'a fine talented, high-principled young man, a very dear friend of Papa's, whose death was widely felt and lamented a few years after'. The date was 9 July 1815, three weeks after Waterloo.

That spring, his 15-year-old sister Anne had been given a donkey by a family friend. On 2 July, a Sunday, Tom was riding the animal, showing off for the amusement of his younger sisters – Anne and little Georgina, aged nine. Somehow, in the course of these games, one of his thumbs was pierced by a thorn, badly enough to have it treated. The doctor was William Hickman,

1    *Thomas Wethered.*

the husband of Thomas's sister Ann; he was readily available since they lived in West Street. According to the younger Anne, 'Uncle Hickman came to see [Tom's thumb] and did something to it – it was very painful – he fainted'.

By the following Thursday he was evidently feeling no ill effects, for 'he played at Trap & Ball in the meadow with the children,' but the next day he was 'not so well, he felt a sore throat and his jaws stiff'. On Saturday, 'Poor dear Tom was very ill … we were very much alarmed in the evening.' Then, on Sunday – just a week after the injury – Tom's sister Sarah noted in her diary,

All the endeavours to restore my beloved brother proved ineffectual, and after a night spent in pious prayer, between 10 and 11 o'clock this morning his pure spirit left a world for which he was too good.

The blow to his parents was severe. Thomas and Sarah had lost two infant children earlier in their married life, and before the Golden Wedding day would lose a second grown son. But Tom had been their special pride and his father's bright hope that he would one day head the family and guide its fortunes. And to die from such a trivial cause[2] … 'Suddenly called in the vigour of youth and health,' as we can read on his memorial tablet in All Saints' church. 'Suddenly called … from the fond bosom of domestic happiness.'

With his gifted elder son taken from him, Thomas had no choice but to make his second son Owen his principal successor in the business. Owen at that time was not yet seventeen and may still have been at his boarding school in Ealing. On at least one occasion he, like Anne, had been dependent on Tom for getting him home. 'Dear Brother', he writes from Ealing when he is a bossy 11-year-old and Tom about twenty,

… I have a design which I hope you will put in execution. I hope you will come in the Gig to see the play & Mrs Standon will give you a bed, next morning you can take me home with you. Give my love to all the family, mind and be here at 5 o'clock on the 12th …

It is tempting, though probably unfair, to play the *What if … ?* game at this point. What if the much credited Tom had lived to fulfil his father's hopes? Would he, for example, have set about expanding the family business into something more ambitious than a relatively small country brewery? Or would he have been content to let it grow, more or less at its own pace, as Owen and his successors were to do? Of course there is no way of knowing. Only the scraps of contemporary writings offer anything in the way of clues, and what follows is no more than an impression of the brothers formed over the years.

Where Tom made friends easily and had a wide circle of them, Owen was cautious about where he placed his trust; where Tom found that success came naturally, Owen had to work hard for it; where Tom was outgoing and self-confident, Owen was less sure of himself and self-effacing; where Tom believed in getting fun out of life, Owen took a more sober view of it. It is hard to imagine Owen's saying, 'Fie! For shame!' in that self-mocking way after coming home late from a party. Of course any view of Tom is coloured by the fact of his early death, and if he comes across as the more attractive personality, that in no way detracts from Owen's essential worth. If Owen lacked his father's undoubted business flair, he was by no means incompetent and made a decent job of whatever he set his hand to, even down to the dolls' furniture (still extant) that he carved for his sisters with his penknife. His own family thought the world of him.

Although Owen and his younger brother Lawrence William were now full partners with Thomas in the brewery, it would be another seven years before Thomas retired for good. At almost 77 he was still remarkably active for his years. As he would write proudly to his sister-in-law six months after the Golden Wedding party,

2   *Sarah Wethered.*

> I thank God Sally and I are both pretty well – I am going to dine with Owen Today, and on Saturday he and I are going to attend a meeting in Aylesbury where the Duke of Buckingham intends to take the chair, after which I must return home to a dinner party at ½ past six, so you see there cannot be much the matter with any of us.

All day, visitors had been arriving at Remnantz to offer their congratulations to Thomas and Sarah. More than anything, though, it was a family occasion, a time for intimacy and for watching the grandchildren play on the lawn. The older Faussett boys – Henry, Willy, Robert and Tom, ranging in age from 14 down to eight – sent up a hot-air balloon which, however, 'soon caught fire, much to their dismay. The Childn. then had tea, fruit & cake in front of the drawing room windows, the little Faussetts, Hickmans, Aldridges[3] & our own – with their nurses.'[4]

In years to come, group photographs dating from about the 1860s would show many of those present that day, assembled with their offspring outside those same windows. And while there are no photographs of Thomas and Sarah, they did sit for their portraits and these give us a fair (probably no more than fair) idea of what they looked like in middle age. It is easy to imagine them, grown older, in the centre of such a group or presiding over the dinner to which 31 members of the family sat down that evening.

The seating plan for that dinner has been carefully preserved, as indeed have those for the 55th and 60th anniversaries that followed. The tables were arranged in the form of a T, with the top table as the cross bar. At the foot of the table and off to one side was a smaller table for five of the older children, including the four older Faussett boys. Their little sister and brothers, aged seven, five and three, were allowed to join the party for dessert. In time to come, young Willy Faussett would marry his cousin Sarah Elizabeth, the second daughter of Owen and his wife Anne, then aged four and asleep in her bed in the Brewery House. Willy's brother Robert would marry Sarah's sister Ellen-Anne, the tenth of Anne's 12 children and still eight years away from being born.

Between them, the eight surviving children of Thomas and Sarah had bought a magnificent silver loving cup which they had presented to their parents that morning. It stands 14 inches high and is surrounded with an elaborately chased pattern of flowers and hop leaves, a single hop forming the knob on the lid. On one side is engraved the Wethered coat of arms, granted to Thomas as recently as 1834, and on the other, the words:

Presented to
THEIR BELOVED PARENTS
Thomas & Sarah Wethered
on the fiftieth anniversary of
THEIR WEDDING DAY
by their affectionate & grateful
CHILDREN
31st July 1838

The meal concluded, the cup was passed round, and then the Rev. Professor Godfrey Faussett, the eldest of the couple's sons-in-law, stood to propose a toast. It is a pity that there is no record of what he said as he was well accustomed to public speaking, both as a preacher and as a university lecturer. Nor was this by any means the first time he had addressed an audience at Remnantz, for in younger days he had been an instructor at the college there. In fact the friendship between the two men – one a self-made brewer, the other an eminent scholar and divine – went back many years before Godfrey had married Thomas's daughter Sarah.

There was common ground between them on two of the great issues of the day: churchmanship and the education of the poor. In December 1811, while curate of the small parish of Holton near Oxford, Godfrey had preached 'before the University' a sermon 'On the Necessity of Educating the Poor in the Principles of the Established Church'. This was the declared purpose of the new National Schools that had been started that year (They did teach other things as well.) He would have warmly endorsed – even if he himself did not prompt – Thomas's gift of land for the National School in Marlow, which opened in April 1813 with Thomas as the first Treasurer.

By the time of the Golden Wedding, Oxford was embroiled in the controversy surrounding Dr E.B. Pusey and the Catholic-leaning Oxford Movement, which Godfrey, 'an uncompromising champion of the Church of England', was said to have 'attacked with the vehemence of a mediaeval zealot'. Thomas would have been equally uncompromising. For one thing, he was a dedicated Anglican; for another, allegiance to the Church was a cornerstone of Conservative Party doctrine.

A Golden Wedding is a time for thanksgiving, and Godfrey would have found much to be thankful for in the lives of Thomas and Sarah: their 50 years of happy marriage, their large and devoted family, their many good works (and the means to carry them out), and the affection and respect of the community. If there were blemishes in this rosy picture, and inevitably there were some, they did not appear that evening as the cup went round and the candles glowed on the faces of the several generations: Owen and Anne; Anne's parents, the senior Peels, and Anne's younger sister Ellen, a girl of 20 and very conscious of Owen's younger brother Florence whom she was to marry next spring; Sarah's sister Martha, many years a widow; old Dr William Hickman, 29 years a widower since the death of Thomas's sister Ann, and their son George, a surgeon like his father, who had survived the horrors of Wellington's Peninsular campaign as Assistant Surgeon to the Royal Horse Guards, the Blues; the three married daughters, Sarah Faussett, Elizabeth Ellen Young, and Georgina Aldridge, each with her husband, and the unmarried Martha and Anne; Lawrence William, the youngest of Thomas's children, who would become Owen's partner in the brewery; Thomas's great-nephew, the sad Charles Wethered; and so on down to the Faussett grandchildren, their heads nodding as the hour grew late.

No one who should have been there was missing. As old Thomas rose to reply, it would have been with a heart full of affection and pride.

## 2

# 'Extremely Bright and Remarkably Pleasant'

Thomas Wethered was born on 16 August 1761. His father George was in a small but apparently successful way of business, primarily as a maltster but with a brewing interest as well. Originally from Penn, a few miles up the road, George had made his home in Marlow, marrying a Marlow girl, Elizabeth Gibbons, in 1744. Whether or not drawn there by love, the move may well have saved his life: within five years of the wedding an outbreak of smallpox in Penn had carried off both of his brothers and two of his three sisters. His marriage to Elizabeth brought rewards of its own, for the malting business, if not the brewing, would have come to him through her father, whose plant is believed to have been on the site of the late 18th-century Old Malt House that now stands in St Peter Street.

Elizabeth died in 1754 having borne a son named George after his father. On 22 September 1757 the elder George remarried. We know little of his second wife, Ann, except that she was the daughter of 'Thomas Reynolds of Co. Oxon, Esq.'[1] which suggests that she was from a family of some standing. The couple were married at All Saints' church in the village of Bisham, George signing his name in the register but Ann managing only a rather wobbly cross.[2] She was some five years older than her husband and nearing forty when her first child, a daughter Ann, was born. Three years later, Thomas Wethered came into the world.

The earliest Wethereds of whom we have any record were living in Berkhamsted, Hertfordshire, in the late 15th century. The best researched family pedigree appears in John Edwin Cussans' three-volume history of that county published in 1879-81. Early references are inevitably sketchy, but the evidence suggests that two distinct branches of the family stem from a William Wethered who, in 1487, was living in the parish of Berkhamsted St Peter. If that is so, then he was the great-grandfather of a Francis Wethered who began the short southward migration via the Missendens and Penn which, four generations later, would bring them to Marlow.

When a man achieves a position of prominence his descendants are likely to be named after him. So it was with Thomas Wethered, and so too with another Francis[3] who in 1628 was Chief Burgess of Berkhamsted St Peter and the owner of Ashlyns,[4] a fine hilltop mansion with sweeping views over the valley below.

He died during the rule of Cromwell. The appointment of his son Francis as Comptroller of Works to Charles 11 shows that he and his family were for King rather than Parliament. The font in All Saints' church, Berkhamsted, was presented by the son in 1662.

A painting by Jan Wyck (1645-1700), possibly commissioned by the Comptroller, shows the view from a neighbouring hill with Ashlyns in the distance and the town with St Peter's church in the valley between.[5] In the foreground stands an elegantly attired huntsman, an eviscerated hare dangling from one hand, while his hounds, according to a writer in *Country Life*, 'look on silently as if awaiting his blessing after a sermon'.

On the Comptroller's death in 1668 Ashlyns descended to the next Francis who, however, did not live long to enjoy it, dying in 1673 at the age of twenty-three. His youngest sister, Elizabeth Craddock, was the last member of the family to own the property; by her will dated 10 July 1703 she directed that Ashlyns be sold. The Wethereds were remembered in Berkhamsted as 'an Ancient and Worthy Family, of good report for Hospitality, Probity & Piety [and] for unshaken Fidelity to the Crown'. So says the memorial tablet to Elizabeth erected in St Peter's church. She herself is described rather condescendingly as, 'not unworthy of the Stock from which she sprung, by the Liberal & Pious Provision she made to the Poor of this Place, to whom she bequeathed Four Hundred Pounds'.

Touched by the thought of her goodness, the late L. Wethered Barroll, of Baltimore, wrote of her, 'the light of her life is not in her tomb but in the hearts of her children'.[6] It is a lovely sentiment, if a metaphorical one, for it seems that the Craddocks had no children of their own. The only issue from Elizabeth's generation were the two daughters of her elder sister Judith. As far as the Hertfordshire Wethereds were concerned it was the end of the line.

A short distance away in Buckinghamshire the descendants of a humbler Francis were supporting themselves on the land. In January 1703 – the year in which Ashlyns was ordered to be sold – his great-grandson Edward, described as a husbandman, or tenant farmer, married a Susannah Eldridge in Little Missenden. Not long afterwards they moved to Penn where all their six children, including Thomas's father George, were born. Both of them lived to a fine age for the time, Susannah dying at 73 in 1748, Edward a year later at seventy-seven.

Even at this distance one can grieve for Edward during his last year of life. To his will, dated six months or so before Susannah's death, he now had to add a codicil leaving her portion to a married daughter, another daughter having already succumbed to the ravages of smallpox. By the end of November a second codicil was needed to take account of the death of his eldest son, Edward, from the same cause. By now he was, as he says, 'sick and weak', unable even to form the E that had served as his mark until then. No third codicil was possible although another son, William, had been felled by the disease before Edward himself died in December.

George Wethered had passed his 30th birthday when he married Elizabeth Gibbons in 1744 and came to live in Marlow. Small market towns like Penn and Marlow were wholly dependent on the agricultural economy, of which farming and malting and brewing were all a part. If George had farmed the raw materials with his father, he now joined his father-in-law in manufacturing the finished product, continuing on his own account after Mr Gibbons' death. By the time of his own death in 1783 he was able to leave his children well provided for.

His elder son, George, now 37, had already taken over the running of one of his father's malthouses. It was on the east side of the High Street and there was a dwelling house that went with it. The lease on this property, along with 'the Stock, Utensils and Implements' of the trade was George junior's principal inheritance from his father.

On the west side of the High Street stood a second malthouse and kiln, land and buildings leased from William Clayton, lord of the nearby manor of Harleyford. These and their accoutrements were bequeathed to 22-year-old Thomas, together with 'all my stock and Utensils in the Brewing Business …' No brewhouse as such, then, but, like his father, Thomas was equipped for both trades. Where the latter business was carried on, whether on the same site as the maltings or elsewhere, is not known. But by 1788, the year of his marriage to Sarah, Thomas had leased another Clayton property on the west side of the High Street for £18 a year and had started building his own brewery.

Before the rise of the commercial or 'common' breweries in the 18th century, brewing was more or less a cottage industry, carried on by the better-off households and by the beer houses and taverns that sold it. These small-scale brewers were not necessarily maltsters or vice versa. Malting required space, a wooden floor to spread the grains; these were seeped in water to start the germination process before being roasted in a kiln – the process that turned them into malt. So the home brewers would buy their malt from the maltsters and the two industries existed side by side.

By the 1750s, however, the increasing size of vats and utensils was giving the common brewer the advantage of economy of scale, enabling him to squeeze out the smaller man. The larger vats began appearing in the 1720s with the production in London of the dark, strong beer known as porter, allegedly drunk by the London porters. At the end of the century there appeared a temperature-controlling device called an attemperator, which allowed brewing to continue through the summer, thus reducing the need for storage capacity. In the meantime the size of the vats had in some cases been carried to extremes. In 1790, it was claimed, in a vat designed for 10,000 barrels[7] at Richard Meux's Griffin Brewery, two hundred guests sat down to dinner, and a further two hundred dropped in and drank to its success. But in 1814, at the Horse Shoe Brewery off Tottenham Court Road, tragedy struck when another of the huge vessels burst under pressure:

The flood swept away walls in the brewery, inundated the crowded basements in the vicinity and caused several tenements to collapse, with the death of eight people by 'drowning, injury, poisoning by the porter fumes or drunkenness'.[8]

The enthusiasm for super-vats waned after this calamity, and porter itself lost favour as the 19th century progressed. It had only ever been a product of the big London breweries, small country brewers staying with the traditional lighter ales.

It is sad that no one – any former partner or director – has provided us with a formal history of the Wethered company. The closest thing to it is a 22-page typescript headed 'Salient Features in the History of the Marlow Brewery, 1758-1929'. It was evidently written by a senior employee of the 1920s who may have signed it on a missing last page but whose name we shall probably never know. He is informative about the development of the brewery (and most respectful towards the family), and if all he gives us are the bare bones we can be grateful to him for those.

The accepted date of 1758 for the founding of Thomas Wethered & Sons – proclaimed on every bottle and beer mat – has puzzled local historians. Thomas, after all, was not born until 1761. The late Piers Danvers Power, a great-great-grandson of Thomas and chairman of the brewery from 1942-9, offers a misprint theory: the actual date was 1788, i.e. the year Thomas started building on the present site, and at some point an '8' got mutated into a '5'. But our anonymous employee states quite plainly that the brewery 'was founded by Mr George Wethered in 1758'. That being so, it seems that Thomas decided to keep the original date while changing the name to his own.

**3**  *A large brew house in 1764. Note, top right, the sack of malt being carried to the top of the building while workers stir a vat on the lower floor.*

**4** *High Street frontage of Thomas's brewery.*

There is also a case for believing that Ann Reynolds brought money into the family when she married George in 1757, and that he used it to diversify his business the following year. For it was Thomas, not the older, more experienced George, who inherited the brewing side of the business. And it was Thomas, not George, who was their father's residuary legatee, receiving 'the Remainder of my Goods, Chattels, Drays, Cattle, ready Money, Book and other Debts, Rights, Credits and personal Estate and Effects'. And finally it was Thomas, not George, who was named as George Senior's sole executor. All of which suggests, either that Thomas – young as he was – was thought to be the one with the business acumen (which indeed he was) and more likely than George to improve the family fortunes; or that a large portion of their father's estate had come to him through his marriage to Thomas's mother; or, very possibly, both.

Two commemorative stones inscribed 'TW 1788' and 'TW 1791' show that Thomas wasted no time in erecting his 'new brewhouse, stable, storehouses and premises'. The 1788 building, known as the Old House, fronts on to the High Street to the left of the gates. The 1791 brewhouse with its 'fine, restrained Neoclassical' architecture (English Heritage) faces you as you look in from the street. The title deeds describe the property with unconscious humour as, 'Formerly Miss Freeman's boarding school and the Three Tuns Tavern'. Thomas had taken a 99-year lease on it from William Clayton for a monthly rent of £18. In 1795 Clayton sold it to Thomas Williams, 'the Copper King',[9] and it was from Williams that Thomas bought the freehold for £400 in 1796. His distribution at this time was done by means of five draught horses, two wagons and a cart.[10]

The early 18th-century White House to the right of the gates was leased by Thomas from one Anne Trash, or her successors, in 1791. He is the most likely person to have installed the pretty bow-fronted fascia – an early 19th-century addition – since he went on to buy the freehold in 1820.

The 18th century had seen a rapid rise in the number of breweries, large and small. According to one authority,[11] if the premises were rented the outlay needed to start a business was modest enough. The expense 'lay in the circulating capital – the stocks of malt, hops and beer on hand – and here the small brewer was fortunate in that he might buy malt and hops on credit, but sold in the main for cash.' In the brewing process the milled grain is mixed with water, converting the starch to sugar (maltose) and producing an extract known as 'wort'. This is boiled up with hops, both to give flavour and to act as a preservative. The addition of yeast causes the maltose to ferment, giving the beer its alcoholic content. The process is gravitational, with the raw materials going in at the top and the finished product emerging at the bottom. Hence the height of the traditional English brewhouse.

In the early days of his brewery Thomas was his own head brewer and as meticulous with his quality control as he was with his bookkeeping. 'Too bitter,' he says of his mild ale on 13 January 1799, 'and not quite bright or pleasant.' On 25 February, 'it now drinks very worty and is not quite fine – think this is not so good as any mild ale that has been brewed this season altho' it is very full and strong ...' But on 5 March the ale 'is now extremely bright and remarkably pleasant – it is now clear to me that the fermentation was not carried far enough to drink at a month but just right for 6 or 8 weeks.' What these entries also show, of course, is how hit-or-miss brewing was at the time. In years to come, the guesswork would be replaced by more scientific methods.

The time taken for each part of the process is recorded in Thomas's small, neat handwriting. But on 8 August he notes, 'Watch stopp'd whilst the 2 Wort was boiling & the 3rd Mash on the Goods & I am not quite sure as to the time of boiling and Mash laying ...' A case of guesswork being resorted to as a result of mechanical failure. A broken pump rod and a saucharometer (*sic*)[12] that had to be sent to London for repair were among other minor problems that year, but in the bigger picture the brewery was doing well.

It was not unusual in the late 18th century for a brewer to act as banker for his local community. It is a measure of Thomas's financial independence that he was doing this as early as 1788, the year of his 27th birthday, when he was taking on the responsibility of marriage as well as for the building of his brewery. Loans of several hundred pounds over terms of five or seven years are recorded in his private ledger. The usual rate was 5 per cent per annum, but small loans, especially to relatives, sometimes turned out to be interest-free.

One of Thomas's debtors was a blacksmith named Charles Clark. Mr Clark had fallen on hard times. He had mortgaged his house to Thomas for £200 and had given his bond for a further hundred. Beneath these entries in the ledger appear the following notes:

> I have given Chas Clark a verbal promise that the Interest of the Bond given me for £100 shall cease 'till July 30th 1790, and after my departure [i.e. his death] the Principal.
>
> Memdm. Feb 23, 1791. I have not taken any Interest since July 30th 1790, as above. Neither must my executors from that time as it would greatly distress the family unless any great and unexpected success should happen to him, the whole from the above date shall be given to him.

Even as a banker, Thomas was not without a heart, and of course there was no head office looking over his shoulder. Mindful of how suddenly death could strike, he even anticipates his own demise. He was 29 at the time; he lived to be eighty-eight.

Increasingly towards the end of the century brewers were buying up public houses, thus gaining control of the retail end of the chain. Often this happened when the publican was in arrears with his payments to the brewery and selling the lease or the freehold was the only way to settle the debt (Thomas's ledgers contain pages of bad debts.) Two of Thomas's first pubs, acquired in the 1790s, were the *Swan* in Maidenhead, for which he paid £800 plus the cost of conveyancing and numerous improvements, and the *Black Lion* at Little Marlow. The latter was cheap by comparison, costing only £240, but, as Thomas notes somewhat ruefully, 'I have also to pay [the publican's] Mother an annuity of 4/- a Week during her life'. How long the old lady survived is not known.

An attempt to buy the *Green Man* at Flackwell Heath in 1793 failed because the title was flawed or, as Thomas put it, 'too doubtful to risque a trial'. The disappointment was the greater because he had travelled, by the mail presumably, all the way 'to Shoreham in Kent' to find the owner, a Mr Blackwell or Blackall. Thomas's expenses, including the cost of the journey (£2 2s. od.) attorney's fees (£29 5s. od.) and even a present of two guineas to Mr Blackwell, were considerable. Only much later was he rewarded for his pains. A note dated 22 June 1821 shows that he had successfully completed the purchase of the pub.

A man whose business interests spanned two or more trades could be expected to divide them between his sons at his death, especially when the products were interrelated as with malting and brewing. In his will George senior had stated his 'earnest desire and request that my said Sons do deal with each other in their several Businesses as I am fully persuaded it will be to their mutual benefit and advantage'. And they may well have done so. That George junior should name his younger son George Thomas after his half-brother, and also make Thomas an executor of his will, shows that their relationship was cordial at least. The trouble was to come in the next generation.

As George junior approached his 60th birthday he declared his intention to hand over the malting business he had inherited to his elder son Charles. This set George Thomas to wondering how much the rest of their father's estate would be worth when he died, and how much he could expect to get out of it. The fairest thing, he decided, would be a pooling arrangement: whatever the two of them received from their father, whether during his lifetime or by his will, must be divided equally between them. He managed to persuade his unworldly brother, and on 25 October 1805, while the news of Nelson's victory at Trafalgar was still on its way to England, George Thomas and Charles entered into an agreement that would cause the downfall of both.

**5**   *Thomas's brewing notes.*

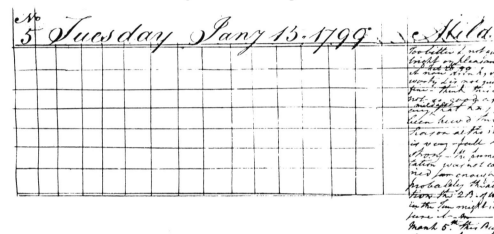

Charles was engaged to be married to a young woman named Mary Ann Bell. In June 1807 George deeded his High Street properties, including the malting business, to Mary Ann's father, William Bell, in trust for himself and the couple until their marriage should take place. They would then take over as George's lessees until his death, when the properties would become theirs. The intention behind the arrangement was to provide George with a continuing income and ensure that the business would not be sold during his lifetime.

It seems clear that Charles was no businessman, but he also had bad luck. With many breweries now producing their own malt, time was against the small independent maltster. By the end of 1809, the marriage having taken place, bad harvests and the swingeing tax on malt had combined to put Charles heavily in debt. To tide himself over he borrowed £800 from a certain John Roads, using as security a property at the north-east end of the High Street which had been jointly acquired at some time by George and Thomas and subsequently deeded by them to Charles.

Four years later Charles was again in trouble. Though he had managed to keep up his interest payments on the mortgage, the principal was overdue for repayment and was being called in. It was a case of pay up or forfeit his interest in the property. However, there were always people in the moneylending business who were happy to take over a debt. Charles turned this time to a man named Richard Reading who advanced him the £800 needed to pay off Roads, against a mortgage on the property as before.

In March 1820 George Wethered died at the age of seventy-four. His portrait, painted a few years earlier, shows a kindly, rather bland face like that of a benign schoolmaster. Altogether lacking is the alert energy one takes from a companion portrait of Thomas. When the contents of George's will became known it was clear to George Thomas that his portion was greatly outweighed by what Charles had already received. Hardly had their father been buried before he invoked the equal-shares agreement of 1805, insisting that Charles make up the difference. Already in debt and with part of his property mortgaged, Charles was in no position to comply. In an act of supreme foolishness George Thomas issued proceedings against him and Mary Ann. The case was to drag on for eight years at a cost one can only guess at, to be heard at last in the High Court of Chancery.

Meanwhile Charles's financial struggles were continuing, made desperate now by his brother's legal action. He was faced with ruin or even imprisonment if the court's decision went against him. But in 1825, with judgment still pending, Charles was offered a partial way out. It would not be easy, for he and Mary Ann would almost certainly be dispossessed of most of their inheritance. On the other hand, Charles would not only be relieved of the worrying debt but, by the terms of the agreement, would be indemnified against 'all Costs Charges Damages Claims and Demands whatsoever' made by his brother George Thomas.

The arrangement was made with a father and son, both named Henry Pigeon, of Southwark. As the elder Pigeon died before negotiations were complete, it fell to the younger one to sign for the Pigeons. Interestingly, the agreement was witnessed by Florance Thomas Young, the husband of Thomas's second surviving daughter Elizabeth-Ellen. Young, like the Pigeons, owned property in Southwark and it is likely that he made the introduction.

Besides taking over the original debt from Richard Reading, Henry Pigeon junior gave a mortgage on Charles's maltings for £2,200, a sum it would never be within Charles's means to pay off. It is worth noting that in his agreement with Pigeon Charles is no longer calling himself a maltster but a liquor merchant.

The arguments in the case were heard on 25 January and 23 February before His Honour the Vice Chancellor, Sir L. Shadwell. As the defence argument ran, the equal-shares agreement was instigated by George Thomas in order to defraud his father 'of his parental control over the Plaintiff and his right to dispose of his property' as he saw fit. Further, the defence claimed, the brothers had concealed the agreement from Mary Ann Bell and her father who were purchasers under the marriage settlement 'for a good and valuable consideration, namely the marriage of the Defendants and the marriage portion of Mary Ann ... which was duly paid by William Bell to the Defendant Charles Wethered.' The agreement, even if otherwise binding, should not be enforced against them.

His Honour was not impressed. It was quite clear, he said, that if Charles's father had meant to restrict his gift to Charles's 'personal enjoyment', he would have so devised. As he had not so devised, he intended that Charles ' should have the full enjoyment of the property, and that it should be liable to all his antecedent debts and all his antecedent contracts'. In other words, Charles might encumber it in any way he wished.

So George Thomas won his case and was no doubt fully indemnified by Henry Pigeon the younger of Southwark. What became of him is not known but we hear no more of him in Marlow. Charles and Mary Ann, their livelihood gone, wound up their affairs in Marlow and moved to Windsor where they resumed trading as wine and spirit merchants in rented premises in Sheet Street.

It was left to Thomas to pick up the pieces. He had been peripherally involved in the case as a former part-owner of Charles's property and was even named by George Thomas as a defendant in the law suit, although in no way was he liable. When the dust had settled he bought up the maltings on the east side of the High Street which had been so disastrously handled by his nephew Charles. An entry on the debit side of his ledger for 4 July 1829 reads, 'Malt house late G. and C. Wethered, £2203.3.0', the amount of the mortgage plus, perhaps, stamp duty. For many years the malthouse and the dwelling that went with it remained in the ownership of Thomas's company. As late as 1862 bills are being paid for 'Repairs to Malt House and Premises late Charles Wethered'.

Thus Thomas ended up with the whole of his father's business interests. But there is a postscript to the story of Charles and Mary Ann. They had a son, Charles Thomas, who became a favourite of Thomas's family and was the only one of George's descendants to attend the Golden Wedding party in 1838. Eschewing the malting trade that had proved so unlucky for his father, he became a schoolmaster[13] and in 1844, probably through Thomas's influence, was appointed headmaster of Sir William Borlase's School across the road from Remnantz at a salary of £30 a year. Six years later he died at the age of 40, the victim of a pulmonary infection. All his possessions, including his watch, he left to 'my dear Mother, Mary Ann Wethered', who was also named as his sole executor. Her address at that time is given as Aylesbury, whereas her husband is listed as Charles Wethered of Slough. It seems that with all the misfortunes suffered by this sad couple, their marriage had finally broken down under the strain.

By 1820, the year of George's death, Thomas's brewery was well established as the town's leading industry and employer of labour, and it was continuing to grow. That year he added more stabling and barrel storage, a confident decision at a time of severe economic depression and deprivation among the poor. Stabling had been claiming more and more space in the brewery yard, for as the number of tied public houses grew so did the number of draught horses needed to service them. There were now nearly forty on the books, each with its own provenance, description and name. Military names such as Colonel, Drummer and Trooper were popular; there was also a sad-sounding mill horse called Blind Captain. It would be 16 years before steam power would replace the horses that drove the brewery's machinery.

Rounds of the Marlow pubs such as the *Hare and Hounds, Red Lion, Two Brewers* and *Complete* (*sic*) *Angler* were made by the town drayman and his mate, those farther afield by the country draymen and their mates. With pubs as far from Marlow as the *Duke's Head* at Farnham, the *Bank of England* at Wendover, and the *Ram Inn* at Uxbridge, Wethered's was extending its reach.

# 3

# *The Gentlemen Cadets*

On 17 May 1802, Remnantz opened its doors to 16 of the British army's new 'gentlemen cadets'. They were aged between thirteen and fifteen and were to be the guinea pigs in a bold scheme to provide officer cadets with a general education and at the same time to prepare them for the military life. Ahead of them lay three years of intensive instruction and (supposedly) rigorous discipline, after which, if they satisfied their examiners, they would be commissioned in the army without purchase.

A watercolour painted that same year shows them in their scarlet tunics and fez-like black caps (later to be replaced by shakos) relaxing in little groups outside the house. Remnantz in those days was still as it had been built *c.*1720: a rather fortress-like three-storey block with two parallel wings jutting out from the south side. The number of boys would eventually rise to four hundred, when other large houses such as Thomas Archer's Marlow Place and Alfred House in the High Street would be needed to accommodate them.

The college was the brainchild of a remarkable officer who, had he lived, would surely have reached the pinnacle of his profession. John Gaspard Le Marchant was a Channel Islander from Guernsey. His early years were marked by lack of promise. So poor were his efforts at school that his father withdrew him and had him educated at home, mostly, it is said, by the family butler, apparently a man of unusual learning.

With a commission bought for him by his father, the young Le Marchant joined the Wiltshire Militia where he quickly quarrelled with his colonel and even challenged him to a duel. Fortunately the colonel had a forgiving nature. But gambling debts followed and only a loan from another officer – after Le Marchant had promised to give up gambling for good – saved him from having to sell his commission. According to one biographer he kept both his promise and his quick temper, though he never again challenged anyone to a duel.[1] His hard-pressed father was prevailed upon to buy him his first promotion (from ensign to cornet) but subsequent advancement was by merit and cost him little.

His ideas for a school for officers came to him during a journey by mail coach in the autumn of 1798. Now 32, a lieutenant-colonel in the 7th Dragoons, Le Marchant had achieved distinction in several fields. He had shown himself to be a fearless commander and a horseman and swordsman of the first rank. His manual of *Rules and Regulations for the Sword Exercises of the Cavalry* had received warm praise from King George III, to whom Le Marchant owed his present rank. The king had also admired some of Le Marchant's paintings for he was a talented draughtsman and watercolourist, important qualifications for a field officer in the days before photography made its appearance.

Military academies were nothing new. Frederick the Great's *Kriegsschule* in Berlin had been founded in 1765, France's *Ecole Militaire* in 1756. The Royal Military Academy, Woolwich, a specialist school for artillery officers, dated from 1741. That Britain was slow to recognise the need for a general programme of training for its officers is said to have been due to a tradition of amateurism, a sort of gentlemanly aversion to professional armies. War, according to one source, was seen as 'fox hunting carried on by other means'.[2]

Le Marchant was fortunate in his patrons. In the Flanders campaign of 1794 he had served with distinction under Frederick Duke of York, the favourite son of George III, who in 1795 had been appointed commander-in-chief of the army. The duke was supportive of Le Marchant's proposals for a military college though doubtful at first that they would succeed. Undeterred, Le Marchant drew up detailed plans which he sent to senior members of the military establishment. One of these was William Huskisson, at that time Under Secretary for War. Huskisson was impressed; he secured an interview for Le Marchant with his chief, Henry Dundas, the Secretary of State. Le Marchant came away from the meeting with a promise from Dundas to recommend the scheme to the Prime Minister. Before long he was writing to his wife Mary: 'I think you may begin to see the sunshine of fortune opening out on my new projects. Mr Pitt has read my book and has promised to support the Plan.'

At Pitt's suggestion a committee chaired by the Duke of York, and with Le Marchant as a member, met to do what we would call a feasibility study. The result was a Royal Warrant issued on 24 June 1801, establishing the principle of a Royal Military College. The committee set a budget of £146,000 for the provision of suitable buildings. Several possible sites were discussed but the choice was surely clear from the start. As A.R Godwin-Austen wryly notes, 'It was proposed that the buildings should be erected on land at Bagshot Heath, the greater part of which, it was found, could conveniently be purchased from Mr Pitt. One passes this coincidence by without comment.'[3] The imposing porticoed building known today as Sandhurst was designed by the noted architect Sir James Wyatt, then Surveyor to the Board of Works. But with the delays and cost overruns not unusual with public works it would be some years before the college was ready for occupation. In the meantime temporary quarters had to be found, and these turned out to be in the Buckinghamshire market towns of High Wycombe and Marlow.

Besides his school for officer cadets, Le Marchant's plans included another 'for the improvement of the Staff', offering advanced courses for young officers. This senior department, which would later evolve into the Staff College at Camberley, already existed in embryo form in High Wycombe. There, at the

**6**  *The Gentlemen Cadets at Leisure. On the left of the picture is Remnantz as originally designed. The two lighter coloured buildings were purpose built for the college.*

*Antelope Inn* in the High Street, a course of lectures was being given by General Francois Jarry, a royalist *émigré* whose c.v. included the governership of the *Kriegsschule* in Berlin. With the issuance of the Royal Warrant this operation was expanded and brought under the aegis of a Supreme Board with the Duke of York at its head.

As governor of the college the Board appointed General Sir William Harcourt, soon to be Lord Harcourt, with Le Marchant as his deputy or lieutenant-governor. At 58 Harcourt was nearing the end of his military career. To him the governorship was a well-earned sinecure, a reward for past services rather than a fresh demand on his energies. This insouciant attitude would contribute to the inevitable difficulties of any new venture.

The day-to-day running of the junior department was to be the responsibility of the commandant, Lieutenant-Colonel James Butler, deprecatingly described by Alan Shepperd as 'an elderly gunner officer with no experience of active service'.[4] A proud, self-important man, Butler resented the authority of the younger lieutenant-governor and would go over his head to Lord Harcourt whenever possible. Shepperd continues: 'Between Butler's obstructive tactics and fierce independence, and Harcourt's studied indifference, Le Marchant found his authority undermined and all his future plans for the college endangered.' Add to this volatile mixture Le Marchant's own proven irascibility and the potential for trouble can well be imagined.

Marlow's chief attraction as a temporary home for the junior department was its proximity to High Wycombe where Jarry's school for staff officers was already established. Of the several large houses that were available Remnantz was a natural first choice. Its six-acre field would make a serviceable exercise and parade ground and there was space for the erection of additional buildings. Its owner, Stephen Remnant, had come into the property through his marriage in 1747, but with an iron foundry to run in Woolwich it is doubtful that he spent much time there. Now almost 80 and in poor health, he was to die at his home on Shooters Hill before the lease with the army was signed.

With the issuance of the Warrant things moved fairly rapidly. On 10 December 1801, the Supreme Board met at Horse Guards with the Duke of York in the Chair. Harcourt and Le Marchant were there, as were the new Secretary for War, Charles Yorke, the Adjutant General, Sir William Fawcett, the Quartermaster General, Sir David Dundas, and Barrackmaster General, Oliver De Lancey. Since the Board's last meeting on 19 November, Harcourt with De Lancey and Le Marchant had been down to Marlow and looked at several properties there. They reported 'that the House belonging to Mr Remnant, if it could be procured, would answer the purpose'.[5] De Lancey had subsequently been to see 'the Person who had the authority to let it', and had 'made an agreement for the same, together with the adjoining Grounds, comprising in the whole about ten acres, for the term of three years ... at the rate of £120 per Annum'.

During a series of lettings the house had been neglected by its absentee landlord, for repairs were needed to every floor of the building as well as to the exterior. Other work included the provision of living quarters in the stables: a dining room at ground level and sleeping quarters in the hayloft overhead. To the rear of the stables was a small lean-to billiard room; this was to be 'fitted up', along with the brew house, wash house and wood house, over which would be space for servants' sleeping rooms and a kitchen. The total cost would be £400 7s. 11d., De Lancey told the meeting. He was authorised to put the work in hand without delay.

Another item on the agenda was the seemingly minor matter of the cadets' beds. This was not delegated to some subcommittee as one might expect, but apparently received the attention of the full Board:

> Lieutenant-Colonel Le Marchant ... presented to the Board a drawing of a Bedstead proposed to be provided for the use of the Students of the Junior Department at Marlow, and some alterations therein being suggested, the same were approved of, and the required number directed to be provided ... together with such bedding as may be approved of by Lieutenant-Colonel Le Marchant.

There, then, was the commander-in-chief of the British army with four of his most senior staff officers plus a Cabinet Minister, studying a drawing of a bedstead with a critical eye, and indeed making alterations to it. It is to be hoped that the beds won the approval of the cadets as they had that of HRH the Duke of York.

And so the cadets came to Marlow. With them came their officers, their professors and instructors, and the college servants including a housekeeper. For the next decade Marlow was a garrison town, its streets brightened by scarlet tunics and fresh-faced youth. And if the cadets' high spirits sometimes got out of hand, this was offset by the greatly enhanced social life of the townspeople – including members of my family, as we shall see – and the lasting friendships formed between them and senior members of the college.

In the early part of 1802 the Supreme Board issued, as part of the Royal Warrant, its *Rules, Orders and Regulations … for the junior department of the college.*[6] Despite its formidable title, this little book runs to only 36 loosely printed pages, yet it contains an excellent distillation of Le Marchant's plans for the department. It was the intention from the beginning to provide not only for 'those, who from early Life are intended for the Military Profession', but also:

> for the Orphan Sons of those Meritorious Officers who have fallen, or been disabled in the Service of their Country, as well as for the Sons of those Officers in our military service, who, from pecuniary difficulties, might not otherwise be able to give them an adequate education.

The 16 first arrivals in that May of 1802 were assigned to the first of four planned companies of 100 cadets each. Each company was to be made up of three 'establishments', varying both in numbers and in fees according to its members' circumstances. The 'sons of noblemen and gentlemen' – 30 in each company – were charged £90 a year, as were the 20 cadets preparing to serve with the East India Company; the sons of serving officers – another 20 – were charged £40 a year, while those whose fathers had been killed in action – 30 – were to 'receive their Education, Board, and Clothing, free from Expence'. For paying students the cost of clothing (as distinct from 'Necessaries' such as shirts and underwear) was included in the fees. Each cadet was provided annually with

> One Scarlet Infantry Jacket, with blue Cuffs and Collar, looped with Silver.
> One Scarlet Waistcoat, without Sleeves.
> Two Pair of Blue Pantaloons.
> One Felt Cap.
> Two Pair of Short black Gaiters.
> Two, or more, Pair of Shoes.

Every three years he would be issued with 'One Blue Greatcoat'.

The boys were given a rigorous daily routine, starting with a parade and inspection at six a.m. At six-thirty there were prayers followed by two hours of study. Not until nine did the cadets get their breakfast, after which they studied again from ten to twelve. Then came 'fencing, riding, swimming[7] and the sabre'. Dinner was at two o'clock, and then it was study until five-thirty when there was an hour of military exercises. At eight-thirty they had supper, followed by prayers and 'the Retreat' at nine.

Military subjects were pre-eminent in the curriculum and included Fortification, Gunnery, Tactics, 'the Drawing of Plans, Military Movements and Perspective [and] Military Geography and History'. But there were also classes in Mathematics, French and German (Oriental Languages for the East India Company cadets), and 'Frequent Lectures … on Natural and Moral Philosophy'. Not listed here, although taught by three masters at least, were the Classics. All in all, it was a well-rounded education.

Little has been written about the teaching staff or the quality of their work. Hugh Thomas comments disparagingly that the latter 'was no worse than at most public schools at the time',[8] but there is reason to believe that it was of a higher order than that.

The most distinguished academic was the then young Rev. Godfrey Faussett, later to become Lady Margaret Professor of Divinity at Oxford and a canon of Christ Church Cathedral. His subjects at the RMC were History, Geography and the Classics. He remained there for just two and a half years, but when he departed in 1807 to take up a curacy at Holton, near Oxford, he left behind in Marlow a young woman who had lost her heart to him. She was Sarah Wethered, eldest daughter of Thomas Wethered the brewer. Sarah eventually found happiness with him, but their story belongs in another chapter.

Isaac Dalby was a Fellow of the Royal Society. A Cornishman of humble origin, he was a mathematician of genius and worked on the first Trigonometrical Survey of England and Wales. Le Marchant had engaged him in 1799 as an assistant to Jarry in High Wycombe, but with the coming of the junior department he began riding over to Marlow twice a week to teach Mathematics to the cadets. They are said to have held him in considerable awe, for he was a demanding teacher, intolerant of careless or unfinished work. However, his exacting standards applied only to his own subject; other subjects did not interest him. R.H. Thoumine[9] tells how one day, to his disgust, Dalby was asked to examine a class in History.

> It was a happy stroke for the candidates, for he brought with him a small book of dates and a quite uncharacteristic mood of careless gaiety. One student who was boggling over the date of the Armada was rallied most cheerily with, 'Come along, never mind a hundred years or so, give me a good round guess!'

For the first half of the Marlow period the chief drawing master was William Alexander, who left to become First Keeper of Prints and Drawings at the British Museum. His salary from the college was £200 a year (about £12,000 in today's money) which, while not princely, did carry some perks: a rental allowance for his house, six bushels of coal a week, candles and writing paper. In 1806, he and his young assistant William Delamotte – a well regarded painter in his day – were joined by William Gilpin, who had just completed a two-year term as president of the Royal Society of Painters in Water Colour. However, an attempt by the Board to recruit John Constable to the drawing department failed, Constable declining on the advice of the president of the Royal Academy, Benjamin West. 'It would have been a death blow to all my prospects of perfection in the art I love,' he told a friend.

The Rev. James Pears was on the staff from 1806 to 1810, with the title Professor of History. He had been educated at Winchester and was admitted to New College, Oxford, at the age of sixteen. A born educator himself, he went on to become headmaster of Bath Grammar School. For a time after leaving Marlow he ran a preparatory school for the college in Maidenhead Thicket; among his pupils were the sons of the Duke of Clarence – the future William IV – whose chaplain he became. His next move was to Windlesham in Surrey where he continued to prepare boys for entrance to the RMC, now at Sandhurst.[10] It was at that house in Windlesham that he coached Thomas Wethered's third son, Florence (a name then given to both boys and girls), who was doing poorly at Eton. As Mr Pears reported to Thomas:

> Florence is well, but I fear he will be sick of this place & heartily glad to get back to Eton, for I find he is not used to much work there. He is on a very bad System, but I will do all that is possible in so short a time with him.

So much for the education at Eton in the early 1820s!

On 25 July 1809, two men, both in their 40s, one a French army officer, the other an English brewer, set out from Marlow and rode through the leafy lanes to Blackwater in Surrey. They wanted to see for themselves how the building work on the new military college was progressing.

The Frenchman was Charles Fontaine de Mervé, formerly a lieutenant in the elite *Garde du Corps du Roi*, King's Bodyguard to Louis XVI, but now a teacher of French to the cadets at Marlow. Mervé's adventures before and since that date would fill a book, but until it is written, brief summaries will have to suffice. With the coming of the Terror and the deposing of Louis XVI, and incidentally of his little son (Louis XVII), Mervé had escaped across the German border, possibly with his new master the Comte de Provence, the future Louis XVIII, or at any rate in the same year, 1791. For 18 months he served in the counter-revolutionary 'Prince's Army' of Louis' distant cousin the Prince de Condé, finally joining up with, of all things, a Highland regiment, the 79th Foot, which had retreated into Germany from the battlefields of Flanders. When the regiment crossed over to England, Mervé went with it.[11] In England we lose sight of him until 1805, the year he took up his post in Marlow, although his service records show that he was 'at the King's side' throughout this time.

If anyone thought that the cadets' rigorous work schedule would put a brake on bad behaviour, they were soon to be disabused. Reports reaching Le Marchant's headquarters in Wycombe told of drunken scenes in the streets of Marlow, with stones being hurled at professors, women being insulted, and shops pilfered. The lieutenant-governor's complaints to Colonel Butler were met with hostility and an indignant defence of the cadets.

Things reached their nadir in August 1804 when a handful of cadets who considered themselves to have been unfairly punished attempted to take over the college. Their plan was to set fire to a haystack in the hope that the college armoury would be left unattended while the guards ran to put out the blaze. Muskets in hand, they would then confront the lieutenant-governor with a list

**7** *General Le Marchant in the uniform of the Dragoon Guards.*

of demands including the dismissal of the two offending staff members and the abolition of the 'Black Hole', a detested form of confinement imposed for even quite minor offences.

That the plot failed seems to have been due to one of the conspirators having turned informer. R.H. Thoumine names him as J.W Cole, a bright 13-year-old who passed his qualifying exams in 16 months instead of the usual three years and was subsequently gazetted without purchase. His former accomplices were expelled from the college after being stripped of their army insignia and having their swords broken over their heads.

The episode brought discredit on the college and drew much criticism from the national press. Le Marchant, naturally, blamed the uprising on Butler's failure to maintain good order and discipline, an accusation that Butler hotly denied. The point was reached where Harcourt was forced to refer the matter to the commander-in-chief. There followed a formal enquiry at which Le Marchant, thanks to his habit of meticulous record keeping, was able to cite chapter and verse of the incidents behind his complaints. The panel of three generals was plainly impressed and Le Marchant found himself effectively vindicated. As a result, Harcourt undertook not to communicate directly with Butler but only through the lieutenant-governor.

The ensuing weeks and months saw a marked improvement in Butler's performance and consequently in cadet discipline. That he retained the confidence of the Supreme Board became evident in 1811, after Le Marchant had been promoted to major-general and, too senior now for his position at the college, joined Wellington in the Peninsula with his own brigade of dragoon guards. The lieutenant-governorship then fell into Butler's lap.

Nor should it be thought that there were no good apples among the bad in the ranks of the cadets. Two early entrants to the Third (or £90) Establishment, one the son of a 'gentleman', the other of a 'nobleman', were to bring credit both to their fathers and to the college. Both as it happened had connections with Marlow itself. Cadet William R. Clayton had been admitted to the college in July 1803, at the age of sixteen. His father, Sir William Clayton, Bart., was lord of the next-door manor of Harleyford. On obtaining his commission young William joined the Duke of Wellington's army and fought in the Peninsula and at Waterloo. Later, as General Sir William, he served as an M.P. for Marlow for 13 years.

Edward Charles Cocks was the eldest son of John, 2nd Baron Somers and Lord Lieutenant of Herefordshire (Another line of Somers Cocks was a leading family in 19th-century Marlow.) In 1821 the baron was created Earl Somers and Viscount Eastnor, but Edward was never to inherit his father's titles. He was killed during the failed attempt to storm the castle at Burgos in October 1812. Wellington declared that 'if Cocks had lived, which was a moral impossibility, since he exposed himself too much to risks, he would have been one of the greatest generals we ever had.'

The next major crisis was not of the college's making but that of the commander-in-chief himself. It grew out of a scandal surrounding the Duke of York's mistress, Mary Anne Clarke, who had been using her influence with him to secure promotions in the army. It was not uncommon then for promotions to be obtained by 'favour' instead of the more usual purchase. But with or without the knowledge of her royal lover, Mrs Clarke had been taking payments from the officers concerned. Her method was to undercut the official rate so that a captain aspiring to the rank of major, say, would pay only about £1,000 instead of the customary £2,500. For him of course it was a bargain, but for her it was pure profit, to be put away against the day when the duke would tire of her undoubted charms.

This occurred in 1806 and it was the moment the duke's enemies had been waiting for. Chief among these was another of George III's sons, Edward Duke of Kent, who would one day father the future Queen Victoria. His part in what followed is unclear; not in doubt is the enmity between the brothers nor Kent's resentment of York's command of the army.

In 1809 Mary Anne was called to answer charges in the House of Commons. Her interrogator was Colonel Wardle, M.P. for Okehampton, who was widely believed to be in the Duke of Kent's camp. From the floor of a packed House she reportedly gave a good account of herself and, says Hugh Thomas, 'her gaiety and saucy directness endeared her even to so strict a man as Wilberforce'.[12] No action was taken against her, nor was any move made to reform the system of promotion by purchase.[13]

Meanwhile a printed pamphlet had appeared which was as fulsome in its praise of the Duke of Kent as it was derogatory towards the Duke of York and the army under his command. It came from the pen of a notorious muckraker named Pierre Franc McCallum, who singled out 'the seminary at Marlow', describing it as 'an absolute mockery of anything like military education' and the governor, Harcourt, as 'totally ignorant of every branch of military science'.

Somewhat to his embarrassment, no doubt mixed with relief, Le Marchant was specifically excluded from McCallum's indictment of the college personnel. The commandant, Butler, on the other hand, was accused along with the housekeeper of misuse of college provisions. Finally, after pointing out some cases of venereal disease among the cadets, McCallum rated the college 'a seminary of vice, pollution and immorality'.

While most of McCallum's invective could be dismissed as empty bluster, it contained enough grains of truth to hit home. And in Whitehall as in Marlow the effect was devastating. At the urging of the Duke of York's secretary, Colonel Herbert Taylor, Le Marchant wrote a strong letter to Harcourt dissociating himself from McCallum's attack on the governor and offering to co-operate in any way to uphold 'the honour and character' of the college. But a move by the Board to prosecute McCallum for libel came to nothing; the college was shy about having its affairs made public.

The pamphlet, along with Mary Anne Clarke's revelations, handed victory to the Duke of York's enemies which was nevertheless short-lived. Although compelled to resign as commander-in-chief, he was subsequently reinstated.

Among some sections of the public there was a feeling that Parliament, which had censured him for negligence but failed to prosecute him for corruption, had allowed his royal status to stand in the way of its duty. Many no doubt shared the view of 14-year-old Thomas Arnold, whose elder brother Matthew taught at the college and later corresponded with the Wethereds. Writing home from school at Winchester, the future headmaster of Rugby expressed his opinion:

> I think the Ministry go too far in their defence of the Duke when they say they see no fault in his Conduct. What? No fault? Is then the permitting of a Mistress to intermeddle at all in military affairs no fault?

What Mervé and Wethered thought of the construction work at Sandhurst is not recorded, but by 1812 it was near enough complete for the college to take up its permanent quarters. Mervé continued his teaching there until April 1814 when, suddenly and urgently, he was called to the side of the king. Peace had been declared and Louis XVIII, whose last years of exile had been spent at Hartwell House in Buckinghamshire, was returning to France to claim his throne. Mervé was one of just eight members of the *Garde du Corps* to accompany him and his court to Paris.

John Le Marchant did not live to see the full flowering of his creation. He was killed at the Battle of Salamanca on 22 July 1812, the very year that the gentlemen cadets moved to their grand new home at Sandhurst. He had won battle honours at Ciudad Rodrigo, La Granja and Villa Garcia before leading his dragoons in a thunderous charge against the French infantry at Salamanca, scattering their lines with the weight of the attack. Wellington and his cavalry commander, Sir Stapleton Cotton, had watched the action from a nearby hill. 'By God, Cotton,' Wellington told him, 'I never saw anything so beautiful in my life. The day is yours.'

In the act of regrouping his own forces Le Marchant was struck by a French musket ball which severed his spine, killing him instantly. When news of his death reached England it is said that that the Duke of York wept.

Like its founder, the college had made an uncertain start, but also like him it went on to achieve great things for the British army.

# 4

# *Going Their Ways*

Behind them in Marlow the cadets left many memories, along with a small
harvest of musket balls and uniform buttons to be unearthed with the aid of
metal detectors by future generations. Most intriguing of all their legacies,
though, is a handsome silver salver inscribed with these words:

From
THE GENTLEMEN CADETS
of the
ROYAL MILITARY COLLEGE
to
THOMAS WETHERED ESQ.
25th October 1809

The reason for the presentation is not known. My mother, ever the romantic,
was sure it was a thank-you for some misdemeanour discovered by Thomas but
not reported to the authorities. More likely, I think, is some perfectly above-
board act of kindness: the use of his fields for sport, perhaps, or helping to
keep the beer cellar well stocked, for unboiled water was not fit to drink. But
whatever the explanation, the salver still conveys the warmth of feeling that
existed between the family and every department of the college.

Several of the officers' names crop up in correspondence: a Captain John
Otter, for example, and a Captain Thomas Abraham, who sent touching messages
of condolence to the family on Thomas's death in 1849. But it was among the
instructors that the Wethereds formed the closest friendships, and since some
of these continued beyond the college's time in Marlow, we can follow the
people concerned as they go their separate ways.

Most noteworthy of course is the Rev. Godfrey Faussett, who in time will
become a member of the family himself. Has he any idea in those early days
of the feelings he has aroused in Sarah? Probably not. She is not yet seventeen
– hardly more than a child – when his name starts appearing in her diary:
'1806, June 15, Mr Faussett dined here; June 16, Mr Knolles¹ & Mr Faussett
gave a very handsome Ball & supper where we went'. And at a later, unspecified
date: '1st Assembly. I danced with Mr Faussett (3).'

Godfrey, on the other hand, is a man of 27 and about to obtain his first curacy at Holton, near Oxford. What he needs is a woman of his own age, and in 1808, the year after leaving Marlow, he finds one in Marianne Bridges of St Nicholas Court, Thanet. They marry and proceed to raise a family. Thomas, though nearly 20 years his senior, clearly liked Godfrey and admired him, sharing the younger man's interest in education. We know from Sarah's diary that the two families kept in touch. In July 1813, on their way back to Holton from the Faussett's family home at Heppington in Kent, 'Mr and Mrs Faussett took an early dinner here'.

To augment his curate's stipend Godfrey took in pupils at an annual fee of £200. He also gave lectures at the university. By 1815 there was no longer room in the Holton house for both the pupils and the children, of whom there were now five. That year the Faussetts moved to a larger place at Harefield in Middlesex, where two more children were born to them.

By now Sarah was 25 and more than ready for marriage herself. But if there were suitors they were unsuccessful: if she couldn't have the man she loved, it seems, she would have no one at all. Meanwhile, as was his custom with his children, girls as well as boys, Thomas seems to have entrusted her with various missions requiring tact and a head for business. A letter survives, which she sent him in 1818. It is written in an educated hand, and one wonders how much his care for his daughters' education – Anne attended a boarding school, as we have seen – was due to his mother's schooling having been neglected.

And there were occasional diversions, as on 21 June 1814 when 'Mr Pears drove us to Guildford & Godalming & we saw the Emperor of Russia, King of Prussia etc. on their road to Portsmouth.' [2] Or when she was invited to stay in London with her sister Elizabeth-Ellen's future in-laws, the Florance Thomas Youngs. So the years passed, and Sarah's youth with them. The two families continued to exchange visits: in March 1818 Sarah, her parents and sister Martha stayed overnight at the Harefield house with its 'sixteen upstairs rooms and large garden'. Godfrey and Marianne paid a return visit in May, and then, just under a year later, news reached Marlow that 'poor Mrs Faussett' had died.

For Godfrey there followed four years of widowhood when his sisters took turns to come and stay with him and look after the children. For Sarah of course they were four more years of spinsterhood, but Godfrey continued to visit, sometimes bringing a child or one of his sisters. Finally, on 19 April 1823, Sarah could write in her diary, 'This morning I was united to the dearest and best of Men …' She was thirty-two.

The marriage lasted for 30 years, until Godfrey's death in 1853, and seems to have been a very happy one. As we know, it was Godfrey who gave the toast at Thomas's and the senior Sarah's golden wedding in 1838. And, despite the many years of waiting, Sarah was by no means past child-bearing age, adding a further seven children to the seven of Godfrey's first marriage. The time would come when two of Sarah's sons would marry two of her brother Owen's daughters, with similarly happy results.

On his father's death in 1825, Godfrey inherited the family's estate at Heppington in Kent. But although this was periodically the couple's home, most of their married life was spent in Oxford, for Godfrey was quintessentially a don. He gained his doctorate of divinity in 1827 and was elected Lady Margaret Professor the same year, which carried with it a canonry of Worcester. It was that year, too, when Godfrey moved his family into the city of Oxford, first to a house he had bought at No 55 St Giles, and 13 years later to the cathedral close. There Godfrey died in 1853.

Godfrey is buried in Christ Church Cathedral with Sarah beside him. She survived him by 22 years, dying in 1875 at the age of eighty-six. They are commemorated by a handsome wall plaque which describes Godfrey as *'Vir Strenuus Probus Sincerus'* (a vigorous, honest and sincere man), and Sarah's life as *'Pia Pulchra'* (pious and beautiful).

8    *The Rev. James Pears.*

Music was James Pears' passion, as one might guess from the hour at which young Tom and his sister Sarah returned home from that musical evening at his house during the college days. As a schoolboy at Winchester, Pears had bought an old virginal which he kept in the 'sick house', and would sometimes feign illness in order to spend time playing it. At Oxford, where he is said to have been made a Fellow of New College at 16, he studied musical composition under the musical prodigy William Crotch (1775-1847), who was shortly to become Professor of Music at the age of twenty-two.

Performing in Oxford at that time was a singer, Mary Radcliffe, as much admired for her beauty as for her musical abilities. To James the combination was irresistible and he quickly fell in love with her. He was 19, she a year or two older, and neither had any money. Fearing that his father, a well-to-do Oxford builder, would object to the match, James persuaded her to run away with him to London and be married. The year was 1797.

In the event the young couple were welcomed into his parents' household at Woodperry House near Wheatley. There they stayed for several years while James rode and shot and had himself ordained in the ministry. In 1803 he took up the curacy at Holton, but only for three years because in 1806 he swapped places with Godfrey Faussett, the latter moving to Holton while

James was appointed Professor of History at the RMC. One wonders who influenced whom.

For most of what we know about James Pears we are indebted to his daughter Mary Anne Goodman, who was born the year of the move to Holton and later (1867) recorded her memories of her parents in a letter to her younger brother Arnold. Interestingly, at the time she wrote, the house in the village of Hurley, near Marlow, where James and Mary had gone to live, was now the rectory of the Rev. Florence J. Wethered whom James had so despaired of when coaching him in the 1820s.

Here is her affectionate portrait of her father:

> He certainly was singular in his power of securing life-long affections wherever he went … All the Marlow circle of young professors (Matthew Arnold,[3] your Godfather, one) and the Wethereds clung to him as long as they all lived, and loved him. From Hurley they moved to Marlow, and lived there in a bow-windowed house close to Mr Wethered's brewery, and there Charles Wethered [Pears] was born on the 16th July 1807. Mrs Faussett (Miss Wethered) was his Godmother. We moved afterwards to a house lower down the street; there Tom was born on May 9th 1809, and christened Thomas after Tom Wethered, the eldest son, a fine talented, high-principled young man, a very dear friend of Papa's, whose death was widely felt and lamented a few years after, caused by a thorn in his hand which produced locked-jaw.

Those were the days when the river was regularly overflowing its banks:

> I remember a voyage in a tub with James [her elder brother], attended by the commissariat, represented by a boy and bread-and-cheese in another tub, starting from our backyard and exploring a lane outside! It was a great overflowing of the Thames, long marked with great black lines on walls and houses, and I think the Church, and comically referred to by many people, years after, as the 'flood'.

In 1816 the family moved to Windlesham, where James 'had a small farm which he inherited from his mother, and he bought a small house which he greatly enlarged'. Here he continued to prepare his pupils for entrance to the RMC, now at Sandhurst. But the college, according to Mrs Goodman, 'had been sinking into nothing' since the end of the Napoleonic Wars, and the connection with it was a disadvantage rather than otherwise to the School, and the eight boys were an expensive luxury'. The outlook improved a few years later when James attained the position of headmaster of Bath Grammar School. With it went the rectorship of the nearby village of Charlcombe, which became the Pears' new home.

Their troubles were not over, however. First came news of the death in India of their son Henry, a lieutenant in the Madras Engineers. Then it was rumoured that Charles Wethered Pears, a midshipman in the Royal Navy, had died of a sickness in Burma. Luckily this proved to be unfounded, for Charles returned home in 1827, and in December 1829 James was writing to his friend Thomas Wethered, 'Your godson Charles is made a Lieut. and appointed to a ship in the Mediterranean'.

Thomas had been named as one of three executors of the will of James's mother Elizabeth, James himself being another. Elizabeth had died in 1816, but her estate was so full of legal thorns – including money owed by 'a Gentleman whose affairs have been many years in Chancery' – that it would be 1841 before everything was settled and Thomas could be released from his obligations. Most of the extensive correspondence between him and James has to do with the disposal of the Woodperry House property, but there is one sidelight on Thomas's affairs. Early in 1819 he took advantage of 'a great reduction in the price of barley' to buy in as much as he could. In consequence he could not agree to advance £350 to James's stockbroker in the time required.

James died in 1853. About the same time his son James returned to Windlesham and founded the preparatory school that continues to this day.

Two more instructors from the college deserve a place in this story. Both were on friendly terms with Thomas and his family, and both were involved, if only marginally, in the great events taking place on the Continent.

In 1811 Matthew Arnold (the godfather of Arnold Pears) had been admitted to holy orders. Like James Pears and Godfrey Faussett, his tenure at the college was relatively short – probably less than three years – and he had resigned his post there before the move to Sandhurst. He must have acquired a taste for the military life, however, for when we next meet him, aged 27 in the autumn of 1812, he is a chaplain with the British forces in Sicily.

His letters to Tom Wethered, two of which have survived, were written against the background of Wellington's Peninsular campaign. Ten thousand reserves under Lord William Bentinck were stationed in Sicily, that kingdom being one of Britain's few dependable allies. Major powers such as Prussia and Austria, having already been mauled by Napoleon, were hedging their bets while watching the progress of the British in Spain and Napoleon's *Grande Armée* in Russia.

Matthew's first letter was written from Palermo and dated 14 September, the day Napoleon entered Moscow. After chiding Tom for not writing to him (in fact their letters have crossed), he launches into an entertaining report on places he has visited and sights he has seen: the theatre at Taormina and the theatre and baths at Catania, 'now underground having been covered with Lava at the time of the great Eruption which destroyed the old City'. In company with an artillery officer he has climbed to the top of Mount Etna, where 'the streams of Sulphur made me feel as if I were beastly drunk, violent Sickness, Head Ache and all the worst Symptoms …' As A.R. Godwin-Austen might have said, one passes over the clergyman's apparent first-hand knowledge without comment.

His descriptions of the local people and customs are colourful and often amusing. The Sicilians, he says,

> are very glad to accept any invitations but rarely make any return. They go with Delight I am told to Lady William Bentinck's Evening Parties … but never think of opening their own Houses in a similar way. The reason they give for it is the very numerous Quarrels and the violent party Disputes among themselves.

But if the Sicilians cannot forget their quarrels for long enough to entertain guests for an evening, there are at least other diversions in Palermo. Matthew reveals the dark secrets of Sicilian opera:

> The instrumental Musick is good, but everything else very inferior to what is in London. The stage only is lighted so that the rest of the House has a very gloomy Appearance, but as many go there for the purpose of intrigue, the Darkness suits them.

Following each performance the audience repairs to the 'Conversazione Room' to play Pharo and *Rouge et Noir*. The English are invited to go along, and 'many have paid very dearly for it', Matthew says pointedly. He himself went one evening 'to see that as I would any other sight', but, not being a gambler, 'I found it exceedingly dull and I do not think I shall go again'. He is mystified by the popularity of the Sicilian horse races, which are run along one of Palermo's main streets, the crowds of spectators giving way as the horses pass and then closing in again behind them.

> The Horses were without Bridle, Saddle or Rider. Small pieces of Leather were stuck on different Parts of them with Pitch and to these were attach'd Bladders with Pins or something sharp in them [which] made them act like a perpetual Spur. The Races did not seem to me to afford much Sport. The Horse that took the Lead kept it every Time, nor did the others appear to endeavour to pass him. The Natives however seemed highly delighted ...

But despite his having 'met with a great deal of Hospitality and Civility from the Army', one senses that a chaplain's life could be a lonely one. Matthew misses the comradeship of the college and the social gatherings in Marlow. A former colleague on the Staff, John Buckland, has written about a farewell ball given for the college at Medmenham Abbey. Matthew can picture the scene with the music and the dancing, and he tells Tom: 'I dare say you will think me a great Fool for my Pains but I could not help laughing and crying at the same Time when I read his Narrative.'

Especially he misses female companionship, a subject he returns to more than once. Sadly, all the English women he meets seem to be married, and as for the 'Sicilian belles – as I am but a bad hand at speaking their Language my Bashfulness prevents me from attempting a Conversation with them'. Matthew begs Tom for news and nothing is too trivial to interest him. He has enjoyed Tom's account of how another chaplain, a man they call 'the Poet', soon to join the army in Spain, has absent-mindedly walked into a pond.

> He must take care not to let the Muse or an absent Fit carry him into the Enemy's hands, tho' by way of Comfort you may tell him that a Mr Parker, a chaplain with Lord Wellington, was once taken Prisoner and sent back again as being no use to any one.

There is scant reference to the war, but in the second letter, dated 24 October, we learn that reinforcements are to be sent from Sicily to Alicante where a previous expedition led by General Maitland has failed to create a diversion on the Valencian coast. The general in fact has returned to Sicily suffering from nervous anxiety, his place taken by General W. Clinton. It is rumoured that Lord William Bentinck himself may soon go to Spain, in which case, Matthew confesses, 'I hope he will not take me with him, for tho' I should have been glad to have gone at first I am now better pleas'd to remain where I am'.

Where he would really like to be is back in Marlow, 'that delightful Neighbourhood', as he calls it. In his closing paragraph he finds a friendly word for each of Tom's brothers and sisters. The eldest sisters, Sarah and Martha, he hopes will be his dancing partners once again. To Elizabeth-Ellen, aged just 16, he offers 'a little of the Old Parson's Advice' and hopes she will let me 'blend Amusement with Instruction'. And so it continues. Ann and Georgina, aged 13 and six, get arch messages about marriage and kisses, and there's a promise of old coins for 14-year-old Owen, who is evidently a collector. Matthew apologises to Edward, aged 11, for not going fishing with him, and hopes that five-year-old Florence has not forgotten him. As for the two-year-old Lawrence William, Matthew admits, 'I cannot expect [him to] know anything about me'.

Mat Arnold, as he signs himself, comes across as a sensitive, easy-going sort of man, perhaps more likeable than his famous younger brother. Thomas Arnold was 17 at this time and had followed Matthew to Corpus Christi College, Oxford. Despite Matthew's obvious fondness for women, it seems that he never married, for the announcement of his death describes him as a Fellow of Corpus, and Fellows were not permitted to have wives.

Matthew died in a sailing accident off Gosport in 1820, some months short of his 35th birthday. Two years later, when a son was born to his brother Thomas, the boy was named in memory of his uncle. The second Matthew was to prove the most famous Arnold of them all.

On the evening of 19 April 1814 a letter reached Sandhurst addressed to M. le Chevalier de Mervé, a teacher of French at the college. It was dated the 17th and signed by Le Duc d'Havré et de Croy, close companion and adviser to the man who, since the deaths of his older brother and the brother's young son, was entitled to call himself King Louis XVIII.

For the past five years of his long exile from Revolutionary France, Louis and his court had had the loan of Hartwell House, near Aylesbury in Buckinghamshire. It was there that his queen, Marie Josephine, had died of dropsy. And it was there, according to legend, that this man of learning had enquired of a nephew of the Duke of Buckingham whether he spoke Welsh, as he wanted to know the meaning of the Prince of Wales's motto [*Ich Dien*]. But now, with Napoleon's abdication and banishment to Elba, the latest King Louis was preparing to return to Paris and claim the throne of the Bourbons.

The letter was in effect a call to the colours. Charles de Mervé was a chevalier in the elite *Gardes du Corps du Roi*, the King's bodyguard, in which the Duc d'Havre was a *capitaine*. Havré's letter was both urgent and diplomatic. Mervé had been selected as one of a small number of *Gardes du Corps* who were to accompany the King to France. He must therefore apply at once for a leave of absence from the college.

The old diplomat hopes that this request will not be a problem for a country that has behaved in so noble, so generous, so affecting a manner towards France ... But there is no time to lose. The King will leave for London in two days, and for Paris two days after that.

In fact, Mervé had anticipated the call. On 14 April he had written to Colonel Butler, now Lieutenant Governor of the College, asking for a six-month leave of absence. He was anxious not to sever his ties with England or the college, not knowing what he would find on his return to France. 'My property is irrevocably lost,' he wrote, 'and all my friends mowed down by the Revolutions.' He asks for an early reply 'as I am likely to be called on immediately'.

A leave of absence from Sandhurst was conditional on the teacher's finding someone to take his classes while he was away. But on reading Havré's letter Mervé knew that time had run out. He wrote a brief letter of resignation, informing Butler of his intention to leave after lessons the following day. Mervé had been with the college for nine years and was a valued member of the staff. On receiving his second letter Butler sent an urgent message to the Governor, General Sir Alexander Hope, explaining the situation. He recommended that another Frenchman, Alex de Colville, be asked to take Mervé's classes 'for the present'. De Colville had himself applied for leave to go home but this appears to have been refused.

Hope replied to Butler the same day:

> The order from the King makes this a different case from any other. If you think Mr de Colville can do duty till the vacation I will grant leave to Mr Mervé to declare his intention by the 15th July. A. H.

After an exile of more than twenty years Mervé was on his way home.

He arrived in Paris with the King's party on 3 May, and on the 5th he wrote a long and cordial letter to Butler giving his impressions of post-Revolutionary France. Louis has been received with enthusiasm, both in Paris and on their way through northern France. To Mervé's surprise, in the countryside there is no evidence of war, 'not a tree cut down nor a single field uncultivated'. But no young men are to be seen in the villages, only old men, women and a few children.

Mervé has been extraordinarily quick to assess the mood of the country. Although people in general seem glad to see the Bourbons restored, 'there are many Cities and Communes who are disaffected, and as long as Buonaparte lives there will be no security for this ill-fated Country'. 'The Usurper' or 'the Corsican', as Mervé calls him, has left the country's finances in a dreadful state. It is, he says, *une contrerevolution manquée* and, in common with many other Frenchmen, he fears they are heading for a civil war.

In the army loyalties are divided, with the marshals and other officers drawn to Louis by the praises and promises he has heaped upon them, and the mass of the soldiery remaining more or less loyal to the Emperor. The 'old troops', as Mervé calls them – that is, the remnants of Napoleon's army – 'are bad, very bad. Not a night passes but several lives are lost in the streets of Paris by fights between the old and the new troops.'

The French people are 'exasperated' by the victorious Allies, with the exception of the British. 'The British name,' it seems, 'is blessed everywhere by every rank and every party.' And Mervé is sure that Wellington, who arrived in Paris last night, 'will be hailed with as much enthusiasm almost as the King when he shall make his appearance in publick'.[4]

There are questions in Mervé's mind about his usefulness to the King. All that is asked of him at present is that he accompany His Majesty when he goes to chapel. If there is no real need for his services he will not stay in France beyond two or three months. For 'nothing … can compensate for the happy tranquillity and security which I enjoyed in England.' And he promises to pay the college a visit as soon has he can.

Almost as an afterthought he mentions his wife. 'I found [her] waiting for me at my arrival, & unless affairs assume a better appearance she is determined to sell what property she saved & to accompany me back to Sandhurst.' Did he leave her behind in France when he made his escape? Has she been waiting for him all these years?

In the false dawn between April 1814 and March 1815, when Napoleon came storming back from Elba, the English flocked to Paris in such numbers that the welcome noted by Mervé quickly cooled. Among the visitors was young Tom Wethered, a guest of the Chevalier and Mme de Mervé, who showed him 'great kindness and hospitality' during his stay. Mervé made a short trip to England and no doubt paid his respects to Butler. There is no record of what passed between them but it seems that Mervé's separation from the college was to be permanent.

The King with his small band of followers left Paris for the north on 20 March, just hours before Napoleon entered the city. Ten days later, after a miserable journey in pouring rain, they crossed the Belgian frontier and arrived in Ghent. There, while the rest of his household troops caught up with him, he was installed in a splendid mansion lent by a friend, from which he continued to make policy and issue decrees as if he were still at his desk in the Tuileries and in no danger whatever of capture or worse.

As always in time of war, the demand for transport exceeded supply. Horses were at a premium and Mervé turned to his Marlow friends for help in finding some. After all, breweries have horses, don't they?

But it seems that dray horses are not what he is looking for. On 29 May, two weeks before Waterloo, Tom writes back on behalf of his father and himself. He tells Mervé regretfully that, situated as they are in the country,

> it is next to an impossibility to meet with three such horses as you describe …
> or with any indeed that would be worth the expence and risk of sending [them
> on] the Voyage, except at a price *very far* above what you have named.

He explains that prices have risen steeply owing to the demand caused by the cavalry going overseas, and the horses Mervé wants are likely to cost 50 guineas apiece. The best advice Tom can offer is for Mervé to put himself in the hands of a reputable dealer, with the sensible caveat that the horses 'are *not to be paid for until delivered.*'

About the future of France, however, Tom is optimistic. In a young man's rather stilted prose he writes:

> We trust we may confidently congratulate ourselves on the prospect which is fast opening upon us for the reestablishment of your excellent Sovereign to the Throne of his Ancestors, and the total extirpation of the horrible family of Bonaparte.

Tom lived just long enough to see the fulfilment of his hopes for France, dying on 9 July, three weeks after the Battle of Waterloo.

Two years and some months later, his sister Sarah received a letter from Mervé in response to one she had written to him. He has been rewarded for his loyalty to the Crown, for he is now the Comte de Mervé and, at 53, is about to be promoted from the rank of colonel to that of major-general. He has managed to recover a small part of his property, and he and his wife would be living in reasonable comfort were it not for continuing uneasiness about the state of the country and fears of being 'launched out again in new wanderings'.

As with all the college friends, there is nostalgia for the Marlow days and gratitude for kindnesses shown by Sarah's family 'at a time when I thought happiness was forever banished from me'. And there is renewed sadness over the death of Tom, who it seems had endeared himself to the Mervés' friends: 'I can assure you, my dear Miss Wethered, that ... those of my country men who had only seen him a few hours shared in our grief when they heard of his untimely fate.'

It appears that Owen, now 19, has been growing too fast for the good of his health. Mervé writes:

> If a change of air was thought advisable, pray my dear Miss Wethered, beg your Papa and Mama to send him over to us as soon as possible. We'll nurse him tenderly and I am certain he will soon grow strong.

He concludes with messages to Sarah's parents and asks to be remembered to all her brothers and sisters, one sister in particular:

> I dare say Georgina does not even recollect my name, although I did not forget her. I teased her some times and her 'have done!' still rings in my ears.

Georgina by that time was about eleven years old.

# 5

# *The House that Peters Built*

'The Parish of Great Marlow contains nearly 4000 Inhabitants nearly all poor. The Tradespeople with a very few Exceptions are of the lowest order and almost all of them necessitous. The Houses in the Town and Parish which formerly belonged to Opulent owners, are without Tenants, having been let to Government during the time Royal Military College was established here; when that was removed they were nearly all in bad repair and consequently are not likely to be again inhabited …'

Letter dated 17 May 1814 from the Secretary to the Committee of Marlow's National School to the Secretary to the National Society,[1] seeking funds for the establishment of a girls' school.

Even allowing for some embroidery in a begging letter, this presents a sorry picture of Marlow following the departure of the college. All the colour and excitement have gone, and with them the trade the town had come to rely on. Important houses stand empty and in disrepair, apparently abandoned by their owners, and the town itself has descended into poverty and decay.

As the first of the houses to be tenanted by the Army, Remnantz was certainly in as bad a condition as any. The owner at that time was an eleven- or twelve-year-old boy named John Richard Groves. He had inherited it from his father by default, because the will leaving it to his mother had been declared invalid having been signed by only two witnesses rather than the statutory three. We can assume that John lived in his mother's house near Bath, so whether or not Remnantz was occupied before Thomas bought it in 1825 remains a question. If we are to believe the Secretary to the National School, which is to say the Rev. J. Turner, curate of Great Marlow, it seems unlikely. In any case, who would have had the money to spend on it?

We cannot tell with certainty who designed or built the rather severe box-like structure which a century or so later, under Thomas's guiding hand, would undergo such a welcome transformation. But thanks to his insistence on a thoroughgoing title search we do have some excellent clues. The story opens on 15 May 1718 when negotiations began that would lead to a certain Stephen Peters, described as a merchant from London, buying property from a tallow chandler named Samuel Sells (also spelt Sills) and Christiana his wife. The property is described as 'all that Messuage or Tenement and Malthouse with the Appurts … in a street called the West End in Great Marlow'. Peters

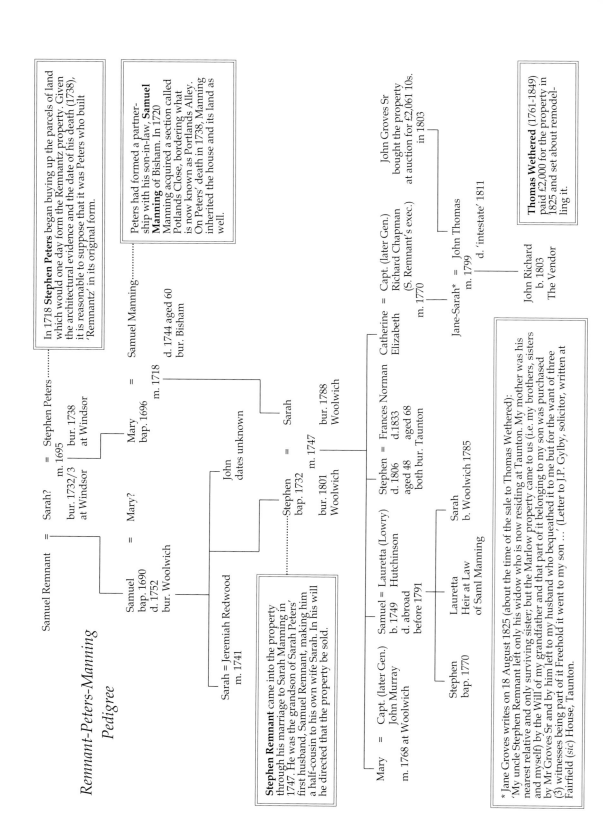

*Remnant-Peters-Manning
Pedigree*

In 1718 **Stephen Peters** began buying up the parcels of land which would one day form the Remnantz property. Given the architectural evidence and the date of his death (1738), it is reasonable to suppose that it was Peters who built 'Remnantz' in its original form.

Peters had formed a partnership with his son-in-law, **Samuel Manning** of Bisham. In 1720 Manning acquired a section called Potlands Close, bordering what is now known as Portlands Alley. On Peters' death in 1738, Manning inherited the house and its land as well.

**Thomas Wethered** (1761-1849) paid £2,000 for the property in 1825 and set about remodelling it.

Samuel Remnant = Sarah?
m. 1695
bur. 1732/3
at Windsor

Stephen Peters
bur. 1738
at Windsor

Samuel Manning
d. 1744 aged 60
bur. Bisham

Samuel = Mary?
bap. 1690
d. 1752
bur. Woolwich

Mary =
bap. 1696
m. 1718

Sarah = Jeremiah Redwood
m. 1741

John
dates unknown

Stephen = Sarah
bap. 1732
m. 1747
bur. 1801
Woolwich
bur. 1788
Woolwich

**Stephen Remnant** came into the property through his marriage to Sarah Manning in 1747. He was the grandson of Sarah Peters' first husband, Samuel Remnant, making him a half-cousin to his own wife Sarah. In his will he directed that the property be sold.

Mary = Capt. (later Gen.)
John Murray
m. 1768 at Woolwich

Samuel = Lauretta (Lowry)
b. 1749    Hutchinson
d. abroad
before 1791

Stephen = Frances Norman
d. 1806    d.1833
aged 48    aged 68
both bur. Taunton

Catherine =
Elizabeth

Capt. (later Gen.)
Richard Chapman
(S. Remnant's exec.)
m. 1770

John Groves Sr
bought the property
at auction for £2,061 10s.
in 1803

Stephen
bap. 1770

Lauretta
Heir at Law
of Saml Manning

Sarah
b. Woolwich 1785

Jane-Sarah* = John Thomas
m. 1799
d. 'intestate' 1811

John Richard
b. 1803
The Vendor

*\* Jane Groves writes on 18 August 1825 (about the time of the sale to Thomas Wethered):
'My uncle Stephen Remnant left only his widow who is now residing at Taunton. My mother was his nearest relative and only surviving sister; but the Marlow property came to us (i.e. my brothers, sisters and myself) by the Will of my grandfather and that part of it belonging to my son was purchased by Mr Groves Sr and by him left to my husband who bequeathed it to me but for the want of three (3) witnesses being part of it Freehold it went to my son …' (Letter to J.P. Gylby, solicitor, written at Fairfield (sic) House, Taunton.*

paid £200 for it, and with it came a garden, an orchard and about an acre of pastureland. The long, narrow strip with its existing messuage, or dwelling, and malthouse (interestingly enough) was the first piece of land that went to make up the estate, and it is the piece on which Remnantz now stands.

Other acquisitions quickly followed. Two more pieces, similar in size and shape to the first, one to the west of it and one to the east, were bought by Peters during the two succeeding years.

Peters and his wife Sarah had a daughter, Mary, who in 1718 – the year of the first land purchase – had married a local man named Samuel Manning. He now joined Peters in his property dealings, buying a large section to the east of Peters' holdings known as Potlands, bordering what is now called Portlands Alley. This piece was to become a walled kitchen garden and would remain as such until sold for development in 1994.

If it was Peters who built the house – and why else would he have so carefully assembled the adjoining plots? – that suggests a date not too long after 1718. Based on architectural evidence, Pevsner plumps for c.1720, while English Heritage is more cautious with 'the 1720s.' Running down the east side of the house, most inconveniently, was a narrow strip of rented church land; a sudden increase in the rent between 1720 and 1721 suggests a rise in the value of the property, with the inference that building had taken place. So visitors to the house are told '1720', which is as close as anyone is likely to get.

As one who believed in leaving nothing to chance, Peters in his will tried to cover every contingency. Upon his death the property was to go to his son-in-law Samuel Manning, who was of course already a part owner of it. On Manning's death it would pass to his widow, Peters' daughter Mary, and after that to Mary's daughter Sarah 'and the heirs of her body lawfully begotten forever'. But, says the will, if Sarah should happen to die without issue, then the estate should pass to 'my late wife's son Samuel Remnant'.

This is where the Remnant family enters the picture, and it happened because Stephen Peters' wife Sarah was a widow when he married her, having previously been married to a Samuel Remnant senior. Her son Samuel was forty-six or so when Peters made his will, but given the number of those named ahead of him it seemed unlikely that he would ever inherit.

As it turned out, the two families were united in 1747 through the marriage of Samuel Remnant's son Stephen and Peters' granddaughter Sarah, she who had stood to inherit ahead of Samuel. To Peters it would have seemed a highly satisfactory outcome, only by that time he was in his grave.

Samuel and Stephen Remnant were from Woolwich: partners in an iron foundry behind the gunwharf, near the corner of Surgeon's Street and Bell Watergate.[2] The Royal Ordnance Depot was close by and would once have been even closer, but its old site on the gunwharf had been too cramped to meet the demands of a standing army and in 1671 the Depot had moved to Woolwich Warren. The open spaces of the Warren were already being used for the proving, or test firing, of guns (a hazardous operation since from time to time the guns would explode), and it was there that a much expanded operation had grown up. In its previous existence there had indeed been a rabbit warren on the 30-acre site, and it continued to be known as the Warren until 1805 when George III renamed it the Royal Arsenal.

It was reportedly in 1730 that Samuel Remnant took charge of the gunwharf foundry.[3] By mid-century he had become a well-established supplier to the Royal Ordnance, as O.F.G. Hogg explains.[4]

> Mr Remnant, a master smith … had many contracts with the Board [of Ordnance], and contributed much in the way of ironwork to the construction of the Warren. Although a private founder, who contracted to supply the Crown and foreign princes with ordnance and shot, he was more of an agent than a manufacturer and acted in the former capacity for some of the largest founders in the Weald … Many hundreds of guns passed through his hands on their way to proof at Woolwich. He was thus a man in a big way of business.

Unfortunately he was a man in a shady way of business as well. Allegations of misfeasance began surfacing in 1749. An investigation followed and a report by the Surveyor General, who was responsible for Government property, showed that stores to the value of £10,370 – a very large sum for the time – had been illicitly sold to Mr Remnant by the storekeeper and clerks at the Depot. Twelve items are listed in the report, a few of them cases of fraudulent weights, e.g. for round shot, but most of them things like shells, guns and ironwork which it can be assumed Remnant sold on at a profit, some no doubt to 'foreign princes'.

Several dismissals and reprimands were meted out to guilty employees of the Depot and Counsel's opinion was sought as to how to proceed against Samuel Remnant. In the event no action against him was taken, or if any was begun it was not followed through. Samuel was already a sick man, and within eighteen months of the report's being issued he was dead. He is buried next to his wife in a vault in Woolwich churchyard. According to his obituary in *The Gentleman's Magazine*, 'He was always apprehensive he should die in his grand climacteric, or sixty-third year, and so it happened'.

The following year, 1752, his son Stephen and daughter Sarah Redwood, who were Samuel's co-executors, agreed to repay what the Crown had lost through his misappropriations. With an estate said to be worth £100,000 they could well afford to do so, and the records of the Office of Ordnance show that the full amount was paid on 8 March 1753. 'Just debts and funeral expenses' are of course the first call on any estate, but in Samuel's case the words have a certain bite to them.

Of course Remnant was by no means the first, nor would he be the last person to be guilty of diverting stores at Woolwich. William Acworth, a storekeeper at the dockyard, was in and out of trouble on charges of embezzlement between 1658 and 1671. 'I know him to be a very knave,' wrote Samuel Pepys in June 1664. That Pepys, who held an important post in the Navy Office, remained on good terms with him may have been due to his confessed attraction to Acworth's wife.[5] Hogg, in *The Royal Arsenal*, excuses Acworth's behaviour on the

**9**  *Stephen Remnant's practice gun carriage.*

grounds, more or less, that 'they all do it', whereas Remnant's was considered to be 'fraud on the grand scale' and 'a scandal of the first magnitude'.

Was Stephen implicated in his father's crimes? He was not yet thirty when the truth emerged; possibly he had been kept in the dark about what was going on. In his will, dated 22 October 1751, Samuel states that his partnership with Stephen has been dissolved, perhaps hoping that by that action he has cleared his son of any liability. A suggestion at the end of the will that his executors put to arbitration 'any Debt Duty matter or thing relating to me' (as distinct from 'my Estate') was not pursued. By making amends as he did Stephen was able to close his father's account and resume trading with the Ordnance. In 1761 he patented a 'skeleton' iron gun carriage which became a model for carriages of that type. It was designed for drill purposes to save wear and tear on the operational carriages.

Samuel's wife Mary had predeceased him, which left Sarah, Stephen and the youngest child. John, to inherit the bulk of his very considerable estate. The source of the family's fortune, the foundry at Woolwich, was left five-eighths to Stephen, three-eighths to John. There is no evidence of a partnership between the two so Stephen may have bought out his brother. In any event he continued to manage the business, bequeathing it to his heirs at his death in 1801. The Woolwich property included two houses, one of which was occupied by Samuel's 'faithful clerk and agent' Owen Whitehead (surely he was privy to what was going on). Under the will he was to receive £300 and 'mourning' and 'be continued at his present salary of £50 a Year with Coals and Candles' until the Woolwich property was disposed of or he was otherwise provided for.

**10**    *Remnantz: front hall and staircase.*

There were legacies of cash and investments for John, and for Sarah and her husband Jeremiah Redwood, who also inherited the lease of Samuel's London house in Bread Street. But it was Stephen as the elder son who was the main beneficiary. The rest of his father's freehold or leasehold properties either came to him directly or else reverted to him and his heirs. The latter was the case with an estate at Palace Green, near Sidcup in Kent, which the Redwoods were to 'enjoy' for three years, before it went to John for his lifetime and ultimately to Stephen or, more likely, to his heirs. Stephen also inherited six leases on properties in the village of Bisham which Samuel had acquired from Sir Philip Hoby, Bart., lord of the manor and owner of Bisham Abbey. The rents from these were to be used for the care and maintenance of Stephen's widowed mother-in-law, Samuel's half-sister, Mary Manning.

Samuel's numerous servants are remembered in the will, and there is an intriguing acknowledgement of the convivial side of his nature: 'To Mrs Jane Papworth, Mistress of the George and Vulture Tavern, Cornhill, and to every Member of the Wednesday Club held there, Vere Warner one of the Members only excepted, Rings to the Value of one pound each.'[6]

What had Vere Warner done to cause offence? He was the lawyer who drew up Samuel's will. Perhaps, when he saw the size of the bill, Samuel considered that Mr Warner had done well enough without a £1 ring.

Stephen Remnant is important to this history, not only as the owner of Remnantz for more than half a century, but as the one who almost certainly ordered the interior decor that is still the chief glory of the house today. Until very recently the name of the designer was unknown to us, but the architectural historian Richard Garnier has identified him as Sir Robert Taylor, a distinguished architect whose work includes the rebuilding of Harleyford Manor, c.1755. Taylor was thus in Marlow at a time when Remnant is on record as having bought up large pieces of farm and other land, evidently with the intention of making Marlow his home.

In keeping with Remnant's situation was Taylor's choice of clientele as those who had recently come into money. He also liked to redecorate houses whose style had fallen out of fashion, as Remnant's might well have done over the course of 35 years. But it is in the mouldings and other architectural detail that Garnier recognises Taylor's individual hand. High rococo was Taylor's period, with a fondness in his case for marble chimney-pieces and 'almost overscaled pedimental doorcases'. The entrance hall at Remnantz has fine examples of both, the fireplaces there and in the dining room closely resembling one designed by Taylor for No. 35 Lincoln's Inn Fields. The Venetian window overlooking the garden (originally with a Diocletian window above), and the wooden staircase made to look like cantilevered stone, are both typical of Taylor's work.

The wonder is that after several lettings, periods of neglect, ten years of occupation by the army, and who knows how many coats of paint, the plaster and other work – e.g. the 'arts of peace and war' motif above the stairwell – should be as well preserved as it is.

In February 1753, about the time he was paying off his father's debts, Stephen and his wife Sarah entered into an agreement with Henry, 8th Baron Paget and 2nd Earl of Uxbridge.[7] The Pagets had held the manors of Marlow and Harleyford in the 16th and 17th centuries, owning much of the land round about. By now many of these holdings had been disposed of and the earl, whose family seat was Beaudesert in Staffordshire, was keen to sell off the rest. The properties were extensive, totalling well over five hundred acres and included some of the best-known farms and houses in the parish: Copy Green Farm, Low Grounds Farm, Forty Green, Highfield and Court Garden, to name a few. A price of £9,300 was agreed and the conveyances were signed by both parties. But the money was never paid and in 1758, while George Wethered was busy starting up his brewery, the agreement was annulled and Stephen Remnant returned the accumulated rents.

One can think of several reasons for Stephen's change of mind. He had seen himself briefly as a member of the landed gentry, as a man of rank and privilege, living on his rents and with a fashionably redecorated house. But that was not really his *métier* and Marlow was not his world. His mother-in-law Mary Manning had died in 1754 so had not long enjoyed the income from the farms or cottages in Bisham. With her death came a loosening of his and Sarah's ties to Marlow. Nor, like Lord Uxbridge, did he see himself as an absentee landlord paying an agent to oversee his large estates. Moreover, £9,000 was a lot of money. Stephen was a wealthy man but his assets were tied up in various ways; he may not have found it easy to raise the necessary cash; better that he cut his losses and return to his business in Woolwich.

It seems strange that Uxbridge was willing to indulge him for five years without receiving a penny for his holdings, but that is what he did. It is significant, however, that the ink was hardly dry on the instrument relieving Stephen of his obligations than another buyer stepped forward. He was Dr William Battie, Physician of St Luke's Hospital for Lunatics in London, that building on whose 'gloomy façade' were carved the 'Hogarthian figures of Melancholy and Raving Madness'.[8] Dr Battie's hospital had received a legacy of £100 under Samuel Remnant's will, and that being the only charitable donation in the will we can conclude that the two families were friendly. A scholar and classicist as well as a distinguished physician, Dr Battie at this time was a fellow of the College of Physicians and on his way to becoming its president. While supervising St Luke's Hospital he also owned and ran a large private lunatic asylum near Islington. His evidence on such places before a committee of the House of Commons contributed to an Act for their regulation in 1774.

Having acquired the Uxbridge properties Dr Battie chose Court Garden, formerly a part of the Harleyford estate, as the site for his new home. It is a part of Marlow lore that in a fit of absent-mindedness he omitted to include a staircase, which had then to be installed at the far end of the building. But the word 'batty', if indeed he gave it to the language, would have had had more to do with his medical speciality than with any lapse of memory. Staircases in the 18th century were not always given positions of prominence, if the owner of the house wanted more space for entertaining on the ground floor.

Court Garden remained in his possession until his death in 1776. It was then sold to another physician, Dr Richard Davenport, who remodelled the house to his own taste. Davenport's land extended across Pound Lane, taking in the southernmost part of what would later be the Remnantz estate. In 1792 an order was made by the Justices of the Peace to divert Pound Lane to the north, where it would have met Portlands Alley higher up and saved 'foot passengers' from West Street '10 poles', or five-and-a-half yards, on their walk to the church or the bridge. What lay behind the order is not clear; nor was it ever carried out. Had it been, it would have appreciably reduced the size of what would become, successively, the cadets' parade ground, a meadow where

Guernsey cows once grazed, and the present-day housing development known as Wethered Park.

At some time or other Stephen Remnant had leased a house in the village of Shooters Hill. It was evidently a substantial house with gardens, and although only two miles from the waterfront at Woolwich, there on the hilltop to the east of the Common it would have seemed a world away from the heat and fumes and crashing din of the foundry. He may have moved there with his family in 1758 or shortly afterwards. In January of that year, when he signed his annulment agreement with Lord Uxbridge, he was still giving his address as Great Marlow. By 1761, as we know, he was back in Woolwich patenting his practice gun carriage. In the early 1770s he was casting ornamental railings for a rebuilt Royal Brass Foundry, and in 1777 he supplied 10 iron lamp brackets for the new Royal Artillery barracks which had become his neighbour on Woolwich Common.

Stephen Remnant died in 1801 at the age of seventy-nine. He was survived by a son, Stephen, and two married daughters, Mary Murray and Catherine Elizabeth Chapman. Both sons-in-law were army captains and both must have been well-to-do since they ended their careers as generals. The father's fondness for Marlow seems to have stayed with him to the end, for although his wife of 40 years lay buried in the churchyard at Woolwich, it was in Marlow or Woolwich that he wished his own body to be laid. Very properly, the family buried him at Woolwich.

The Woolwich property naturally went to his son Stephen, along with 'all my Work utensils, Materials and Effects … belonging to my trade and business as an Iron Founder'. But the new owner did not run the business for long, if at all, for this Stephen outlived his father by only five years, dying at his home in Taunton aged forty-eight. He is commemorated by a plaque in the church of St Mary Magdalene[9] in that town.

Freehold properties such as Palace Green and a former Manning property at Westerham in Kent, likewise the leases on dwellings in London, Bisham and Shooters Hill, were to be distributed between Stephen and his sisters (in the latter case the husbands being specifically excluded). Remnantz was the only exception. That was placed in the hands of a trustee, Frederick Booth of Booth & Harlewood, Attorneys of Craven Street in the Strand, to be sold 'at such time as he shall think proper or convenient' and the proceeds invested and held in trust for the testator's grandchildren. Until then, all rents and profits were to be used for the grandchildren's maintenance and education.

Meanwhile the house had been undergoing a series of lettings. Details of these are sparse and the only tenant we know by name is a Mr Joseph Dalmer who, according to the land tax records, was in occupation between 1783 and 1795. Four years later the property was leased by the army, and the college was in occupation when Remnantz was sold by public auction, along with Albion House Boarding School and other properties in 1803.

The successful bidder – at £2,061 10s. – was a John Groves, of Pimlico, who despite being no relation himself was evidently determined that Remnantz should remain in the Remnant family. In 1799 Mr Groves' son, John Thomas, had become married to Jane Sarah Chapman, daughter of Catherine Elizabeth and her husband Richard. She was thus a direct descendant of Samuel and the elder Stephen. In due course John Thomas inherited, only to be declared 'intestate' after his death in 1811.

In the course of their title searches in 1825, the firm of Allen, Gylby & Allen of Carlisle Street, Soho, wrote to John Thomas's widow Jane for information about the inheritance. At the time, Jane was staying with her uncle Stephen's widow in Taunton. She replied as follows:

> My Uncle Stephen Remnant left only his widow who is now residing at Taunton. My Mother [Catherine Elizabeth] was his nearest relative and only surviving Sister; but the Marlow Property came to us (i.e. my Brothers, Sisters and myself) by the Will of my Grandfather and that part of it belonging to my Son was purchased by Mr Groves Senior and by him left to my Husband who bequeathed it to me but from want of three witnesses being part of it Freehold it went to my Son …

Meanwhile, John Richard Groves had grown to manhood. The 22–year-old owner of Remnantz was now a 2nd lieutenant in the Rifle Brigade. Implicit in the mother's letter is the hurt of finding that her husband's wishes had been flouted by a technicality (as she would see it) and her inheritance denied her. Her reply to a second letter from the lawyers contains a postscript: 'Pray request Mr Charles Allen to let me have the accounts for the last half years rents and whether there is any more money owing to us.' Poor Jane, it seems, was depending on her grandfather's bounty to make ends meet.

The conveyancing agreement was signed on 25 October 1825. Lieutenant Groves was stationed in Cork at the time and his signature was witnessed by a brother officer. For the avoidance of any future disputes, the signatures of Mrs Groves and of another granddaughter, Lauretta Hutchinson, described as 'Heir at Law of Samuel Manning', were also added. Everything was settled at last and Thomas Wethered had become the new owner of Remnantz.

He cannot have been drawn to the outward appearance of the building, for Remnantz then was without architectural charm and he immediately started remodelling it. What it offered was a comfortable family home of proportions suited to his status in the town, and with easy access to the brewery. This was gained through matching doors on either side of Portlands Alley: in no more than four paces from the bottom of his garden, Thomas could be at his place of work via the bottom of the White House garden.

The energy of the 63-year-old Thomas was impressive. To start with, he had the short west wing taken down while lowering the height of its twin, so that instead of a shallow U the plan of the house became an L. With the west wing gone, he extended the line of the main building by 16 feet to form the south facing drawing room with its bay window and French

of pulling or fighting against it'. Tom was at one time master of the Pytchley Hunt in Northamptonshire, an exalted position in any county, but gave it up when he could no longer afford to keep hounds. For the same reason, he tells Owen Wethered in 1840, he has declined an invitation from Lord Cardigan to ride with that hunt, and one from Miss Chamberlayne and Lord Palmerston 'to hunt the Heaverley Country between Southampton and Stockbridge'.

Among the other brothers, Edward, with a commission in the navy (and a boat cloak costing one pound, seven shillings), sailed to South America in 1820 in HMS *Hyperion* and brought home £10 of his pay and £11 in prize money to give to his increasingly hard-pressed mother. But the brass memorial plaque in Shalden's small flint church[4] shows that in the years that followed Martha was to suffer far worse than financial woes. In 1826 Edward had attained the rank of lieutenant-commander when, on 27 August, his ship, H.M. schooner *Magpie*, was caught in a squall off Cuba and went down with all but two hands. In December of that year, Francis died while in India, a first lieutenant in the Bombay Artillery. They were aged twenty-eight and twenty-two. Their brother Frederick, a Sandhurst graduate, had died in India three years earlier.

Then, in November 1827, Martha's daughter Sarah, aged 31, and her youngest child Arthur, who was just 20 and a student at Balliol College, Oxford, died within five days of each other. They were buried at Shalden in the same grave and on the same day. Within four years Martha had lost five of her children, all but Sarah still in their twenties. Another, Augustus, an ordained minister of 28, died of pleurisy in 1834.

Martha did not always do the begging herself. In 1821, when she was trying to fend off Mr Ward, her son William was in difficulty with his bills at Lincoln College, Oxford. With his mother unable to help, William, who was one of the youngest and a favourite at Remnantz, wrote a tactful request to his uncle Thomas. 'I am compelled having no other alternative,' he says, 'to presume on your kindness again …' 'And', he insists, 'I would not on any plea have made this request at present were not the College so strict and peremptory as to its bills.' It appears from the correspondence that this and future bills were met for the time being by Thomas.

At the end of the year before his finals William was invited to spend part of the vacation at Remnantz. 'But,' he explains in a letter to his cousin Sarah, 'in truth I am afraid of the place for I am sure my Greek & Latin have never prospered there yet – and by this time next year I shall have taken my degree and my prospects will have been determined.' Is this a back-handed compliment to his fair cousins? William followed an elder brother Samuel into the Church, and the next we hear of him is in 1849 when he is vicar of the village of Overbury near Tewkesbury.

In the early summer of 1820 an advertisement had been placed in various national and local newspapers, including *The Times*, *The Post* and *The Morning Chronicle,* and handbills carrying the same announcement had been distributed:

# Shalden Lodge & Farms,

A particularly desirable Residence for a Sportsman,
COMPRISING TOGETHER, NEARLY
220 ACRES OF LAND

with

SUNDRY COTTAGES AND GARDENS,
IN A FINE SPORTING AND PICTURESQUE PART OF
HANTS

The house, Shalden Lodge, is described, rather incongruously, as 'a white, modern cottage villa'. 'Cottage', here, must mean small as villas go, but within the low whitewashed building were 'Three Best Bed-Chambers, Two smaller ditto, Dressing-Room, and three Attic Bed-Rooms', so it seems there was room for everyone, even when they were all growing up. 'An elastic house', one member of the family called it.

But despite the wide coverage given to the advertisement, and the very considerable cost, little was actually achieved by it. An offer of £3,000 for the whole property by a James Carter, a man they called 'the Quaker' and who addressed them in his letters as 'thee' and 'thou', was not accepted. A 38-acre piece known as Weston Common was bought by a neighbouring landowner, Edward Knight,[5] for £800, although Martha had hoped to get £1,000 for it. (It was this money that her son-in-law James Ward generously allowed her to use to defray other debts.) Apart from that it was a fruitless exercise and the Smiths were thrown back once more on their own resources. They spent the next 30 years either borrowing from each other, in the words of the song, or engaging in sometimes rancorous debate about what should be done.

Caught in the middle of all this were Thomas Wethered and his son Owen. There was no one else for them to turn to because Tom Smith's brother Samuel had died in 1818, and William Lee, the third trustee, four years before that. Although Thomas did not resign his trusteeship until about 1840, when he was nearly eighty, he had earlier turned most of the trust business over to Owen and it had become a different story. Until then the correspondence had been mainly between Martha and Thomas, or Martha and her sister Sarah, and the brothers for the most part had kept a respectful silence. But Owen was of their own generation and as such was fair game, a legitimate target for any need or grievance that might arise.

One of the Smith petitioners was in a category of his own. Owen's cousin Charles – one of those who was tutored by Dr Nicholas – was seen by everyone, his brothers and sisters included, as a special case, as someone to be treated differently. Was he handicapped in some way, mentally or physically challenged as we would say now? Apart from a rather bizarre reference, in a letter to Owen, to a book he is writing to prove that the Smith family were descended from the god Apollo, there are no signs of serious mental disturbance. His letters are crisp, often witty, and one begging letter in particular, addressed to Owen in December 1826, must stand as a classic of disarming *chutzpah*.

> It has always been my wish to preserve the intercourse between us on terms of equality, and no difficulties pressing upon me at any time have induced me to forfeit that condition. However, the subject before me cannot be spoken of with any sort of grace, so away with words. I am in need of fifteen pounds …

Two and a half years later, in a hastily pencilled note, Charles writes, 'I cannot speak but necessity makes me write.[6] Is it *possible* for you in the course of *this or next week* to furnish me with twenty pounds until I am able to repay.' Owen notes at the top, 'Advanced the sum of twenty pounds to Charles Smith Aug 6 1829'.

As a young man Charles had made regular visits to London, and from his subsequent leasing of chambers in Middle Temple it is clear that he had been studying with a view to a career at the Bar. But as Owen says in a letter to Martha Marx, the second of Charles's three sisters, it is 'a profession which scarcely ever produces any emolument for the first few years'. In Charles's case he might have added, 'if at all'.

By 1832 Charles had fallen behind with his rent for his chambers and pro-ceedings against him were begun. This time £70 was owing. Another desperate plea followed, and Owen and Martha Marx between them came to his rescue. Like her mother, the younger Martha had been widowed, and it seems that her first husband, Colonel Arthur Johnson of the 19th Regiment of Foot, had left her well provided for when he died in 1824, for she was evidently a woman of independent means. Little is known of her second husband, a Mr George Marx, but his address at 81 Eaton Place suggests that he, too, may have been in possession of a good fortune.

To keep Charles solvent a fund was set up at Owen's suggestion, to which six of the better-off members of the family provided an initial sum of £20 each and an undertaking to pay £10 a year thereafter. The original benefactors were Charles's sister Martha, his brothers Tom and Sam Smith, Thomas and Owen Wethered, and an anonymous 'friend'. It was a kind and generous gesture, and of course the saving of Charles, but it was typical of the Smith family that, in only the second year of the scheme, Sam had to borrow from Owen in order to honour his pledge to Charles.

It fell to Owen to keep things on the rails, to remind people to make their payments, to mediate in any disagreements – especially when it came to the final settlement of the estate – and to seek legal advice when necessary. The family's debt to him was enormous, and there is no reason to doubt their gratitude even when his counsels were unpalatable. With two of the brothers, Tom and Charles, the correspondence sometimes strays beyond matters of inheritance and becomes chatty and entertaining. As we have seen, Tom's abiding interest was sport, everything from cricket to fox hunting to the 'Fancy', i.e. prize-fighting. In a letter to Thomas he describes a fight he had witnessed in 1821:

> I met Mr Wethered the other day at the fight between Spring and Neal.[7] I wish it had been you as you never would have forgotten it, such a *gentlemanly* sort of fight. Fancy only, two of the finest men in the world, probably (at least Spring is), and they are both above 6 feet high, for 7 minutes in the finest attitudes imaginable without a blow being struck, and not a syllable uttered by the 30,000 present. The whole list of the Fancy were present, old Cribb[8] as second to Spring was fine to a degree: I marked his attitude and his age, both of which could not have been more worthy of notice had he been fighting himself, so great was his interest ...

With Charles it was politics, or rather, political banter. In 1850, the year after Thomas's death, Owen had spoken at a Protectionist meeting in Marlow, where Disraeli was present as the M.P. for Buckinghamshire. Charles had read a news report of the meeting and, after signifying his approval of Owen's speech, made the following comment:

> Pray do not have any more communion with that mischievous boy Mr D'Israeli, for depend upon it he is all a sham. He knows as well as you and I do that he is deluding his party to no purpose, whilst our cousin Robert [Peel] deluded it to a very considerable purpose indeed.

He means, I suspect, that while Peel had 'deluded' the government into abolishing the Corn Laws in 1846, his adversary Disraeli was fighting a rearguard action he knew could not succeed. To be an anti-Corn Law 'Leaguer' in Buckinghamshire, however, would have been political suicide. Charles, incidentally, is incorrect in referring to Robert Peel as 'our' cousin; he was a cousin of Owen's grandfather and therefore of Owen's (at two removes) but not of Charles.

For a while, in 1838, there had been hope of an appointment for Charles as a receiver of rents for estates in Chancery, but it seems to have come to nothing and he had continued to live on his family's charity. At last he was forced to give up what William described as his 'worse than useless Chambers', and move down to Shalden where he had the use of a house called Anstey Knap Cottage on the estate. Owen sent him a gift of an 'easy chair'. It had 'scroll elbows covered with claret coloured Morocco leather', and Charles was delighted with it. 'One of the happiest days I have had for many years,' he wrote, was that when you and your kind hearted sister [Sarah?] and sweet daughter [Anne Maria?] came up here to the Knap, and the beautiful chair which you have given me is a most pleasing reminiscence of it ...'

Despite his apparent fecklessness, his willingness to live on the charity of others, and a strong mulish streak (which was to cause anguish over the final disposition of the Shalden property), one can see why Owen was fond of Charles. There is an engaging, take-me-as-I-am quality about his letters, even his begging letters, which is hard to resist. Sobersided people like Owen sometimes enjoy a little teasing. Charles's good-natured sallies were invitations to Owen to take himself and his preoccupations a little less seriously, and they lightened his day.

11 *Portrait of Owen Wethered.*

Martha Smith died on 6 December 1852 aged eighty-six. She had been widowed for 41 years, seen half her large family predecease her, and eked out a precarious existence on rents from the farms and some assistance from her son Tom and her namesake and second daughter Martha. Now, with her death, the estate must be wound up.

Tom Smith and Martha Marx were their mother's executors, Owen still acting as trustee of their father's estate. He now called in his solicitor, C.J. Bloxham of Bloxham & Ellison, 1 Lincoln's Inn Fields, and a valuation was arrived at. Golden Pot Farm was set at £2,700, and the Shalden Lodge Farm, including its cottages, at £3,017. The latter figure was probably accurate enough, but it was also tailor-made to match the £2,300 owed by the estate to Martha Marx, plus the legacy of £717 that she was to receive, in common with her remaining siblings. Under an arrangement made in 1839, long before her mother's death, and apparently agreed by all concerned, the debt would be offset against the Shalden Lodge property, which would then become Martha's. The plan was for this to take effect soon. Golden Pot Farm, which was under lease, would pass to Tom on his making up the difference between the valuation and what was owing to him from the estate.

In practice these things seldom go smoothly, and the Smiths were not the family to change that. Charles had never been happy about the arrangement, claiming he had not been properly consulted. He told a family gathering that his mother 'must remain undisputed mistress of Shalden' (translated by Tom as 'Charles must remain master'), adding, 'such is my determination'. Charles's consent was essential, so when it seemed that he would continue to dig his heels in even after his mother's death, she was persuaded to write a codicil cutting him out of her will unless he withdrew his objections, which presumably he did.

However specious his arguments and however unreasonable his attitude, it is clear that the unmarried Charles adored his mother. 'Her image is ever with me', he told Owen after her death. 'She was the only thought that I ever had of happiness.'

Another problem was Tom, who was pulling every string he could to meet the cost of Golden Pot. First he argued that the farm had been overvalued: £2,400 was a more realistic figure than £2,700. He also believed that the division of assets proposed by Owen and Bloxham was overly generous to Charles. Then a row broke out between Tom and William, with Tom insisting that the cost of William's expensive education (Eton and Oxford) should be counted against his share of the estate – a view that Owen and Mr Bloxham appeared to share. Tom's own education, he claimed, had cost no more than £50, which suggests that he did not complete his course at Cambridge. He made his case to Owen in several letters, one of which he rather foolishly read out to William.

William, who was unwell and about to take a prolonged leave of absence from his living at Overbury, wrote a deeply aggrieved letter to Owen:

> ... that a brother of mine could be found not content with standing selfishly aloof in all my troubles and vaunting his higher station and circumstances – but just at the moment of my natural yearning for some chance of ease and restoration stepping in between me and my just expectations ...

Replying to both brothers in measured tones, Owen proposed a meeting of the parties at Remnantz, 'as one hour's conversation will be more to the purpose than a hundred letters. Mr Bloxham will be there and also Martha.'

At this point Tom appeared to back down, perhaps realising that Golden Pot was never going to be within his means. Declining Owen's invitation, he offers a proposal of his own, which, 'should it not be accepted by you, I fully authorise you to advertise & sell both Shalden & Golden Pot Estates, etc. as far as I'm concerned.' He concludes:

> Give our kindest regards to all of them, and at your house to which I should have much liked to have gone but my feelings on the subject are too strong for me to venture, tho' you are gentle as a lamb and firm as the late Duke of Wellington when necessary.

The story of the Smiths of Shalden reveals more about Owen's character – his fairness and his extraordinary patience – than can be found anywhere else. We might have learned still more about him had he not copied his own letters on to thin, absorbent paper where the ink was as self-effacing as the writer himself.

Martha Marx did indeed become the mistress of Shalden. The window over the altar of the present church of SS Peter and Paul was given in her memory.

# 7

# *Edward Wethered and the Politics of Hate*

Edward's death at the age of 31 was another great sadness to the family. It was caused by 'inflamation of the lung' or, as we would say, pneumonia. To lose a second much-loved son would have been pain enough for Thomas and Sarah, but what followed next was like the twisting of the knife in the wound.

Only two of Edward's letters survive, one to his elder brother Owen, the other to Georgina, at 20 the youngest of his five sisters. In them he comes through as a thoroughly likeable young man, easy-going, charming and amusing, especially about his own shortcomings. Here is what he says about his failure to reply to a letter from Owen's future mother-in-law:

> I am afraid that I must be in Mrs P's black book for not having answered her kind note ... I could not do so till I arrived here and in fact till two days before your wedding and I then thought that Mrs Peel would have other things to think of, and that a letter would be bothering her for nothing.

Realising Owen won't fall for *that*, he adds,

> I believe to tell you the truth that my old enemy 'laziness' had something to do with it – never mind. If I am in disgrace I must trust to your wife to get me out of it.

The 'here' in Edward's letter is the artillery barracks in Exeter, where this captain in the 3rd Dragoon Guards (Prince of Wales's) was currently stationed. Surprisingly, considering the family connections, he had not entered the army through Sandhurst but had evidently had his commission and subsequent promotions bought for him by his father.

His education, in fact, is a bit of an enigma. He entered Eton in 1811 at the age of 10, the first of the family to go there. Yet for three months in the spring of 1814, aged not yet 13, we find him serving as a 'Volunteer lst Class' aboard the warship HMS *Devonshire*. Perhaps he was thinking of a career in the navy, or perhaps this was a sort of Outward Bound course arranged through a friend. He would have been kept closely under the eye of the captain, performing minor services for him. According to a certificate signed by Captain Donnally, he 'behaved with diligence and sobriety and was always obedient to command'. In June of the following year, now nearly 14, he is mentioned in his sister Anne's diary as 'going back' to somewhere called Castle Hill, which suggests another educational establishment.

**12** *Edward Wethered in silhouette.*

Of several postings during his short army career, Ireland was the one he liked least. In his letter to Georgina, an affectionate older-brother sort of letter, written to 'dear Gena' from Cork, he wails about the village of Kilmacthomas in Co. Waterford, comparing it – for sleepiness, presumably – with the hamlet of Well End near Marlow.

> An Irish town is bad enough, but an Irish village – Oh! Defend me from ever being quartered in another ... I had to send 15 miles for bread, and the Guard of the Mail neglecting to bring it one fine morning, I was obliged to ride in to Waterford for it!!!

In Cork, on the other hand, 'there are too many good things at a time, as there are concerts independent of the theatre and Cork will not stand so much gaiety at once'. Musical entertainment was evidently to Edward's taste. On one occasion, after dinner with some friends, he joined in the singing of glees with the two young daughters of the house.

This letter is dated 1 August 1826. It is harvest time but the dry weather has spoiled much of the Irish potato crop (unlike the terrible crop failure of 1845, when it was damp weather that caused the blight). 'If it continues,' Edward writes, 'the distress will be greater than was ever known, for independent of the other crops, Paddy's 'praties' are all burnt up.' As so often, the great and/or dreadful events of history can be seen unfolding, even in casual correspondence such as this.

He ends by teasing Georgina with an account of a young fellow officer whom he greatly admires and calls his 'chum'. 'Perhaps at some time or other I may introduce him to you,' he writes, 'but you must not fall in love with him. I give you this warning, as wherever he goes he is a great favourite both with Ladies and Men.'

Warrington was the officer's name. Whether or not Georgina ever met him is not known. Eight and a half years later, when she was 29, she became the wife of James Aldridge, Esq. of Inholmes, Hungerford, and Princes Gate, Hyde Park. They were married at Bisham as Frederick Inwood's new church in Marlow was still in the final stages of completion. The bride wore 'a beautiful white satin dress trimmed with swansdown, a plain white satin cottage bonnet, & a blond veil 2 yds. Sq. thrown over it.'[1]

That particular letter from her elder brother is of the sort that a sister might well keep. After Edward's death it would have become a treasure.

While still in Ireland, Edward bought a horse that he found did not suit him, and asked his father to find him another. This Thomas duly did, sending it over to Ireland and following it up with a letter.

> I am anxious to know all the perfections and imperfections of the Horse I sent … If he does not suit you I should think, if you have no accident with him, that he would do to carry me and Owen but if too heavy for us that he would fetch a great deal of money for a leader in a Gentleman's Carriage …

The horse was heavily built, then, as befitted a charger for a dragoon. And the dragoon himself? A silhouette of him hangs among others of the family in the library at Remnantz. It shows an extraordinarily aristocratic looking young man with a high forehead and prominent nose and chin, not unlike the profile of the Duke of Wellington. In his dragoon's uniform with his sabre at his side, he would have cut a fine figure as he rode at the head of his men.

In November 1830, the 3rd Dragoons were quartered in the villages of Dursley and Wotton-under-Edge in Gloucestershire, when trouble arose in the nearby small town of Tetbury. 'A Mob' had assembled, and the Lord Lieutenant, the Duke of Beaufort, sent an urgent message to the commanding officer asking for troops to deal with it. A detachment under Lieutenant Edward Wethered rode into Tetbury on the night of the 26th and placed themselves under the orders of a Mr Wolford, the magistrate who had raised the alarm. By then, according to the subsequent letter of commendation, a mob of nearly two hundred had 'assembled in a riotous and tumultuous manner', had 'broken to pieces several agricultural machines', and 'levied contributions from the inhabitants of the Town of Tetbury and its neighbourhood'.

The letter, which was signed by Wolford and 12 other justices including the Lord Lieutenant, praised Edward and his men for their 'prompt, efficient and soldier-like conduct' in capturing 23 of the offenders and conveying them to prison. It was by no means an isolated case. Unrest was widespread in the autumn of 1830, with rioting and machine-breaking a common occurrence, especially in the south. With no police force as yet outside of London, it was left to the soldiers to restore order. That Edward managed it so successfully was a credit to him and his men.

It is sad that not more of Edward's letters survive, for along with the immediacy and freshness is a suggestion of real comedy, as in this passage from the letter to Owen from Exeter. The precentor of Exeter Cathedral, an old friend of Thomas's, had called on Edward 'and talked much about my dining with him'.

> I have not heard more from him on the subject as yet, and I am getting hungry … I should like to dine with him, he has so much the appearance of a man who knows what good living is. I see him in his Stall in the Cathedral every Sunday. The first time I saw him there I must confess that, as my eye rested on his fat portly figure and sleek face my mind reverted more to the good things of this

world than of the next. However, to prevent a similar error on the next Sunday,
I lunched before I went – it had a good effect.

It is the visual impression one carries away: the well-fed priest in his stall (what
was he thinking about?), and the hungry young man in the congregation who
has had to eat before the service in order to keep his mind on things spiritual.
It is a scene worthy of Gillray.

Edward died on Christmas Eve 1832. Ironically, the regiment was in Brighton
when he was taken ill – the town where his mother had once gone to recuper-
ate after an illness. It was Edward's elder sister, Elizabeth-Ellen Young, who
assembled such information as there was and passed it on to their mother.[2]
On 16 December, a Mr Ward,[3] who had been in Brighton at the time, had
entertained Edward to breakfast at his hotel. Edward was reported to have been
'hoarse with a cold', but he ate heartily and that afternoon he and and another
officer went and sat with Mr Ward who was troubled with toothache. Edward's
cold 'did not appear at all serious', but Mr Ward told him to take care of it.
Obviously it was the beginning of something not only serious but fatal.

News of Edward's deteriorating condition must have reached Marlow and
caused Owen to go down to Brighton to be at his brother's bedside. A letter
from Owen to his mother dated the 26th, two days after Edward's death,
welcomes the arrival of Florence, and together the two of them accompanied
the hearse back to Marlow, where Edward was interred in the crypt below the
parish church.[4] The start of the 'solemn and mournful procession' was witnessed
by another friend in Brighton, who, according to Elizabeth-Ellen, 'heard our
beloved brother spoken of by rich and poor with the greatest respect and
regret'. In the regiment, her source was reported saying, 'he was considered
quite the Peace Maker, and whenever any difference arose, he was the person
applied to, to adjust them'. What better epitaph could one have?

Letters of condolence there must have been in abundance, but just one
has been kept. A letter of empathy we had better call it. It was addressed to
Thomas and it came from Benjamin Disraeli.

Bradenham House
January 8, 1833

My dear Sir,
I had hoped to have shaken you by the hand before I left Bradenham for town
and to have thanked you for all your kindness to me, but a melancholy event
has deprived me of this pleasure.

It would be presumptuous in me to attempt to condole with you, and even were
we as intimate as I could wish, fatal experience teaches me that under these
circumstances condolence is of no avail. The consolation of religion and the
course of time, the duties of life, and the engaging distraction of an affectionate
family, can alone alleviate these bitter pangs.
When we meet again, condolence will have mellowed into sympathy.

Believe me, my dear Sir, with sincere regards,
Your obliged friend and servant

B. Disraeli

It seems a curious pairing, the 29-year-old would-be parliamentarian and the 71-year-old brewer: Disraeli, flamboyant and ambitious, with his intellectual Jewish background; and Thomas, the solidly English middle-class family man and man of business. The relationship, moreover, ran more or less concurrently with Disraeli's much talked-of affair with Henrietta Sykes, wife of Sir Francis Sykes of Basildon in Berkshire, conduct that Thomas would certainly not have condoned. 'A truly respectable family' is how, many years later, Disraeli himself referred to the Wethereds!

Nor, on the face of it, was there an identity of political views. Thomas was a Tory, a member of his local Pitt Club and a supporter of the Williams family which held one or both of the Marlow

**13** *Benjamin Disraeli in 1834.*

seats for the greater part of the century. Disraeli, in 1832/3, was standing as a Radical, a group described by Lord Blake as 'an erratic, frivolous, colourful collection of independent MPs with no coherent political philosophy'.[5] His radicalism, however, had a recognisable Tory bias while allowing him the freedom to spurn party labels and to call for such 'radical' measures as the secret ballot, triennial parliaments, and the improvement of conditions for the poor. (The first of these he achieved 40 years later, by which time Thomas's grandson was a Member of Parliament.) On the heated issue of the Corn Laws he straddled the fence with a not very helpful proposition to 'relieve the customer without injuring the farmer'.

On 10 January, just a week after Edward's funeral, a letter appeared in the *Windsor Express* that was deeply wounding to Thomas and his family. The writer was William Francis, a regular correspondent of the Whig newspaper and surely one of the most contradictory characters in Marlow's history. Since 1814 he had held the post of Master of Sir William Borlase's 'Free School', across the road from Remnantz, having previously been headmaster of Taplow Hill Academy in Maidenhead. He came highly recommended for his 'great talents', among them 'an extraordinary Knowledge of Mathematics'; he was described, moreover, as having an 'exemplary moral character'. Francis was also a competent draughtsman and cartographer. In all he produced 12 testimonials, including three from professors at the Royal Military College. Thomas especially, as head of the *feoffees*, or school governors, must have been delighted to get him.

All seems to have gone well until August 1830 when a violent altercation with a local baker landed him in trouble, as we shall see. More important to this story,

**14** *First and last pages of Disraeli's letter of condolence.*

though, is his furious attack on Thomas in the popular press. These were days of almost unrestrained abuse and name-calling in political journalism; Francis himself was described in the Tory weekly, *The Wycombe Sentinel*, as 'the Marlow Cur':

> One Francis of Marlow, the pest of the neighbourhood, and better known as *The Cur*, has been pouring forth his venom against Mr Disraeli in the Windsor Express ... The only proper answer to a thing like Francis is a horsepond or a blanket, but we may be merciful enough to concede him another. Let him beware of the Sentinel's bayonet ...

But there were limits even to this sort of mud slinging and Francis's letter goes well beyond them. Much of it is routine invective. Thomas – nicknamed Perfidy by Francis – 'is accused of 'clandestine and tyrannical interference in electoral concerns', and of being 'the odium of every honest and upright candidate in the neighbourhood'. According to Francis, he is

> Busy in the town with recommending in the same breath both a Conservative and a Liberal candidate;[6] busy in the county to impose two of the most intolerable Tories[7] upon the electors that ever disgraced the shire; busy in the county of Berks in dividing electors from their plighted faith, adding menaces to entreaties; and busy at the election booth in Maidenhead with a renegade tinker attached to his tail ... For the borough of Wycombe he lent his aid to one of the most impudent aspirants after parliamentary honours that ever attempted to burlesque the representative system.

Was Disraeli the 'renegade tinker'? That he was the 'impudent aspirant' there is little doubt. Disraeli was in the race for Wycombe and he clearly had Thomas's support.

But this sort of language, although hugely insulting, was part of the electioneering cut and thrust of the day. Utterly indefensible was the vicious blow that Francis struck at the end of his letter:

Although the laws of the land cannot reach such odious misconduct, the laws of
the Almighty will, and relying upon the sacred truths of the Decalogue, I think
I already see the iniquity of the Sire has been visited on the head of the Son.

In other words, the death of Edward was brought about by Thomas's political
sins. And the letter goes on:

May the anguish he *affects to feel* [my emphasis] ... be real, and may it effect in
him the reform which I much doubt whether anything short of the most intense
personal affliction can produce.

Thomas and his family were appalled. Such an unspeakably cruel libel could not
be allowed to stand. Legal proceedings against Francis were issued at once.

Disraeli had twice failed to get elected for Wycombe and would shortly fail again
in Marylebone. But his power base, such as it was, was in Buckinghamshire
and he needed local men of influence on his side. Still in his 20s he had
already learned to turn on the famous Disraeli charm, and he had turned it
on Thomas to good effect; witness this courtly apology for being unable to
keep a dinner engagement:

> 35 Duke Street, St James
> Apl, 8th /33
>
> My dear Sir,
> I am most grieved that I cannot dine with you on the 10th. Your tall trees and
> sweet flowers haunt me in the midst of this close metropolis. But just as I was
> stepping into my carriage on Thursday for Bradenham, with a prospect of fresh
> air and quiet, I was stopped by a deputation from the Marylebone Election, and
> have consented, with every prospect of success, to become a candidate in the
> event of an expected vacancy. I am now once more in the midst of a canvass on
> a very different theatre to our little market town.
> My kindest compliments to Mrs and the Misses Wethered, whom I hope soon
> to see. Believe me, altho' in haste,
>
> Your ever faithful servant
>
> B. Disraeli

Of far greater importance to Disraeli than the patronage of a country brewer,
however, was that of the Marquess of Chandos, heir to the Duke of Buckingham
and master of Stowe. Lord Chandos was an ardent Tory and upholder of the
agricultural interest, who well deserved his sobriquet of 'the farmer's friend'.
He goes down in history as the author of the so-called Chandos Clause in the
1832 Reform Act, a measure designed to give tenant farmers the vote, although
seen by the Grey Government as simply handing more votes to the landlords.
Both he and – more famously – Disraeli turned against Peel ten years later
when Peel was veering towards the repeal of the Corn Laws.[8]

By the autumn of 1834 Disraeli was firmly in the Protectionist, if not yet quite
in the Tory camp. In a letter to Thomas dated 30 October he announced that
'a grand agricultural Dinner' was to be held in the county hall in Aylesbury,
probably in the first week of December. He has had 'a long conversation' with
Lord Chandos 'and told him that I should consult yourself and a few other

**15**   *The Old Borlase School.*

friends in order to form an estimate of the numbers who wd probably attend from our end of the County.'

Richard W. Davis quotes the *Bucks Gazette* as reporting that 'upwards of 800 persons sat down to dinner, the great majority of whom consisted of the farmers of the county'.9 'By this time,' adds Davis, 'Chandos had switched his emphasis to the repeal of the Malt Tax, which probably had even less direct relevance for the farmers of Bucks than the Corn Laws. But ... by this time, [they] had confidence in the 'Farmers' Friend' and were ready to follow his lead.' Thomas, being a brewer as well as a farmer, and who no doubt attended the dinner, would have supported the marquess on both counts.

The dinner preceded another general election, when Disraeli failed for the third time to get himself elected for Wycombe. It wasn't until 1837 and the election following the accession of Queen Victoria that, with the aid of Wyndham Lewis, a sitting member for Maidstone, Disraeli was finally elected for that borough. Ten years later he was returned for Buckinghamshire.

In his short history of Borlase School, former Senior Master J.C. Davies writes, 'However exemplary Francis's moral character may have been in 1814, it seems to have deteriorated a good deal by 1830.'10 Indeed, such was the savagery of his attacks on political opponents, it appears that his mind had become unhinged. On 14 August that year, between five and six p.m., a baker named William Hatch was chatting with some men just up the road from the School when Francis appeared. As he passed Hatch he said, 'Halloa! Sod!'

Later, at the Quarter Sessions in Aylesbury, Hatch testified: 'I went up to him and said, "What do you mean by calling me Sod?" He was in liquor and staggers up to me and strikes me with his fist on the breast and calls me a sodomite and "Get away from me, you sodomite." '

One of the other men tried to intervene but, in Hatch's words, 'Mr Francis began fighting and a scuffle took place between us.' Hatch was a tall man, over six foot, and he was able to hold him off with one arm while Francis flailed away with both of his.

Under cross-examination Hatch denied that he had insulted Francis first, denied having started the fight, and denied that he himself was drunk. 'I had been drinking,' he said, 'but no more than would do me good. I might have taken beer with my dinner, and perhaps two or three pints – not four pints – I will swear not more than four in the course of the day.'

Each man produced witnesses who swore that he had never laid a finger on the other, but the jury believed Hatch's version and found Francis guilty of assault. He was fined £9 and sentenced to one week in the common jail.

The Tories in Marlow were called Coppers after the trade of the Williams family. Hatch, like Thomas, was a Copper, while Francis was a 'Blue', or Whig. Following the fracas, Francis was dismissed by the governors, but incredibly he refused to go. Even more incredibly, the governors, 'fearing expensive litigation', as Davies puts it, allowed him to stay.

The case of Rex v. Francis – the libel against Thomas – was heard in the Court of King's Bench in June 1834, the Lord Chief Justice, Lord Denman, presiding. Acting for the Wethereds were the celebrated Sir James Scarlett and a Mr Whately. At the time the libel was published the editor of the *Windsor & Eton Express* had been William Henry Reynell. In his evidence he stated that he had published only *part* of Francis's letter, suppressing what he considered to be the most offensive part. (For this he was commended for his 'good sense and humanity'.) Owen appeared for the family, sparing his elderly father more distress, and recited the details of Edward's death. As a final act of spite Francis had subpoenaed Thomas's wife Sarah and one of their daughters; they attended the trial but did not speak. Curiously enough it was a local builder who confirmed that the letter was in Francis's handwriting. The jury wasted no time in finding him guilty.

At the sentencing appearance in November, Francis pleaded that he was in a bad state of health, and at the advanced age of 60 was receiving only a small stipend from the school and had to support a wife, a son and a nephew. The judge told him that the libel contained the most contumelious and abusive language, compared with which the political allusions sank into insignificance. The time was not yet come when a man was permitted to publish such things with impunity. He was sentenced to three months in Aylesbury jail.

This time, although not without difficulty, the governors were able to remove Francis for good. He was still owing rent on a field which he had leased from them, so they seized his haystack by way of compensation. The solicitor's bill for getting rid of him came to £108 11s. od.

# 8

# *Snapshot: 1838*

Over the period of the Golden Wedding, Owen's wife Anne had had her hands full. In addition to the two of them and their four small children (Anne-Maria, six, Thomas Owen, five, Sarah Elizabeth, four, and Owen Peel, one), she had her parents staying, her younger sister Ellen, and two of Owen's Faussett nephews, Robert and Tom. Somewhere in that overcrowded household there must also have been room for Mary Tyler, the children's nurse, as well as for Caroline, the new young nursemaid, and no doubt other female servants too. Caroline had been taken on the previous year, replacing an Irish girl named Eliza who, Anne felt, was 'not sufficiently fond of children'. But 'Tyler' had been with the family since the birth of Anne-Maria in 1831, and would remain with them, a much-loved companion and friend-in-need, for 50 years. Since there cannot have been room for all these people in the White House, it seems certain that the Old House – whatever its normal use at that time – would have been requisitioned by the family for the occasion.

Anne was from the north, a Peel, her father a first cousin of the man who in three years' time would succeed Lord Melbourne as Prime Minister. Not that the cousins were on any kind of terms. The Rev. Giles Haworth Peel had retired the previous year from the small living of Ince in Cheshire. There, on 25 May 1830, he had performed the wedding ceremony for Anne and Owen. There is no evidence that Sir Robert Peel was among the guests.

Now Anne was eight months pregnant with her fifth child. In the normal way she would not perhaps have been appearing in public, but a family milestone like this was not to be missed. Besides, in the daytime at least, Remnantz could be reached quite easily by going through that door at the bottom of the White House garden, across narrow Portlands Alley and through the facing door into the Remnantz property. (The latter was also a handy short cut to Sunday worship and was thus known as the church door.) There would have been no need for her to be seen by all and sundry in Marlow's busy High Street.

In the eight years of Owen's and Anne's marriage, great changes had taken place in Marlow. The High Street, where the brewery gates were flanked by the handsome frontages of the Old House and White House, no longer ran down to a wharf at the river's edge. Instead, it swept on through the arches of William Tierney Clark's fine new suspension bridge linking Marlow with the village of Bisham on the Berkshire side of the Thames. The more modest wooden bridge that it replaced had crossed over a few yards down river, from the foot of what is now St Peter Street but was at one time Duck Lane, so called (it is said) for the ducking stool that stood there.

The upkeep of the old bridge had been in the care of three bridge wardens, William Clayton, Thomas Wethered and Thomas Rolls; they acted as trustees for a number of properties, the rents from which were supposed to pay for repairs. There was never enough money, however, and when the safety of the bridge became a concern the properties were sold to help defray the cost of a replacement.

Work on the new bridge began in 1829, local labour being used wherever possible. The stonemason, Theophilus Clifford, had been employed by Thomas Wethered during the alterations to Remnantz in 1826. So proud was he of his part in the building of the new bridge that, when a daughter was born to him and his wife towards the end of 1829, they had her baptised Charlotte Suspensiana.

The official opening of the bridge drew crowds from both sides of the river. Among them was a young woman named Elizabeth Rockell who ran a small school for lace-making in a cottage where the church hall stands today. Miss Rockell was engaged to an Irish carpenter who had worked on the bridge, and she was determined to be the first one to cross it. She and a friend rose at dawn and with great daring ran across the bridge and back again before the barriers were removed. History is quiet as to whether she already had on the poke bonnet, puce silk dress and cloak lined with canary satin which, as she would one day tell her granddaughter, she wore for the ceremony.

The year the bridge was finished, 1832, was that in which another Marlow landmark began building. For years the lower end of the town had been regularly inundated by the floodwaters of the Thames. The trouble started with the installation of the first pound lock in 1773. Before that time, navigation was made possible by 'flash locks', which were simply removable sections in the centre of each weir, hazardous for barges heading downstream, hard going for those coming up. The new locks did away with the dangerous shallows but created problems for those like the Pears family who had lived near the bottom of the High Street.

Mary Anne Goodman (*née* Pears) was probably right about the 'great black lines' on the walls of the old parish church. That building was indeed in trouble. Norman in origin, with transepts added, probably in the 13th century, it had a square tower 'built of clunch and rough-cast, similar to that of the adjoining parish of Bisham'.[1] At some later date the west door had been blocked except for access to the tower and to the fire engine house and 'dead house' beneath it on either side. Entry to the church itself was via a porch in the north-west corner.

The story is told of a Sunday in 1831 when the water came up so quickly that the worshippers had to be rescued by boat. Among them was a lady noted for her tight purse strings. She was told by her rescuers that unless she paid

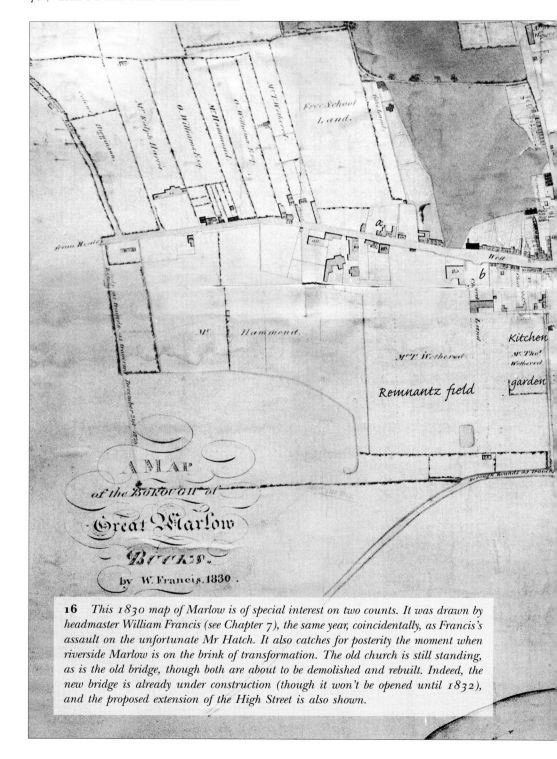

Kitchen

garden

*Remnantz field*

**16** *This 1830 map of Marlow is of special interest on two counts. It was drawn by headmaster William Francis (see Chapter 7), the same year, coincidentally, as Francis's assault on the unfortunate Mr Hatch. It also catches for posterity the moment when riverside Marlow is on the brink of transformation. The old church is still standing, as is the old bridge, though both are about to be demolished and rebuilt. Indeed, the new bridge is already under construction (though it won't be opened until 1832), and the proposed extension of the High Street is also shown.*

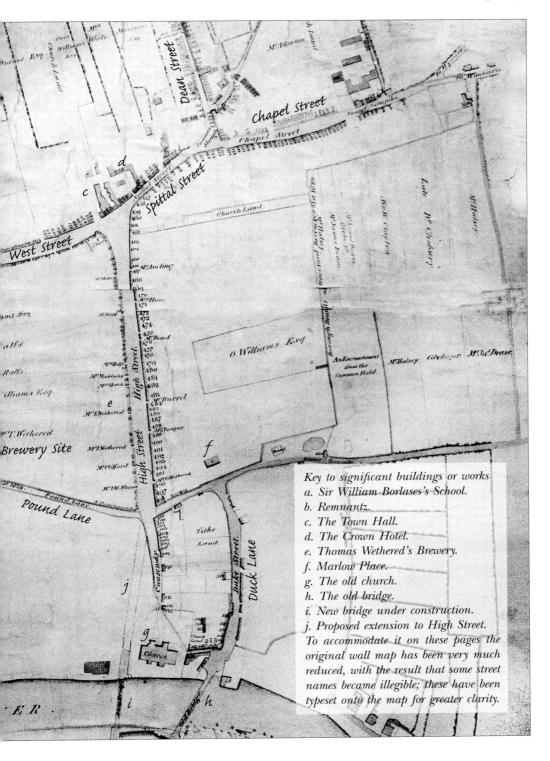

Key to significant buildings or works
a. Sir William Borlases's School.
b. Remnantz.
c. The Town Hall.
d. The Crown Hotel.
e. Thomas Wethered's Brewery.
f. Marlow Place.
g. The old church.
h. The old bridge.
i. New bridge under construction.
j. Proposed extension to High Street.
To accommodate it on these pages the
original wall map has been very much
reduced, with the result that some street
names became illegible; these have been
typeset onto the map for greater clarity.

them a shilling for their trouble they would drop her into the deepest part of the water. She is reported to have paid up.

By 1830, the year Anne came to live in Marlow, the situation was becoming desperate. There was a permanent high-water mark 17 inches up the sides of the box pews, while the church's interior walls were 'extensively cover'd with green vegetation'. These were the observations of James Savage, the architect called in by the churchwardens. In his view the building was not worth saving. Why spend £3,200 – the cost of raising it above flood level – when for another £2,000 the parish could have a new, a bigger and a better church? He thoughtfully submitted some plans to show what he meant.

Savage had made a name for himself as the architect of St Luke's, Chelsea and St James's, Bermondsey, but for some reason his plans for a new All Saints', Marlow, were not accepted. The church that began building in 1832, after Parliament had approved the raising of the money, was designed by Charles Frederick Inwood and cost £15,654. 'Modern Gothic' in design, it was built of brick dressed with Bath stone and, when completed in 1835, looked – in contemporary prints at least – more like a mausoleum than a church. There was no chancel; that and the steeply pitched roof and 170-foot spire came later.[2] A short spire at the west end was balanced by four needle-like pinnacles at the east. Inside, a gallery supported by iron columns ran round the side and west walls. When the present 'Father' Willis organ was installed in 1876 the pipes projected through the gallery floor, 'offering tempting places for the deposit of nutshells and similar trifles to the rising generation in the adjoining pews'.[3]

But if Mr Inwood's building fell short of being an architectural masterpiece it was well enough liked by the people who mattered. It was, said one writer, 'with infinite good nature, greatly admired by the inhabitants'. It opened for business on 2 June 1835, with a service of confirmation conducted by the Bishop of Lincoln.[4] The White House guests on that occasion were Owen's sister Elizabeth and her husband Florance Thomas Young. Remnantz too had visitors who were brought along for the service. It was a beautiful day, and when the church doors opened a little after two, 'the rush for admittance was very great'. Anne put the congregation at 2,000, but it is hard to see how the building could have held much more than a quarter of that number. According to her, the vicar, Mr Thomas Tracy Coxwell, read his portion of the service 'in a most impressive style and uncommonly well, [but] in consequence of the extreme heat & crowd' the Wethereds did not stay for the bishop's address.

What was really worrying Anne as they emerged into the June sunshine was what would happen the following Sunday when the allocation of pews – 'that unpleasant business', as she called it – took place. 'I must own,' she confided to her diary when it was all over,

> I went to Church this morning rather fearing a gt. Confusion for the pews being allotted to the different families at a time so extraordinary. Of course all wd. not be satisfied, probably very few, as it wd. be impossible for 2 persons (Mr Gibbons & Mr Barnes Ch. Wardens) to please a whole congregation; however … the Rem. Family & we had every reason to be pleased for we were shewn into the seats we wished for.

Clearly Messrs Gibbons and Barnes knew where deference was due, and where it was not.

For the three years while the church was under construction, services had been held in a building in Oxford Lane used for the making of satin stitchwork. It was not really big enough for Mr Coxwell's flock, some of whom had taken to worshipping at the Methodist or Congregational chapels. In his sermon that Sunday Mr Coxwell expressed the hope that they would now return to the Established Church, and no doubt a number of them did so. For the Dissenters, although no longer barred from holding public office, still chafed under considerable restraints. As late as 1861 Owen Wethered, as treasurer of the Marlow almshouses, had to refuse an application from a Dissenter because occupation was restricted to members of the Church of England. The applicant was the widow of a respected builder, George Reading, and the incident provoked some indignant letters in the local press. But, as Anne remarked to her husband, 'You must look to the poor of the Church first.'

With the completion of the new bridge and the church beside it, Marlow lost forever the quaint rustic look of the pre-1832 prints. The old wooden bridge had been downstream of the church and the view was usually from that side, showing the weir, the squat church tower with its wooden spire sprouting from behind some thatched cottages and, in the foreground, a couple of yokels pausing for a chat. It was an idyllic scene, but the impression it gave of a sleepy riverside town where no one was in any hurry cannot have been accurate for many years, if indeed it ever was. Long before the 1830s Marlow was a bustling town with its twice-yearly fair, its own well attended race course, and several local industries including paper and copper mills and a thriving river trade.

The grain that made the Wycombe area 'the bread basket of London' was brought to Marlow for its journey down the river. Hence Daniel Defoe's famous assessment of Marlow in 1708 as 'a town of great embarkation on the Thames, not so much for goods wrought here (for the trade of the town is chiefly in bone lace) but … particularly a very great quantity of malt and meal is brought hither from High Wickham.' We can suppose that much of the 'malt and meal' was on its way to the emerging London breweries. The *posse comitatus* of 1798 lists 27 bargemen living in the town (even though one is described as lame and another subject to fits) and a further eight in the outlying parish, as well as three bargemasters. The population then was something over three thousand; by the time of the Golden Wedding it was approaching four-and-a-half thousand, and by then the biggest industry was brewing.

In addition there was a flourishing retail sector, with far more traders, one might think, than a small market town could support. Everyone, it seemed, had something to sell. Along the High Street on either side was just about every kind of business, rubbing shoulders with the houses of the gentry. Five of Marlow's eight tailors had their premises there (the other three being in West Street), and four of its eight grocers. There were three boot-and-shoe makers, three braziers and tinners, and two each of bakers, insurance agents, lace makers, drapers and surgeons. The High Street was home to the building trades, with Thomas Corby's brickyard and Theophilus Clifford's stonemason's yard, as well as three joiners and carpenters (two of them also builders), a cabinet maker-cum-upholsterer, and a painter-plumber-glazier.

Jostling for business with all of these were an attorney, a blacksmith, a fruiterer, a confectioner, an ironmonger, a dealer in china and glass, a furniture broker and appraiser (who was also an estate agent and auctioneer), a millwright and brass-and-ironfounder, a pawnbroker, a poulterer, several taverns, and a 'news and billiard subscription room' where you could drop in for a game of billiards or just to read the local newspapers.

For the weekly food shopping, West Street was the place, especially if you happened to live there. Trading there in 1838 were three bakers, three butchers, two grocers, a fruiterer, and one of several shops in Marlow purveying 'groceries and sundries'. You could get a chair made in West Street, or a barrel, a basket, a straw hat, a man's suit, a pair of boots, and almost certainly a lady's dress. There were also two satin stitchers, a saddler, a draper, a shop selling china and glass, an insurance agent, a straw plat dealer, and a printer, in addition to several schools.

Spittal Street on the other side of the Market Place boasted the only bookseller in Marlow. His name was George Cannon and he was also a printer, a stationer and a stamp distributor, in addition to running a circulating library. Further along Spittal Street, before it ran on into Chapel Street, were two butcher's shops, two grocers, a baker, a blacksmith and a boot-and-shoe maker. A Mr J. Creswell was licensed to let post horses.

Chapel Street was the street of boot-and-shoe makers. There were six of them, all cottage businesses to be sure, but, together with the five elsewhere in the town, a reminder that the way we got about then was on foot. A scattering of other shops included a coal merchant and, as we can read above the door of No. 4, a small house facing north up Dean Street, a shop 'Licensed to sell beer by retail and deal in tobacco'.

Dean Street was the poor quarter, but if, as we are told, the police had to walk in pairs with truncheons drawn it must have been at another time, for the town had only one constable, and one for the outlying parish of Great Marlow. The street's few shops were unremarkable except that it had the only tobacco-pipe maker, one Jeremiah Humphreys, and no fewer than six retailers of beer.

What is clear from all this activity is that Marlow in the period 1838-42 was humming with commercial activity of one kind or another.[5] Of course the pattern changed as shops failed or closed for different reasons, and others took their place. Away from the town centre, many were probably no more than the front rooms of cottages, and could even have been seasonal with the trader employed on a farm in the summer months. Bankruptcies were frequent for any number of reasons including bad debts. The 'gentry' were notorious for ignoring their bills.

A traveller back through time would recognise none of the shops that were there in Thomas Wethered's day. But many of the inns and taverns have survived, at least in name, even if rebuilt or resited. Gone now is the *Greyhound* in Chapel Street where the annual dinner for the brewery workers was held, and 'every Tuesday and Thursday evening about five' Samuel Loftin's horse-drawn van would clatter off to Henley. But a pub-crawling visitor from today would find plenty of familiar landmarks. From the *Hare and Hounds* at Redpits he could make his way down to the *George and Dragon* in the Causeway, stopping off at the *Red Lion* in West Street, the *Clayton Arms* in Quoiting Square,[6] the *Ship* and *Coach and Horses* in West Street, the *Cross Keys* in Common Slough (now Spittal Square), the *Chequers* in the High Street, and the *Two Brewers* in St Peter Street. And across the bridge the *Compleat Angler* was in business (*The Anglers* it was then), as was the *Bull* in Bisham.

Standing shoulder to shoulder and dominating the Market Place at the top of the High Street were the town hall and the *Crown Hotel*. It was from the *Crown* that in former times the London Coach would leave every morning, travelling through Maidenhead, Slough and Colnbrook on its way to the *New Inn*, Old Bailey. But now the coach went no further than Maidenhead, where it connected four times a day with the newly built line of the Great Western Railway.[7] The famous broad-gauge track of I.K. Brunel had been opened amid great excitement on Monday 4 June, eight weeks before Thomas's and Sarah's Golden Wedding.

Unfortunately, 'God's Wonderful Railway' got off to an inauspicious start. To begin with, the engines were underpowered and inclined to break down or even leave the track. One hopeful passenger, George Henry Gibbs, arrived at Paddington on 7 July to find the engine derailed and sunk to the axles.

> This led to an accumulation of trains and people and in an attempt to correct the evil another engine got off the line and sank in the same way. The consequence was that many hundreds of people were disappointed and the four o'clock train did not reach Maidenhead till past 10. I was so sick of the sight I made off.[8]

These mishaps notwithstanding, such was the rush that weekend to take the train out from London that by Sunday evening there were no carriages left in Maidenhead to make up the seven o'clock train on Monday morning. Some were hastily assembled and sent on their way down the single track, but without any warning to other traffic on the line. Between Hanwell and West Drayton the engine pulling them collided with a 'ballast carriage' east-bound with a load of gravel. As *The Reading Mercury* told its readers,

> The engine ran against it with such force as to break it to pieces, at the same time throwing the engine with the carriages attached off the line, damaging the engine most extensively, and the three engineers being thrown off by the shock to a considerable distance, without, however, sustaining any severe injuries.

Despite these and many other calamities – some of them much worse – the railways had become the transport mode of choice. No longer need travellers from Marlow endure the jolting four-hour coach journey to London. After a short ride to Maidenhead they could, barring accidents, be in the City in 65 minutes. And there would be other benefits to the town. The Great

Marlow races were expected, at least by *The Reading Mercury*, 'be more fully attended than on any former occasion'. The closeness of the station, the paper predicted confidently, would 'induce vast numbers to visit this beautiful and celebrated Course'.

Whether or not that was the case, it was clear to everyone by now that the age of steam had arrived. Water would soon give way to rail as the freight transport of the future.

Four weeks after the Golden Wedding, on 28 August 1838, Anne gave birth to her fifth child and third daughter. The baby was baptised Sophia, which comes from the Greek word for wisdom. Sophie's remarkable life runs like a plot line through the rest of the 19th century and beyond, but her story must take its place after those of her two big brothers.

# 9

# *Uncle Tom*

He was in fact my great x2 uncle, but my father referred to him as Uncle Tom and that was how he was known in the family. Opinionated, irascible, implacably determined when he needed to be, and in no doubt as to his station in life, he was nonetheless a kindly man at heart and a generous one. 'Blackguard' was a favourite epithet of his. 'The man's a blackguard', Tom would snort if someone had transgressed his code of honour. But for all that, he had a sentimental side, which found expression in the writing of simple little poems and hymns.[1] The many stories that are told about him are like gold dust to the family historian and, as they say in the newspaper world, too good to check, even if that were possible so long after his death.

Born in 1832, the second child and eldest son of his parents, he was named Thomas after his Wethered grandfather and Owen after his father. As a tiny boy his mother found him hard to control (his father had more success with him), although to be fair this seems to have been mainly when he was cutting his teeth. 'He is a remarkably high spirited child,' Anne notes in her diary, 'and will require great firmness in correcting him.' He was just 18 months old at the time. His sister Anne-Maria – A.M. as she was called – was three. Eventually they would be joined by six more girls and four more boys, among them poor Eddy whose head was enlarged and who was subject to fits.

With Thomas and Sarah and the younger members of their family now settled at Remnantz, Owen and Anne were master and mistress of the White House. Owen spent his days working at the brewery, where he and his younger brother Lawrence William were being groomed to take over from their father. Anne's daily routine is confided to her diary:

> It is our wish to be punctual in breakfasting at ½ past 8 o'clock – a thing we have been able to accomplish but seldom. I am almost ashamed to own my idleness has been the cause. The children breakfast at 8 & afterwards come down (A.M. comes down to Prayers) & amuse themselves while we are at b'fast. … After b'fast the two children remain with us till 10 o'clock when Eliza [the Irish nursemaid] comes for them to take them into the garden or up to Remnantz & I go into the kitchen &c. At 11 o'c. when the children come in for their sleep I commence my reading and continue till 12 o'c. from wh. time till 1 o'c. I spend in doing anything wh. requires most to be done; work, writing &c. &c. At 1 o'c. we dine, the servants after us. … In the afternoon various occupations such as receiving visitors, returning calls, writing letters, working &c. afford amusement for me.

**17** *Uncle Tom thanks the voters: an impression by his sister Sophie. Evidently the rioters had dispersed.*

Owen would return home at seven or eight, when he and Anne had their 'tea', the children having gone to bed. Prayers are said at nine 'and the Tray comes in directly after'. At half past ten or so the couple retire to bed. We are left to guess at the contents the tray.

Young Tom was not quite eight when he was packed off to his first boarding school, Rose Hill, near Oxford. Owen and he made the journey by train. The newly built section of the GWR line passed close to Basildon in Berkshire, scene of Disraeli's dalliance with Lady Sykes and now home to Anne's parents, who had taken the splendid riverside property known as the Grotto. By arrangement, the two of them stood on their lawn and waved handkerchiefs to their grandson as his train chugged slowly through the English countryside, giving him plenty of time to respond.

In Oxford the travellers were entertained by Sarah Faussett, two of whose sons, Robert and Tom, were already enrolled at Rose Hill. Sarah, with a younger son, Edward, then drove Tom Wethered to the school in her fly. There the little boy was left, 'not appearing to care at all'[2] Owen spent the night in Oxford, returning to Marlow early the next day.

From Rose Hill Tom went on to Eton where he seems to have done rather better than his uncle Florence. Some of his Latin verse was judged good enough to be 'sent up' to Dr Hawtrey, the headmaster, to be read aloud by him to the school. Next came Christ Church, Oxford, where he matriculated on the same day as the young Charles Dodgson (Lewis Carroll). But whatever pursuits he followed there, they did not include taking a degree. You might say, what would a brewer want with a degree in *Literae Humaniores*?

On 9 September 1856, three years after coming down from Oxford, Tom was married to Edith, daughter of the Rev. Hart Ethelston of Cheetham Hill, near Manchester, and of his wife, Elizabeth, *née* Peel. Elizabeth was second cousin both to Anne Wethered and to her sister Ellen, who had married Owen's brother Florence. To complicate things further, Anne's and Owen's eldest daughter, Anne-Maria, was by now married to the Rev. Francis Peel, a half cousin of the three Peel women.[3] As in the case of the Godfrey-Faussetts, it seems that middle-class families of this sort, once found to be compatible with each other, would often follow one marriage with others. For the daughters of such families, for whom there was no London season and who 'came out' only in their own localities, the opportunities of meeting eligible – and suitable – young men could be limited, especially for those living in small country towns such as Marlow. Any reader of Jane Austen can testify to that.

Perhaps, like Tom's parents, he and Edith spent their honeymoon in the Lake District. They arrived back in Marlow on 4 October. Lawrence William ('Uncle L.W.' to Tom and his siblings) had been invited to dinner that evening to meet the bride. Meanwhile he was a witness to the triumphal homecoming:

> They were met at the other side of the bridge by a large party of the Town's people who took the Horses off the Carriage & ran with it to their door & cheered & sang 'he is a jolly good fellow, etc., etc.' It reminded me of the happy arrival of the previous generation [i.e. Owen and Anne] in 1830 – Bells ringing, cannons & anvils, firing all the evening.

A dramatic enough reception for the heir to the senior partner, you might think. But there was more.

> Poor Tyler the Paralytic was standing near the cannons & received a Galvanic Shock which restored the use of his Paralysed hand and arm – he says he shall never forget Mr T.O.W's wedding!

If any member of the family was to be found acting as catalyst for such a miraculous-sounding healing, it would surely be Tom. But, miracle or not, he was entirely serious about his religion. Tom's God was in his heaven and was, moreover, a Protestant of the Evangelical stripe. Tom's hatred of ritualism may have stemmed in part from a trip to the Continent that he and Edith took in May 1865. While in Brussels, he visited a Catholic church and witnessed a procession where an image of the Virgin, 'all in velvet and gold lace', was carried through the streets. 'A tawdry piece of goods', he wrote scornfully to his mother. Conversely, the attitudes of the worshippers impressed him greatly: their devoutness, and the fact that 'poor *men*' (his emphasis) as well as women attended church on weekdays. 'Sometimes you may see poor old creatures going up to the moneybox in the church and throwing in their mite, unsolicited, quietly and without ostentation.'

Unfortunately, the issue of ritualism was rising to the top of the Church's agenda. Three years later, in 1868, a harvest festival procession at Haydock in Lancashire caused *The Times* to thunder:

> [The Ritualists] imagine it a sign of life in the Church of England that a party in it is no longer contented with prayers and preaching, but has ventured suddenly to put forth processions, with crucifers and 'fathers' and 'priors', figures of patron saints, banners of the Blessed Sacrament, banners of ST CUTHBERT and ST JAMES, banners of the Holy Spirit, titles and initials which suggest inscriptions of Odd Fellows' Lodges over public house doors …

Tom's anti-ritualist convictions may have hardened at this time. They were to be vented years later, when the then vicar, the unfortunate John Light, stepped over the line (as Uncle Tom saw it) between what was and was not acceptable practice in Marlow.

For many years Marlow, with its two Parliamentary seats, had been virtually a pocket borough of the Williams family. It was in 1788 that Thomas Williams sr. bought the copper mills at Temple, and in 1790 he and one William Lee Antonie were returned for Marlow following nearly forty years of domination by the Claytons of Harleyford. Antonie, a Liberal like the Claytons, was related to the Lees of Hartwell. He held the seat for just one Parliament and in 1896 transferred his allegiance to Bedford, leaving the way clear for the Williamses.

Thomas Williams and his son Owen, then Owen and his business partner Pascoe Grenfell – notwithstanding that he was a Reformer – between them retained both seats until 1820, when Grenfell stood down in favour of Owen's son, Thomas Peers Williams. For the next 11 years, until 1831, these two represented Marlow in the House of Commons. But on Owen's death it was the turn of the Claytons once more, and in 1832 Colonel William Robert Clayton, a Liberal, was elected along with T.P. Williams. It was Thomas Wethered's support of both these candidates that so infuriated Mr William Francis.

From then on until 1868 it was a question of who would come second to T.P. Williams in the polls. Clayton hung on until 1841 when he squeaked in just one vote ahead of his Conservative opponent, Renn Hampden. When it appeared that that vote – among others presumably – had been bought, he was unseated on a petition and Renn Hampden returned. However, the evidence before the election commission revealed that the Williams cupboard, too, had its skeletons.

> It showed that the Williams family let their houses at uneconomic, and in some cases almost certainly fictitious, rents to qualify voters. The influence of the Williamses, the largest landlords in the constituency, was backed by that of the Wethereds, the brewers, and far and away the town's largest employers. Indeed, had it not been for the Wethereds, who took over the costs from a financially exhausted Hampden, the petition would never have been pressed to a successful conclusion.[4]

Did the Wethereds know what was going on? Assuredly they did. It was how the system worked.

In 1847 Hampden was replaced by another Conservative, Colonel Brownlow Knox, a cousin of T.P. Williams. Together these two held the constituency through four further elections, right up to 1868. By then, under the Reform Act of 1867, Marlow's representation had been reduced from two seats to one.

If the Conservatives were to hold the remaining seat they needed someone who would appeal to a new breed of voter – the tradesman, the artisan, the religious dissenter – in an electorate that had virtually doubled. It was Lord Derby's 'leap in the dark', and there was cause for worry. The Liberals had put

# 10

# *OPW and the Call to Arms*

The anarchist's bomb that narrowly missed killing Napoleon III and his empress outside the Paris Opera on 14 January 1858 had repercussions in Marlow and on the Wethered family, as well as on relations between Britain and France. The would-be assassin, an Italian named Felice Orsini, was known to have connections in England, and the bomb, it was alleged, had been made in Birmingham. Anger on the part of the French was matched by apprehension on the part of the British. France had been expanding her army and navy; the latter with steam-driven, iron-clad warships, more advanced than anything in the British fleet. The invasion scare, though not on the scale of the 'Great Terror' of 1803, was nonetheless real in the public imagination. At that time Thomas had donned a volunteer's uniform.[1] Now it was to be the turn of his grandsons.

In 1858, due partly to calls on the army occasioned by the Indian Mutiny, Britain's defences were in a weakened state. The response of Lord Derby's Government – apparently unperturbed by French sabre rattling – was to sanction the formation of Volunteer Rifle Corps, to be raised in each county by the Lord Lieutenant.

As in the case with the Military College, the Volunteer movement was not without its critics. The harshest was the Duke of Cambridge, who had succeeded his brother the Duke of York as Commander-in-Chief of the army. Volunteer soldiers to his way of thinking were 'a very dangerous rabble', which, he protested, 'would ruin our army' Down at the local level, Colonel Brownlow Knox, one of Marlow's two M.P.'s, also had his reservations. He believed the idea might founder because 'we are to have a change of government'. (The new Prime Minister was to be Lord Palmerston, up to this point no admirer of Volunteers.) He also grumbled about the expense involved. But since the Volunteers themselves were to bear the cost of their uniforms and equipment, the Government was in a win-win situation. Public fears would be quietened at no expense to the taxpayer. The all-important rifles were to be loaned by the Government.

Colonel Knox aired his opinions at a meeting on 13 June 1859 to discuss the feasibility of a Marlow corps. The twenty or so local gentry gathered in the National Schoolroom included the Crimea veteran Colonel George Higginson, the vicar of Marlow Mr Frederick Bussell, Mr G.H. Vansittart of Bisham, and Lawrence William Wethered. Owen Wethered was in the chair, and Tom, his eldest son, acted as secretary. Tom read out a letter he had received from the Lord Lieutenant, Lord Carrington, expressing qualified approval: volunteers must come forward in sufficient numbers, and the establishment of the corps must be agreed at a public meeting.

Tom's younger brother Owen Peel (known to later generations as OPW) was also present. Like Tom he had attended Eton and Christ Church, Oxford, and had come down the previous year with a pass degree. He was twenty-two. *The South Bucks Free Press* 'believed' that it was these young brothers who had pressed for the meeting (Tom at this time was twenty-eight). Perhaps Knox was irritated by the presumption of such whippersnappers. In his view it was the seaboard counties that would most require defending in the event of attack. Let them take the initiative in forming the rifle corps, and if necessary, at a later date, the inland counties could follow and have the benefit of their experience.

It seems likely that by this time OPW was already drawn to the idea of military service. And the evidence of Lord Carrington's letter suggests that the family as a whole was in favour of raising a corps. Supported by his father, his uncle and his elder brother, young Owen was not to be intimidated by Knox. Some seaboard counties had already taken the initiative, he said. And in any case, these days the railways made it possible to move large numbers of men to wherever they were needed in a very short time. He did not think Marlow should lag behind in so important a cause.

The argument went back and forth, with Knox being accused of throwing cold water on the project, and him denying it. As a military man of 26 years standing he had merely come to offer the result of his experience. He was not at all opposed to the formation of a rifle corps if only it were practicable … Finally Owen, in the Chair, proposed 'That it is desirable that a rifle corps should be formed in Marlow, for the town and its neighbourhood'. His motion was carried unanimously and a committee was nominated to take the matter forward.

Owen was not the only Wethered to find himself chairing a meeting as a result of the bomb. The Honorable John Wethered (1809-88), a Congressman from Maryland's Third District, was with an American delegation in Paris when the attempted assassination took place. Two weeks later they assembled at the Hotel du Louvre for the purpose of framing a congratulatory message to the emperor. John Wethered was appointed to the Chair and the following text (omitting the preamble) was read out and approved:

> Resolved, that we have heard with detestation of the attempt made on the 14th inst. to destroy the lives of the reigning Emperor and Empress of the French. Resolved, that we express our congratulations at the escape which, under Providence, has been accorded to their Majesties from the terrible danger to which they were exposed.
>
> Resolved, that the chairman of this meeting be requested to communicate these resolutions, so that they may be made known to their Majesties.

So John conveyed to the emperor the Americans' pleasure at the failure of the assassination attempt – an attempt that his cousins across the Channel might very well have wished had succeeded.

The congressman was part of the Wethered diaspora, which by the early 18th century had begun to settle in the United States. He and his brother James Sykes Wethered were Quakers and ran a successful woollen-milling business in the small town of Wetheredville (since renamed Dickeyville) at the north-west corner of Baltimore. James was the compiler of a little book, brought out in 1898, called *The Wethered Genealogy*, which traces that branch of the family back to the Wethereds of Ashlyns in Berkhamsted.[2]

John's wife Mary was a friend of Dolley Madison. It must have been a close friendship because when, on 24 May 1844, the widow of the former President was invited by Samuel Morse to send the first ever personal message by his newly invented electric telegraph, it was to Mrs Wethered that she sent it. 'Message from Mrs Madison', came across the wires from Washington to Baltimore. 'She sends her love to Mrs Wethered.'

L. Wethered Barroll tells us that John was in England in 1860, but there is no record of his visiting the family in Marlow. It was left to OPW to take up with the Baltimore Wethereds, but that was much later in this history.

The public meeting required by the Lord Lieutenant was held on 18 August with Owen again in the chair. In the meantime the committee had met and had outlined some conditions for service. Each man on joining would contribute £3 8s. towards the cost of his equipment, the balance to be raised by private subscription. In certain exceptional circumstances (hardship cases presumably) the cost could be met from the general fund. The annual subscription would be 20s. Personal donations of more than £55 had already been received.

A motion was put by Colonel Higginson and carried unanimously:

> That so soon as the number of Volunteers amounts to thirty, the Secretary [Tom Wethered] be requested to put himself in communication with the Lord Lieutenant of the County, with a view to their immediate embodiment as a Sub-Division.

Lengthy bureaucratic procedures, including acceptance by the Secretary of State for War, meant that it was not until 8 December 1859 that the men could be sworn in by Owen Wethered, JP. Nevertheless Marlow was the first of the five Bucks Volunteer Corps to be initially enrolled, the others being High Wycombe, Buckingham, Aylesbury and Slough. Those in the county's southern tier, including Marlow, were organised as the 1st Buckinghamshire Battalion.

The Volunteers' uniforms were dark grey with red facings, their heads being adorned with plumed shakos, later changed to spiked helmets. In Marlow the uniforms were made by a Mr Stockbridge in the High Street and cost £2 5s. each. Before the drill hall in Institute Road was opened in 1887, the men mustered in a small room at the bottom of the east side of the High Street. Drill was held every weekday evening, and in addition the men were expected to attend six company drills and three battalion drills a year.

The infant Marlow corps comprised 33 members and was commanded by Lieutenant G. H. Vansittart, with Tom Wethered as ensign. OPW enlisted as a private. He was to serve in the Bucks Rifle Volunteers for more than thirty years, rising through the ranks to become their Honorary Colonel. He left a brief but lively memoir of those years, which has been extensively drawn on for histories of the Volunteer Movement.[3]

In addition to their drills the Volunteers were mustered for an annual inspection. In 1860 the Marlow corps, still numbering fewer than forty, were inspected by Colonel Higginson. The mayor of Maidenhead, himself a Volunteer, also attended. At the dinner afterwards the mayor gave a rousing speech on the importance of the Volunteer force, which, he said, 'would safeguard our liberty and make despots tremble'.

That the 1st Bucks RV had not yet reached such awe-inspiring heights is well illustrated by OPW:

> The word 'discipline' was of course known to us, but its application in a military sense was a sealed book to us all. We had no staff sergeants, no adjutant to enlighten us; and we amateurs had to grope our way by the sole aid of common sense ... The officers were mortally afraid of offending their men, many of whom were of equal social standing with themselves. I well remember that soon after we commenced our nightly drills, my brother came to my home one evening on his way to drill and said, 'Look here, Owen, I notice that when I give the word "Fall In", many of the men fall in with their pipes in their mouths. Now I'm sure that *can't* be right, so I want you to fall in tonight with *your* pipe in your mouth. I shall then pitch into you, and after that I can blow up anyone else who does it.' The above ruse was duly carried out – I was roundly pitched into – and after that evening pipes were duly pocketed at the "Fall In".

Captain Mainwaring would have recognised the script. The Volunteers went on to confound their critics by their enthusiasm and eventually by their effectiveness, and as the renamed Territorials won honours in both world wars, even if not quite in the way that the Mayor of Maidenhead imagined.

In 1865 the Volunteers started going into camp for a few days each summer. The weather then was as unreliable as it is now, the worst year being 1879 when the whole 1st Bucks Battalion, more than five hundred strong, were camped by the river at Bourne End. The men were woken in the early hours by a violent thunderstorm, which inundated the field, soaking food, clothing and equipment. They were rescued by a Good Samaritan in the person of Alfred Gilbey, who rode over from his home at Wooburn House to see if he could help.[4] With OPW (now a lieutenant-colonel and the commanding officer), this excellent man moved half the men into his own barn and then got another barn and a schoolroom opened up for the other half. They then roused the local bakers and maltsters – anyone with a kiln or oven that would help dry the equipment and stores. The camp was eventually re-sited on higher ground, and continued for an extra two days to make up lost time. And such was the spirit of co-operation of the men that OPW called the 1879 camp 'the making of the 1st Bucks'.

**20**  *Officers of the 1st Bucks Battalion in camp, June 1867. Tom Wethered and OPW are first and fourth from the left, back row. The man in the top hat is Sir Harry Verney, M.P.*

Public support for the Volunteers – and the number of enlistments – rose and fell according to international tensions at the time. The Balkan Crisis of 1867-78 produced a big jump in enrolment, as did the Sudan Crisis of 1885 following the murder of General Gordon. Interestingly, too, there was a small upward blip in 1882 when work was started on a Channel tunnel. Figures for 1861-1908 (when the Volunteers as such ceased to exist) show the highest peak as 288,476; that was in 1901, during the South African War, when a unit of Volunteers was sent overseas for the first time.

The roll of the Marlow Volunteers is replete with old Marlow names – Habgood, Hobbs, Sawyer, Batting, Tugwood ... and Lunnon. The contribution of the Lunnon family was singularly impressive, especially in the vital area of marksmanship. Obviously this was an important part of the training, and there was keen competition between the various corps. In an 1894 match between No. 1 Marlow Company and two companies of the London Rifle Brigade, Marlow was the winner by 775 to 689 points. First out of ten in the Marlow team was Colour Sergeant R. A. Lunnon; second, Lieutenant T. G. Lunnon; third, Lance Corporal R. H. Lunnon ... and sixth, Lance Sergeant W. Lunnon. It was a famous victory for both the family and the Corps.

But if Marlow and the 1st Bucks had their triumphs, there was one blot at least in the battalion's copybook. Seen from this distance the episode may be good for a laugh, but to OPW, so personally involved, it was 'the only really miserable time that I ever passed as a Volunteer'. In 1875 the Duke of

**21** *Colonel Owen Peel Wethered.*

Buckingham, who had succeeded Lord Carrington as Lord Lieutenant, had been appointed to the governorship of Madras. Before departing he held a grand field day at Stowe Park for all the Volunteer forces under his command. For the southern contingents, which had first to travel by train to London and then up to Buckingham, this necessitated a very early start and a four-mile march at the other end. By the time the field day was over and the men could sit down to a sumptuous meal provided by the duke, it was 4 p.m. and they had eaten nothing for nine or ten hours. OPW writes:

> Naturally, the men, almost before they had taken their seats, poured out tumblers of the first liquid handy, and drank them off at a draft. It was not until they had emptied their tumblers that they realised they had been drinking – not light Claret, as they supposed, but neat *Port* ...

The first hint of trouble came after the speeches, when the duke had been thanked for his hospitality and had departed from the food tent with his guests. The men of the Bucks persisted in singing 'For he's a jolly good fellow', even while the band was rather pointedly playing 'Home Sweet Home', OPW continues:

> I shall never forget the march down the long Stowe Avenue, and I trust that I shall never see such a sight again. Man after man staggered to the roadside where they lay like logs – and for these we impressed farm wagons in which they were conveyed to the station like corpses. Many others could just keep their feet, and for these we detailed men to help them along. At least half the Battalion were out of the ranks, either incapable or helping along 'incapables', so that our march through the streets of Buckingham was the reverse of 'Triumphal'.

That night he wrote a very apologetic letter to the duke. The following week he attended special parades of every company in order to explain what he called the 'extenuating circumstances'. He concludes, rather touchingly: 'It speaks volumes for the good sense and kindly feeling of Buckinghamshire that the fiasco of Oct. 6th 1875 has never once been thrown in our teeth.'

Richard Plantagenet Campbell Temple Nugent Brydges Chandos, 3rd (and last) Duke of Buckingham and Chandos, was of a very different order from his father, 'the Farmers' Friend', that staunch upholder of the Corn Laws and patron of the young Disraeli. It was in fact the repeal of the Corn Laws and the consequent fall in the value of land that was responsible, in part, for the collapse of the family fortunes. Another reason was the 2nd Duke's free spending, especially on lavish hospitality. It is said that during a week-long visit to Stowe by Queen Victoria, the bailiffs were already present in the house, though disguised as footmen for the occasion.

The 3rd Duke was by contrast a successful man of business, who was able to restore much of his father's losses and bring Stowe back to something like its former grandeur. He held a number of important positions including, to his father's disgust, chairman of the London and North Western Railway. 'That ever a son of mine,' the 2nd Duke was heard to say, 'should have become a clerk in a railway booking office!' Government posts included Lord President of the Council and Secretary for the Colonies. As governor of Madras he organised large-scale relief against the terrible famine of 1876-7.

OPW's letters to the duke show a deference bordering on obsequiousness: 'I have the honour to inform your Grace …,' 'Your Grace's hospitable suggestion that the Officers should dine at Stowe will be warmly appreciated.' Such cap-in-hand language was quite usual then, and would have come naturally to OPW when addressing someone as exalted as the Duke of Buckingham and Chandos. Even so, he could be quite blunt if the need arose: 'I note your Grace's intention to have enclosed £5 for Capt. Landon, which however *was not in the letter*, and has not therefore come to hand.'

That he was corresponding with the duke at all placed OPW – at least in his own estimation – on a level with 'county' folk. When contemplating his retirement 'on doctor's orders' in the late 1880s, he was anxious that his replacement should be someone of 'high county standing'. Hence his reluctance to recommend a certain Captain Cutler for promotion to major, which would have put him in the line of succession. Evidently Cutler lacked the necessary social credentials. It is a curious fact that brewers alone among those engaged in 'trade' did not carry the stigma otherwise associated with it.

County standing aside, OPW was clear that an officer should also be a gentleman: 'I do not think it would answer,' he tells the duke in 1883, 'to promote anyone who is not a gentleman by education and manners to our commissioned ranks … nor do I think the men would like being commanded by any but gentlemen.'

And in the rigid class divisions of the day, OPW considered what he called 'the artisan chap to be the backbone of the Volunteer Force', rather than 'the agricultural (and other) day-labourers'. The latter, he believes, could not reach proficiency with the limited amount of training available to Volunteers, and are best left to the regular army and militia. He forgets, perhaps, that he himself is the direct descendant of a humble husbandman.

OPW retired in 1891 and was succeeded by Lord Addington. In 1908, after much political wrangling, the Volunteer Forces were reconstituted as the Territorial Force under the supervision of the War Office. And in the end it was with the French and not against them that the Volunteers went into action. As two battalions of the Oxford and Bucks Light Infantry the Buckinghamshire men went off to fight in the trenches: along the Somme, and at Ypres and elsewhere. Their casualties were heavy and many were decorated for bravery.

Their descendants showed equal bravery in the Second World War. One example of it was the defence of the Belgian town of Hazebrouck by the reformed 1st Bucks Battalion between 26 and 28 May 1940. By their courage and tenacity they held up the German advance in that sector for a crucial two days, an action that was described in a German broadcast as 'truly worthy of the highest traditions of the British army'.

That war was really their swan song. In 1958, just a hundred years after Orsini's bomb, a further rationalisation took place and the Oxford and Buckinghamshire Light Infantry ceased to exist, at least by that name. With the King's Royal Rifle Corps and the Rifle Brigade, they were formed into the three battalions of the Green Jackets Brigade, since renamed as the Royal Green Jackets.

# 11

# *Sophie's Story*

If Thomas is to be the hero of this history, which he surely must, then his granddaughter Sophia, the fifth child and third daughter of Owen and Anne, must be numbered among the heroines. Sophie's story, told mainly through her unvarnished letters home from India, has many of the ingredients of some Victorian novel: love, tragedy, pathos, saving grace, and a justly felicitous resolution. There is no villain, at least not a human one; that role is played by the malign actions of fate. As with her elder brothers Tom and OPW, enough has been written by and about her to form a pretty fair picture of what she and her life were like.

Sophie's birth just four weeks after her grandparents' Golden Wedding would have made her 11 years old by the time Thomas died in 1849. Her memories of this essentially 18th-century man must have remained with her throughout her long life, until her own death in 1920. How one wishes that this fluent and impressionable writer had committed some of them to paper. But Sophie was a reporter, not an historian. Nor, as far as we know, did she keep a journal. Her diary is in her sprightly letters and in the talented and often amusing paintings and sketches that she did on her many travels.

We know little of her growing up except that she shared a bedroom, and most likely a bed, with her favourite sister Georgina, 19 months younger than herself. She would have been 18 or so when Owen's family moved into Remnantz after the death of Sophie's grandmother Sarah in June 1856. A badly faded photograph shows the young people playing croquet on the lawn, while an archery target stands nearby. Not surprisingly Sophia loved the house, to the point where, to please her, her soldier husband named his horse Remnantz, no doubt to the amusement of his brother officers.

This charming but poignant description of how the two of them met at an evening party is a later insert by Sophie in her aunt Anne Allen's diary entry for 10 January 1856:

> Captain Fenwick, home from India, was the hero of this little dance, admired by all especially by my sixteen year old self & others. Four years after, when I became Mrs Percival Fenwick, this little party was called 'The Shoe Dance' because while dancing with me, in the thick of a waltz it seems I said, 'Stop a minute, my shoe is coming off.' This casual remark, in the following years, kept sounding

in his ears in Burmah & wherever he went till he felt impelled to come home for some thing more – all too happy & too short.[1]

By the time she wrote this postscript in her aunt's diary, Sophie was home from India and a widow. Percy Fenwick had been born in June 1820, making him 17 years older than Sophie. His family home was in Falmouth in Cornwall. Percy's father, a retired lieutenant-colonel and former governor of Pendennis Castle, had died when Percy was ten, and it was his widowed mother who brought him up. In 1838 she managed from her slender means to scrape together the £450 needed to buy him a commission in the army. Now Ensign Fenwick, he joined the 69th Foot, which was to be his regiment for the rest of his career. Promotions followed but at considerable cost to himself: lieutenant in 1840, £250, captain in 1846, £1,100, major in 1857, £1,400. By the time of his marriage to Sophie in 1861, Percy was a lieutenant-colonel (£1,300), a veteran of several foreign stations and with a magnificent set of mutton chop whiskers. Now he was to command the garrison at Fort St George, Madras.

There could have been difficulties about Sophie's marrying Percy and accompanying him back to India. Memories of the 1857-8 Mutiny and its horrors were everywhere fresh in people's minds. In Marlow, OPW had been treasurer of a fund for the families of victims. But luckily for Sophie, there was a precedent. In July 1859, the month the war was officially declared over, her tall and beautiful sister Sarah Elizabeth had accepted a proposal of marriage from their cousin William Godfrey-Faussett. 'Willy' was the second son of Godfrey ('the dearest and best of men') and his Sarah, widowed in 1853.[2] A major in the 44th Foot, he had served with that regiment in India and was expected to return there. On the day after Sarah Elizabeth's agreement to marry him, he had gone to Owen to seek paternal permission. The following is from the diary of Willy's sister – alas, also named Sarah – for 27 July 1859:

> He went after breakfast to Remnantz to see Uncle Owen – he did not come back to luncheon so hoped all was right, but by the by Mama told me that he was walking alone in the kitchen garden so I went out to look for him in a horrid fright – asked if he had had a satisfactory interview with Uncle O. 'Anything but', said he – it seems he objects decidedly to her going to India, and as Willy knew of nothing else to do he was afraid it must be given up and was in most melancholy mood. I went afterwards to Sarah [Elizabeth] & we groaned together on the untoward state of the affair.

We know nothing of the tears and entreaties that may have followed, but it seems that Owen finally relented. The diary entry for 1 August reads: 'Uncle O. gave consent to a regular engagement.' The wedding took place on 26 January 1860. However, to her family's undoubted relief, it was not until September 1862 that Sarah and their baby boy joined Willy in India. The 44th had been ordered to China where an invasion force of 20,000 troops was engaged in fighting near Tientsin. The men of the 44th arrived too late to take part, but by the time they had been re-routed to Belgaum in south-west India, Percy and Sophie had been in Madras for nearly a year.

**22** *The Colonel and his Lady — Percy and Sophie Fenwick.*

Sophie and Percy were married in All Saints' church, Marlow, on 16 July 1861. Sophia's uncle Florence, vicar of Hurley, conducted the service as he had for Sarah and Willy 18 months before. The bride's younger sisters again acted as bridesmaids along with two Aldridge cousins, daughters of their aunt 'Gena'.

According to the *South Bucks Free Press* Sophie wore a dress of a rich white silk with a veil of Brussels lace. Head dress fashions had changed in the last quarter century: no cottage bonnet for Sophie, but a wreath of orange blossoms, lilies of the valley and jasmine on her red-gold hair. She was given away by her father, anxious though he must have been at losing now a second daughter to the uncertainties of life in India.

Lined up along the walk as the couple left the church were children from the church schools, boys on one side, girls on the other, the girls strewing flowers before them as they passed by. Later, every school child in Marlow was 'gratified with a large bun'. There was a reception at Remnantz with the town's brass band playing outside. And there was a dinner party and ball given that night by Uncle L.W., the bachelor Lawrence William whose home now was the Old House in the High Street.

The days were long gone when a female member of the bride's family would travel with a couple on their honeymoon. During the time they spent at

Ross-on-Wye, Sophie and Percy had only each other, which was all the company they needed. (Their first act on the morning after their arrival was to buy a sketchbook for Sophie to record their wanderings.) But hers was a close and affectionate family, and Sophie was grateful to Georgie and OPW the following October when they braved a rain-swept crossing from Folkestone to Boulogne to start the couple on their month-long journey to India. When they parted from each other at the station in Boulogne, Sophie could hardly believe that the parting might last for years.

Continuing on their overland journey through France, they reached their hotel in the rue de Rivoli in Paris at ten that evening. There, in their room, they fortified themselves with provisions they had brought with them: hard-boiled eggs, sherry (remembering to toast the families at home), and biscuits supplied by Aunt Anne. Downstairs, a ball was in progress; the high-spirited Sophie wanted to waltz in the corridor but Percy managed to dissuade her.

To Sophie's delight there was a letter waiting for her from her sister Sarah. She was soon snatching every spare moment to write her own letters home, including time in the morning before she left her bed. With no adjoining room for Percy to dress in, it was necessary for him to dress first and then disappear so that Sophie could do the same.

They had arrived in Paris on 22 October and were to leave for Marseilles on the 27th. Everything was new and exciting, but in four days of sightseeing there was too much to take in, let alone attempt to describe. In a letter to Georgie she merely listed the sights they had visited, 'for the benefit of those who had seen them': Notre Dame, Ste Chapelle ('which was lovely'), St Etienne, the Pantheon, Gobelin tapestries, and the zoo in the Bois de Boulogne ('I wished the children were all here'). She could do no more than window-shop in the Palais Royal because, as Bobby Fearnley-Whittingstall notes, Percy wisely took her there in the evening when the shops were closed. As much as anything, it seems, she admired the brightly-lit dining room in the Hotel du Louvre, with its scurrying waiters, each 'with a certain number of people to attend to, so that everyone gets [the food] directly, steaming hot'. It is a sad reflection on English hotel catering at the time.

Sophie's 'last words from Europe', probably written in Marseilles, carried a message of reassurance to her mother. 'Percy takes the greatest care of me,' she writes, 'and doesn't let me do too much – dear Man. I like him better every day – I never thought there was such a man out of the family.' Her next thoughts are for her father – a natural transition given her affection for them both and the 17-year gap between her and Percy. At 63 Owen was not well, suffering from what the family called neuralgia but was really diabetes, an excruciatingly painful disease if acquired late in life and before the discovery of insulin. The last Sophie had seen of him he was lying on a sofa, following her with his eyes as she left the house. She would not see him again.

She ends her letter 'with 50 kisses to you and Papa, AM, G, O ...' and all the family, which included, as an honorary member, Tyler, their much loved nurse. Offering or demanding an abundance of kisses was a Sophie trademark over the years. 'I want a thousand kisses', she was remembered as saying as she gathered some small niece or nephew into her arms.

On the morning of the 28th, a Monday, Percy and Sophie 'got up at five o'clock by candle light, put up our things, had coffee & bread & butter in our room, paid our [hotel] bill, drove off – glad to get away'. At the quayside they and their luggage were put into a little boat and rowed across the busy harbour to the paddle steamer *Valetta*. Sophie was delighted with their cabin, which was 'not big, certainly, but very cosy [with] two little white beds, not one over the other but on different sides ... I have chosen the lower bed as the higher one is back to the horses.' Even in the cabin the proprieties were kept to; indeed, there can scarcely have been room for two people to dress at the same time.

Among their travelling companions were a Major and Mrs Drury, who were also on their way to Madras and were to become good friends, and a Bishop Gell and his unmarried sister. The bishop, whom Sophie judged to be about thirty-five, was 'a very tall thin man, looking very much as if he had been drawn through a keg hole' (a good choice of simile for a brewer's daughter). At sea, when bad weather struck down many of the passengers, the bishop looked 'as if he had been buried and dug up'. But he had recovered enough by the next day, a Sunday, to take a church service on deck, which Sophie found 'all very nice'.

Sophie had told her mother, 'I don't dread the voyage in the least and don't expect to be ill.' Unfortunately she was proved wrong, partly no doubt because by then she was two months pregnant. And there were to be other unpleasant surprises:

> After having undressed, a most distressing process in my state of sea sickness, with the ship rolling from side to side, wind roaring & thunder & lightning &c., & laid down on my berth & half closed my eyes hoping for sleep – when I fancied I saw something black creeping up the wall close to me. I started up, gave a frantic grab at my friend – with my handkerchief – gave him a squeeze & flung him to the other side of the cabin (as Georgie can imagine me from frequent beetle fights) ... On recovering, look where I might there was one of these horrid cock roaches, as Percy was obliged to confess them to be. They are the length of beetles, half as wide & hundreds of legs ...

Poor Sophie! However, she 'finally yielded to Percy's persuasions to shut my eyes & think about something else – since then I have lost my very great horror of them.' She did not feel well enough to go ashore when the *Valetta* anchored for a few hours in her home port in Malta, but she was cheered by the bouquets of red and white roses that Percy brought back for her and Mrs Drury. He also bought Sophie 'a lovely Maltese broach [*sic*] & a Maltese lace veil'. Percy had been stationed in Malta for two years and 'he knew where there was no cheating'.

Early on the morning of 4 November the *Valetta* entered Alexandria. Here the passengers disembarked, 'without many regrets', to begin a three-day journey by train, two steamers and horse-drawn 'desert carriages' to Suez. Offsetting the undoubted discomforts of this Overland Route was a saving of several weeks over the sea passage round the Cape of Good Hope. For the Suez Canal, which was under construction, would not be opened until 1869.

Not yet fully recovered from her seasickness, Sophie nevertheless found herself 'in a continual state of wonderment' at the sights and sounds that met her as she and Percy prepared to be driven to the hotel that would be their base for the morning:

> My breath was quite taken away by the swarms of Arabs & blacks of every description, all yelling & fighting & scrambling to get the passengers' things to carry to the Omnibuses and vehicles wh. stood near ... they regularly forced some of the people into their carriages – a great many went on donkeys, such pretty ones there are there. Percy knew how to manage the people & soon got me safe in & we rattled off at such a rate & such a jogging thro' the streets of Alexandria ... our turbaned Jehu keeping up a continual jabber in his highest key to clear the way.

Before leaving Alexandria they had time for a quick tour of the city, taking in the narrow streets and open shop fronts, the Pasha's Palace with 'its grand state apartment', and the 25-metre obelisk known as Pompey's Pillar.[3] Then, 'feeling all the better', she was 'able to eat a good substantial dinner (11 a.m.) & drink a considerable amount of champagne'.

One cannot always rely on Sophie's estimates of elapsed time. But it seems they left Alexandria at about noon and reached the Nile by train and canal boat – 'little naked boys rushing after us on the banks to catch the occasional fish we washed up' – at nine that evening. Once in their steamer, which they boarded by torchlight, they were offered coffee without milk and, according to Sophie, 'made with water taken straight out of the Nile'. The food on board was no better: 'awful stuff – stewed camel &c. we are convinced it was.' Nor was poor Sophie in for a comfortable night:

> There was a saloon below but they said it was so fearfully close, every inch of the floor even being covered with people for the night, that I did not attempt to go down. So we laid down on deck & Percy covered me well over with rugs, & Major Wilkinson, rather a nice man, lent me an air cushion for my pillow ... In the middle of the night Major W., thinking my feet were come untucked, took the rug & wrapped them (as he thought) up very carefully – when to his surprise an unfortunate man's head rose up instead of my feet, thinking someone was trying to suffocate him. We weren't sorry when the morning came.

They reached Cairo at about five-thirty in the afternoon and 'drove to the Hotel [Sheppard's?] through wonderful Eastern scenes, just as you would fancy it was in Bible times'. Percy had telegraphed ahead for a room. It was a relief to sleep in a bed again, the last time having been in Marseilles. After an early night they were on their way again by eight-thirty next morning for a three-and-a-half-hour drive through the desert. Two stops for refreshment were made along the road, when 'cheese and hard biscuits' were available for the passengers, but Sophie preferred to lunch on the seemingly inexhaustible supply of biscuits provided by the good Aunt Anne.

At Suez, a party of French people who had joined them in Marseilles now embarked separately for Mauritius. Sophie was thankful she was not going with them – 'they make such a row'. The passengers bound for Madras were taken aboard the SS *Candia*.

When the *Candia* was put up for sale in 1874 she was described by her owners, the P. & O. Steam Navigation Company, as 'specially worth notice, either as a first-class steamer of great speed, or for conversion into a sailing ship for any trade requiring speed, superior passenger accommodation, and large measurement capacity'. A photograph of her shows a strange, elongated vessel, with a bowsprit, three masts, and a funnel sticking up incongruously in the middle. The age of steam was well advanced by the beginning of the 1860s, but the navy was slow to adopt it. According to James Morris, the 20,000 troops sent to China in 1860 were carried in 173 old-style sailing ships.[4]

Sophie was pleased with her new cabin, which was 'quite twice size of the other [and] very clean – two port holes wh. is a great blessing'. She was relieved to see their luggage come aboard, especially the plate chest 'by some miracle, considering it had nothing in the world by way of direction but "Lt. Col. Fenwick". 'A few days later she was reporting, 'We have not seen many Cock roaches ... I shd. expire if we did for here they are about 6 times the size as the others – the hugest Stag beetles they are like.'

On 12 November they put into Aden at the foot of the Arabian Peninsula, to take on mail as well as coal. The Red Sea had produced 'no end of a swell', which sent Sophie back to her bunk. But there were some compensations: 'Captain Hamilton, the Admiralty Agent, is most polite – he has a very large easy chair [in] which he won't allow anyone but us to sit.' Percy would sit beside her on deck reading Kingsley's *Westward Ho!*, evidently his book for the voyage. In 'his thin costume – white boots & turned down paper collars – he looks killing[5] to a degree.' A 'holland jacket & black skirt' were Sophie's response to the hot weather.

Eighteen days after leaving Suez the *Candia* dropped anchor off Madras. The city has no port as such, and in those days had no man-made harbour either. Everything and everybody had to be rowed ashore in boats, their construction described by Sophie as 'very rough – boards sewn together with string to stand the violence of the surf'. Getting into them was 'very dodgy, the swell being so great that unless you put your foot on the edge of the boat in the very nick of time, the next moment it is down in the very depths ...' The boats were run into the shallows and the passengers carried ashore by the Indian crew:

> I rather looked forward to going over the surf, of wh. I had heard so much ... it came about 20 yards from the shore and gave us a delightful top perfectly straight up in the air, then a series of little waves took us on the sand. I thought it was scarcely necessary to be carried out, not relishing the thought. However, it was the easiest thing in the world – three men raised a plank on wh. I seated myself & put my hands on a shoulder & was carried in state on to the dry sand, Percy following in the same way.

They were met on the beach by Percy's adjutant, Captain Blood, who led them up to the esplanade where Mrs Blood was waiting in her carriage. At 22, even younger than Sophie, Mrs Blood was 'very nice, and nice-looking too; tall and dark hair … and he I like very much indeed; talks a good deal'. Between the Fenwicks and the Bloods a strong bond was to be formed.

In the second volume of his trilogy on the British Empire, James Morris has the following description of the oldest British city of the *Raj*:

> At Madras, beyond the Coromandel surf, the British erected the best of all their city skylines, a romantic extravaganza … like a cross between the Kremlin, a story-book Damascus and St Pancras railway station.[6]

The Fenwicks had arrived on 25 November, but Percy's regiment, the 69th, was in Burma, and not due to take up garrison duties at Fort St George until mid-February. Their destination now was Dent's Garden Hotel on the Island, a small delta formed by two arms of the Cooum river, where rooms had been reserved for them and where the Bloods were also staying. To Sophie's eyes, the Island was 'the Hyde Park of Madras – a delightful green place with paths and drives and trees on each side'. The Cooum, she says, 'is a very pretty river & quite answers to the Serpentine'.

> After about 2 miles we turned into a sort of Park gate – up a drive to a very handsome house with Pillars supporting the verandah all round, very unlike an Hotel – till now it belonged to a very rich civilian of the name of Dent.

The Fenwicks' quarters consisted of a drawing room and dining room on the ground floor, the two divided by a screen, and a large bedroom and a dressing room upstairs.

> My little ayah was standing at our bedroom door & impressed me very favourably at once. I had expected to be horrified & quite dreaded seeing her – she is small and very young & has a nice face – all eyes … & looks innocent.

Bobby Fearnley-Whittingstall has accused Sophie of xenophobia, and there is some truth in this. She undoubtedly had an 'irrational fear' of dark-skinned people, especially in the mass. To her, Indian men are 'creatures', and on one occasion 'black bogies'. It should be remembered, though, that she was only 23 and with little or no experience of foreigners of any kind. Nor would she have been immune to her father's anxieties following the Mutiny. Finally, she was a child of her time, when many whites considered themselves different in *kind* from other races, and had no hesitation in showing it.

In the case of the *ayah* – Marie Mootoo was her name – there was the expectant mother's apprehension about entrusting the care of her child to anyone she had not yet met, no matter who she was. But it is clear that Sophie took to her 'little *ayah*' immediately and without reservation. It seems, too, that the liking was returned, although, according to Sophie, this had more to do with her long red-gold hair, which, when unfastened, fell down well below her waist. Marie loved to arrange it for her, making it clear that none of her former mistresses had possessed such luxuriant tresses.

Among the servants assigned to them were a butler, Babo, and an underbutler, Maty. Babo had 'a yellow & white line down his forehead & nose, showing that he is gt. swell of his kind'. At times when they had nothing to do, they – and Marie too – would simply curl up on the floor and go to sleep.

On going up to bed on the first night, Sophie was startled to see 'a heap of white at the foot of the stairs & thought they were table cloths or something, when our two men jumped up all alive and kicking and lighted us up'.

Next morning, after Marie had brought them 'tea and toast & butter, wh. we devoured in bed', and before facing a breakfast of 'fried fish, mutton chops, grilled turkey, muffins and eggs,' Sophie took her morning bath:

> There was no fastening to the door so I asked [Marie] how I was to prevent all the world coming in. She said, 'Me sit on the other side', wh. I find is the correct thing.

That Sophie adored her husband there is no doubt whatsoever. But she was a home-loving girl and, especially in the early days, missed her family dreadfully. Not that she complains of homesickness, but it is there in her letters, in her hunger for their news, which she reads 'again & again', and in the way she tries to imagine what they are all doing at various times of day. ('When you are at bk.fast you can generally imagine us receiving visitors – at your lunch we are just preparing for our evening drive at 5.') All their birthdays are remembered and duly toasted by her and Percy.

Tucked into her luggage are the small last-minute gifts which her family has given her, and which she now unpacks one by one: her mother's work box,[7] AM's 'little collar & cuffs', Frank's[8] quill pens, Owen's and Georgie's 'pleasing addition to my library', Sarah Fausett's smelling bottle, and 'the little bags you all made me for sandalwood to keep out the red ants', and several more. To her, they are 'pleasing remembrances' of a much loved home.

But Wethered women are known for their resourcefulness and tenacity;[9] in her role as Colonel's Lady, Sophie would need plenty of both and she hardly faltered. Just two days after their arrival, she and Percy made the obligatory call on the Governor and his wife. Percy looked 'very charming' in his 'blue undress uniform – dark blue coat, gold buttons & crowns, red sash, white belt round his waist, white trousers, sword, forage cap covered with white'. As for Sophie, 'after some consideration we decided it was a case for the new bonnet'. This she wore with 'Old Nico's green muslin & black lace shawl – for it doesn't do to be outdone by one's husband'.[10] And so they got into their carriage, 'thinking it great games'.

As Governor of the Presidency of Madras, General Sir William Denison was one of the three most important men in India, the other two being the Governor of Bombay and the Viceroy himself. Sir William had come to his present post in the same year, 1861, having previously served as Governor of New South Wales. He was known to be opposed to the advancement of native aspirants to office. The Indians were incapable of governing themselves – the British had much better do it for them.

The Denisons were at their country house four miles from the hotel. Sophie found the drive 'delightful – not too hot and the country very pretty'. She felt a stab of apprehension as the carriage drove through the gates, 'and I began to hope fervently that we shd. not have to do more than leave our cards'.

> Three native servants appeared & said to my relief that Lady D. did not receive visitors till next Monday, so Percy sent in his card to Sir W. D., to whom he wished to speak, & out comes the Aid [*sic*] de Camp to fetch him in & say that Lady D. wd. be also glad to see Mrs Fenwick. So in we went thro' very handsome halls into the drawing room, where her ladyship joined us ... She is not in the least an alarming person to deal with – rather like Mrs Jackson of L. Marlow, only taller, & nice manners. After talking a little, P. went in to see Sir Wm. Denison, who after a space came in to pay his respects to me – and very soon we departed, very glad to have done it.

Of course there were other calls to be made and visitors to be received. 'People are beginning to return the 40 calls that Percy has made', she tells her 13-year-old sister Emmy, '& invitations to dinner &c. come every day.' Among the early callers were Percy's commanding officer, General McCleverty, and his wife. 'They are nice people,' Sophie goes on, 'she a motherly sort of person, & has some nice little girls your age.' She grew to like the McClevertys as much as anyone; she had reason to be grateful to them later on.

A companionable relationship had developed between Sophie and Mrs Blood, and the two women would sit together over their sewing in the morning. If a caller arrived they would hide their work under the sofa cushions and compose themselves for the visitor. On one such occasion Sophie was cutting down the front of her wedding dress for a dance at Government House, while Mrs Blood mended her husband's socks.

The days passed quickly, and 'very pleasantly, for these are holiday times for us till the regiment comes'. Percy had light duties such as attending a court martial, 'to try some Lieut. who was tiresome enough to knock another man on the head'. Mostly, Sophie had him to herself, 'except from 6 to 8, when he goes out – sometimes to the Club to see the papers, or to look at horses to be sold &c.' But there was one evening of excitement when their husbands were dining at the Fort and Sophie and Mrs Blood were on their own:

> At about 10 we heard someone fr. the verandah above calling out in the most imploring frightened voice, 'Captain Blood, Captain Blood', over and over again. So Mrs B. ran outside while I made up my mind they had got hold of a robber, having heard of one being caught hiding under someone's bed here a few days ago. However, it was that Major Kirby (of the 68th) had poisoned himself by mistake, & was groaning away while his wife screamed & shrieked. Mrs B. went up to him while I went and saw that one of the black bogies outside took up some mustard & hot water.

Eventually Percy arrived,

> & went up himself to the man, who it seemed was suffering more from the effects of drinking his toast & water rather too strong than fr. the imaginary poison. So after making him drink a tumbler or two more of mustard & water, he left him better and his wife consoled – we hear it had the desired effect & hope he will profit by the lesson.

The social round continued, with balls ('I danced Quadrilles & Lancers, but fast dances with none but my husband'), receptions ('the A. D. C. took my cloak and asked me if I wd. play or sing, wh. I speedily declined), and the appearance of an Indian prince, of whom, understandably, she did not approve:

> His Turban was set with diamonds & emeralds, his dress yellow satin trimmed with jewels. I was asked to go and be introduced to him but declined the honour. He was sitting in the compound where were 100s of people looking at the juglers [*sic*] who were doing all sorts of absurd & horrid things in the centre. You should have seen the heap of large round pebbles they brought down from their throats – most unmistakably – & quantities of hair pins &c., put swords ¾ yard down their throats, wh. I couldn't bear to look at, & other things.

Most of what we know about Sophie comes from her feelings about others, or her day-to-day reactions to people and events. Once in a while, though, she makes a revealing comment about herself. 'We have come to the conclusion that the temper I warned [Percy] of is a myth', she tells Georgie, who would know the truth of that if anyone did. 'But I tell him to wait till I have occasion – it's not likely that he will ever suffer from it, such a blessed sweet-tempered creature he is. I beg you not to laugh at me, though I know you will.'

That sweet temper manifested itself one morning in late December when, as Sophie informed her mother, 'Percy woke with a twinge in his left foot, wh. he says is gout … I have been waiting, in vain so far, expecting him to get very grumpy, as one hears is usually the case with gouty husbands, but I think the sensation must be [more] pleasant than otherwise, so very agreeable and amiable does he make himself.'

Earlier that month, orders had come through for Percy to go to Rangoon to accompany the 69th back to Madras. For 24 hours there was consternation as Sophie pictured the weeks spent alone. But all was well: the orders were rescinded. In mid-February the regiment arrived as planned, and Percy and Sophie took up their quarters in the fort.

# 12

# *Sophie's Story Continued*

To the north of the city of Madras, now known by its Tamil name of Chennai, is the original settlement of George Town. Founded by the East India Company in 1639, it was the first British toehold on the Indian subcontinent. Work on the fort began the following year, continued unconcernedly through the English Civil War, and was finished in 1653. Both Clive and Wellington had been quartered there during their respective Indian campaigns, and now it was home to Percy and Sophie.

But Sophie had no time for such ancient history, caught up as she was in the excitement of the move. Of their arrival at the fort, she says:

> the difference of atmosphere we found at once most delightful, the sea breeze blowing straight upon us … Marie & I confined our energies to the bedroom – the easy part of the work, arranging about mosquito curtains, pillow cases &c. while Percy and his army [of coolies] managed the furniture & very soon got the drawing room and dining room into shape. The 4 great pillars help a great deal towards furnishing, with much fewer things than such a huge room wd. otherwise require.

The last Governor but one, Sir Charles Trevelyan, had ordered the fort's outer wall on the seaward side to be taken down. Seated on her veranda, Sophie could write letters or make plans for the arrival of her baby while 'being almost blown away by the sea air' and enjoying an uninterrupted view over the Bay of Bengal. By now she is in her sixth month of pregnancy. She has 'a most dreadfully good appetite, & shd. starve before Tiffin [the midday meal] if I did not devour every morning at bk.fast a great mutton chop, an egg & a dish of muffins …' These are served from the electroplated dishes bought with £30 given them by Owen and Anne, and used 'on every occasion, breakfast, lunch & dinner, Percy having an objection to things being kept only for high days & holidays'.

Sophie's housekeeping duties, such as they were, began immediately after breakfast when the butler, Babo, having been to the market for the day's provisions, brought in his account book for her inspection. Not only was he completely trustworthy but, according to her, he wrote and spelt beautifully, 'as well again as an English manservant'. It was the custom for the butler, rather than the lady of the house, to keep the keys to the storeroom and hand out whatever was needed, also to see that there was no wastage on the part of the other servants. It was customary, too, to bring your own servant when going out to dinner, and Babo was adept at securing food for his master and mistress ahead of the other guests' butlers.

Perhaps Babo was too perfect for Sophie's liking, for, perversely, she preferred to be served by Maty, the under-butler. 'He is so delightfully stupid & anxious to do everything right that he never by any chance does it the first time of telling.'

With the coming of the 69th Sophie as well as Percy had regimental duties to attend to. The soldiers' wives formed a 'working class', sewing clothes under the supervision of Sophie and her 'ladies'. Sophie was appointed treasurer and together with Mrs Porter, the 'Scripture Reader's wife', had to price each garment according to the amount of material used. Not yet familiar with annas and rupees, she finds this 'rather a puzzle till Percy comes to the rescue & settles it in no time'.

Within the fort is the church of St Mary's, which is the oldest Anglican church in India and is in use to this day. The vicar in Sophie's time was a Mr Alcock, 'who is rather like Godfrey Faussett and is liked immensely'. It fell to her to accompany him on his parochial visits. 'I expect you would laugh for a month,' she tells her cousin Louisa Aldridge, 'if you saw me going round with him to see the wives & they all bowing & scraping at the "Colonel's Lady" as he will persist in calling me.'

Sophie liked both the vicar and his church, and remarked to Georgie on the numbers that attended: 'everybody as a rule going twice, wh. surprises me, having heard them spoken of as lax in such respects.' In the same letter she reminds her sister of the strict standards of religious self-improvement expected of them by their mother:

> Our Sunday evenings wd. please Mama I always think – as regularly as clockwork after dinner 'Melville's Sermons' are produced & we read one of them together wh. takes till nearly prayer time. I always think how Mama used to say she wished we had a greater taste for sermons. I certainly think I never did such a thing as read one all through before I took the pledge, & won't promise that I should now without somebody to help me.

Sophie shows a commendable reluctance to conform. Just what the pledge committed her to we can only guess at. Certainly it was not abstinence – champagne seems to have been the remedy of choice for most of her ailments.

Her account of the general's Inspection on 8th April 1862 – the last event of importance before her confinement – is notable chiefly for the references to Percy's mount:

> Yesterday eve. at 5 Mrs Blood drove with me to see the Inspection on the Island, where was all Madras collected ... 'Remnantz' & his rider struck me as objects as worthy of observation as anything on the Field, & the former behaved to perfection & everyone who came to talk to us at the carriage were full of his praises – with his green & gold cloth &c. – & the rider went thro' all the arrangements in most approved style & his voice heard by every creature on the Island. The General, after all was over, came & testified his decided approval to me of all that had been done.

On 12 April Sophie gave a dinner party at the Fort. 'The table looked brilliant, she reported, '& the dinner [was] of a most recherché description'. In a 'black net dress & pink & silver wreath &c., & my dear Carbuncle set of things' – a gift, perhaps, from Percy or her parents – she must have made Percy very proud. When the gentlemen rejoined the ladies after dinner, there was music. 'Mrs Wood plays very well indeed & Mrs Blood nicely, & I had to play no end.' At the Governor's reception she had 'speedily declined' to play or sing, but now, and at home, she had no such inhibitions. One senses a new confidence about her as she grew into the various roles expected of her – wife, first lady, and very soon the role of mother.

Sophie's baby was born on 23 May. She had known intuitively that it would be a girl, and some weeks before had spelled out the name *May* in pins on her pincushion. She was attended by a Dr Gordon, a physician attached to a nearby hospital, and by her friend Mrs Wood, who appears to have been a professional *accoucheuse*, attending other ladies as well. In a letter headed 'Private for the Dear Mother', Sophie begins an account of the birth, before remembering her sisters and adding the words, 'only for selected female eyes'.

> Mrs W. digging into my back was such a comfort & tugging at the sheet with my hands. I felt it was almost better not having people I cared for with me while the pains were going on – Percy came in now & then – Mrs W. says there were over 50 pains & then the blessed release came, the delight of that first cry showing it was a live child.

Sophie does not say that any form of pain relief was offered, and it is probable that none was. There was still some resistance, on medical and/or religious grounds, to the use of anaesthesia during childbirth, although Queen Victoria's taking of chloroform during the birth of Prince Leopold in 1853 had made it more acceptable. Even then, according to one writer, it was reserved for 'cases of difficult and exceptionally painful labour'.[1] It is a measure of Sophie's courage that she could tell Georgie, 'I was able to keep to my determination & did not utter a sound thro'out – in fact Dr G. says I enjoyed it rather than otherwise.'

To her, the baby that had been placed in her arms was 'the most ducky little fat dumpling I ever saw … The colonel's rapture was a bit more restrained he 'proclaimed it at once a "decidedly jolly baby"'. But Sophie was pleased that little May took after her father: 'I shouldn't like her half so well if she had taken after me'. To which she adds, 'May she be like him inside.'

Other likenesses were noted: the 'round smooth clear face, big eyes and little wee round mouth' were those of Tom's and Edith's daughter Ethel, while the baby's 'pretty bright brown hair' was just the colour of Georgie's when she was a small girl.

The customary lying-in period was observed, in Sophie's case lasting about ten days, although advice manuals of the period recommended 'strict rest for at least four weeks'.[2] During this time no visitors were allowed, apart from Mrs Blood who came nearly every day to sit with Sophie and hold the baby. Even

**23** *Sophie's drawing of the butler carrying 'the most ducky little fat dumpling …'.*

letter-writing appears to have been restricted, since a letter to Georgie dated 3 June begins by saying that 'permission' has been given. A fever, 'which took a great deal of strength out of me', accounted for several extra days in bed beyond the expected ten.

The wife of one of the soldiers was taken on as a nurse for the baby, and Mrs Woods continued her visits until after May's christening on 13 June. The date was that of Percy's birthday, and Sophie wrote asking that her three youngest sisters – Ellen, 15, Emma, 13 and Mary, 11 – be given 'a whole holiday to keep the two events'. Evidently they were being educated at home. In time, Sophie herself would take over as head nurse, assisted by the admirable Maria. She found she was well able to breast-feed little May although her breasts appear to have been smaller than the norm. 'Tell G. [Georgie] Baby has fortunately a very small mouth', she writes to her mother. 'She used to laugh at me on *that account* & say I shdn't be able to nurse a baby.' This sisterly teasing clearly rankled.

On 1 July came the news of her father's death. Her mother had sent the letter to Percy so that he would be with Sophie when it was read, and for this she was grateful. Owen had died in London, in his sister Elizabeth-Ellen Young's house in Great Cumberland Street, chosen for its proximity to Harley Street and its doctors. The end had come on 27 May, just four days after the birth of Sophie's baby. Apart from Sophie and the chair-bound Eddie, all his children had been with him, as had Frank Peel, AM's clergyman husband.

While the sad news was taking its time to reach her, Sophie was responding cheerfully to earlier hopes that Owen was showing some improvement, and this of course she now regretted. The thoughts in her letter back are somewhat jumbled, but their meaning is clear:

> This morning I have been reading all the letters of the last months – with all
> the ups & downs & hopes and fears – & now nothing but rest & happiness – but
> a *happy* death even one cannot help dreading … when it is over you can think
> of it & be thankful.

And she recalls what a 'smooth happy life (as this world goes) dear Papa's
has been, and that he felt it was so … "always finding diamonds among the
pebbles" (to use his own expression)'.

Sophie's words of comfort to her mother are not as trite as they may sound
to a modern ear. Sophie believed unquestioningly in the resurrection of the
body and the life everlasting. Her father had led a good life and was now
among the angels, an inheritor of the kingdom of heaven – there was every
reason to be happy for him. Yet convention decreed that Sophie should at
once garb herself in deep mourning, which would be relieved only by stages
in the months to come.

In the same letter to her mother she describes how her black silk dress is to
have 'one deep piece of crape round the skirt, the little flounce at the bottom
of it of course taken off'. Having no suitable bonnet, '[I] sent for a black net
shape – the oldest possible fashioned one – I added about 3 inches to the front
& Mrs Porter is kindly trimming it, so I shall do very well'.

This of course was the age of the crinoline, a style which, mourning
or no mourning, would always retain its elegance and flair. Later, Sophie
finds she needs a silk cloak. 'So if any of you are in London,' she writes to
Georgie, 'I should be much obliged if you would choose one for me … The
mourning, by the time I get it, will have lasted 5 or 6 months so you will
know how deep it ought to be.' The shade of the silk would be determined
by how long ago the death had occurred, something Sophie's sisters would
be expected to know.

Her views on bereavement must touch a chord with all who have lost someone
near to them: 'It is a mistake, I think that the first grief of the blow is the
worst … I think one never realises it all till that is over & you settle down to
your usual ways & thoughts.' Because, in Sophie's time, death could strike so
suddenly, and often so unaccountably, it held a stronger grip on the imagination
than perhaps it does today. More than once in her letters she voices the hope
that her little daughter will not die.

Towards the end of July, Sophie began to look forward to her sister Sarah's
arrival in India in a little over a month's time. Percy had discovered that the
journey from Belgaum to Madras, should Sarah manage to get away, was 'the
simplest thing alive – a few hours steamer work & train & you are at this Station
& will find our carriage awaiting you – I shd. jump out of my skin I think'.
In the meantime, as an experienced traveller, she offers Sarah some practical
advice for the journey:

> I trust you will have a good voyage, no seasickness – take salts, eau de Cologne,
> fan, sal volatile in your travelling bag, very light clothing for the Red Sea, &
> *interesting* books to read, & [needle] work ditto. Also choose either the top or
> bottom dish/joint in the Steamer at dinner – the side ones are always cold &

tough. Make friends with the Purser & he will be very civil & let you have any little delicacies for you or [little] Willie. Eat plum pudding, raisins etc. when you feel sickish ... Do get your own place at dinner, if you can amongst English people – not French – they always took away any power of eating I might have.

Whatever it was that she found so repugnant about French eating habits, she does not say.

Sophie ends the letter with the news that 'Baby was vaccinated yesterday ... & I took the opportunity of doing myself with a needle'. And then, alarmingly, she adds, 'Do you remember, cruel girl, snipping a hole in my arm with scissors for that purpose, the mark of wh. remains to this day?' One hopes that Sarah – two years older than Sophie – was very young when this unsisterly act took place. Neither of the vaccinations took at the time. but a repeated attempt with May was successful. 'It was done from a black child,' says Sophie, rather unfeelingly, 'after being assured that she would not change colour in consequence.'

It had been almost six months since the arrival of the regiment and the end of those weeks of idleness at Dent's Hotel, and Percy was due for two months' leave. On 12 August he and his little family took up residence in Bangalore, in hilly country about 220 miles to the west of Madras. The first leg of the journey was by train, but for the last 80 miles they travelled in a horse-drawn 'transit'. This vehicle was covered like a carriage but was in effect a bed on wheels, eight feet long by four wide, with 'just room for two to lie straight down'. For comfort it left something to be desired:

I immediately found crinoline must be dispensed with so I took it off & put it under our pillows wh. we brought with us – & off we jolted, Baby laid in my lap. It was all very well the first hour but one got very stiff & cramped after that – not pleasant at all – changed horses every 5 miles, wh. waked Baby tho' she was soon off again ... Very pretty country we passed – moon shining enough to see out of the little windows as we lay - great hills to go up & several times the horses stopped for more than ½ an hour, being yelled at by the driver & runners, wouldn't stir a step, poor things.

With its pleasantly cool climate and fertile soil, Bangalore – today a thriving city – is known as 'the Garden of India'. In the Fenwicks' time there was a large cantonment, and 'no end of Regts [which] seemed to be considerably worked now that the Chief is here'.[3] In the field next to the house where they were staying, cavalry exercises were going on:

Percy & I look at them over the hedge wh. is rather amusing – they have imitation heads stuck on poles & some on the ground, & they have to cut them off & pick them up on the end of their swords going at the rate of 20 miles an hour in turn, Sir Hope Grant at their head.

The Fenwicks had been lent half of a bungalow belonging to a Captain Bagot, and it was there that they spent most of their leave. Bagot was engaged to a young woman named Miss Prosser, who was expected to arrive from England in October. It had been arranged that she should be married from the Fenwicks' house in the fort, and that Percy would give her away. The engagement had been a lengthy one and the couple had not seen each other for nearly six years. Did they really care for each other? Sophie wondered, 'as there was nothing particular to prevent her coming before'.

As the time for Miss Prosser's arrival drew near, the captain began showing signs of nervous agitation. 'Capt. Bagot is marching up and down under the porch talking about his wedding &c.', Sophie wrote to her mother. 'Such a talker he is, & rather louder than is necessary. So panicky was he that he actually asked Percy to go and meet Miss Prosser off the steamer. Sensibly, this was refused and Bagot persuaded to go himself.

As it turned out, his fears (Will she have changed? Will I feel the same about her?) were misplaced:

> At 5 o'clock this morning Cap. Bagot went off to the steamer to fetch Miss Prosser, our carriage met them on the Beach. She is so decidedly nice looking, & young & blooming, can't be more than 5 or 6 & 20. We have now sent them up to a room at the top of the house, which has just been painted &c. & has a pretty view of the sea & all the country. They are both very cool & collected & well behaved considering they have not met for nearly six years … Little May is to be Miss Prosser's bridesmaid! – the only one, as there isn't a creature in the shape of a girl she knows here, & we cdn't ask a stranger.

What makes Sophie's letters so readable is that she never repeats herself from one to another, knowing that all of them are being passed round the whole family. Bagot's pre-wedding jitters and his reunion with the lovely Miss Prosser are serially described in letters to her mother. The wedding itself comes in a letter to her youngest sister, Mary, dated 6 November.

> The wedding took place this morning at ½ past 9, up to which time we were very busy, arranging flowers for the Breakfast table, dressing the Bride &c., Mrs Porter helping … We met all the rest at the Church, Percy marching her up, her bridesmaid Miss May Fenwick dressed in blue & white, carried by Mrs Porter in the rear. She (Baby) behaved with great propriety, & fell asleep during the ceremony … That deed done, in the most composed manner by the parties concerned, all returned to our house.

The Fenwicks' second Christmas in Madras was very different from their first. That had been marked simply by a church service in the morning – with the Sacrament, as Sophie calls it – and a quiet dinner with the Bloods in the evening. Marie, the little *ayah*, had given Sophie a rose. Now, Sophie had the men and their wives to think about. She and Mrs Porter made a 'monster plum pudding' which they mixed in two large washing basins, '& Oh! The plums & currants & spice, & when baked fulfilled our fondest hopes, as black as your hat with goodness'. Some of the men had taken the pledge, so no beer was to be provided. 'I was wicked enough to suggest a glass or two with their cheese, lemonade & cheese would be so very horrible, but they think none at all would be wisest.' Her 'wickedness' notwithstanding, she had praise for Mr Porter and the vicar, Mr Alcock, who between them ran a Bible class with about forty regular attenders every evening.

In late January 1863 little May, now eight months old, developed a cold and cough which Sophie, in a letter to her mother, attributed to a damp north-east wind. Some three weeks later Sophie is writing to Georgie that 'Baby's cough got worse & worse, fits always coming on when she was just off to sleep & seven times she has regularly hooped [sic] … Dr Gordon (who has never heard one of her fits) declares it is not hooping cough, and I hope he is right.'

Percy was away at this time on a two-day 'musketry' exercise. Angered by Gordon's insouciant attitude ('nothing to signify' was his comment on most of his patients' complaints), Sophie asked Mrs Wood to have dinner with her 'that she might give her opinion about Baby who generally has a bad fit at that time. She said, on hearing it, that it was hooping cough without a doubt'.

A few days later she reported that the cough was 'much better … so I am in hopes it is a very mild attack'.

Despite Sophie's triumphant riposte to Georgie on the subject of breastfeeding, she had actually been having some difficulty with it. At about six months it was decided to wean the baby, and May was now taking 'nothing but Cow's milk'. The alternative would have been to hire an *Armah*, or Indian wet nurse, an idea that filled Sophie with horror. By 27 February there was a new concern over May's health. 'She was in a high fever with diarrhoea', Sophie tells her mother. Dr Gordon had told her that teething was the cause.

> The fever is gone but not the other, however that is rather a comfort to me as they say it is a safeguard against convulsions wh. is my great dread. Dr Gordon gives her powders & says there is no cause for anxiety, but she is so pulled down by it her little arms are half the size they were. Mrs Porter is the greatest blessing to us. She comes in every day & stays with her to enable me to go out. I go much more by her than by Dr G., he isn't at all a baby doctor, in fact his place is more at Balls & parties &c. Percy believes in him however …

Sophie does not paragraph her letters so the switch from one topic to another can be abrupt. From the passage just quoted she turns to sundry matters such as her sister Mary's persistent (consumptive?) cough, the wedding of the Governor's eldest daughter, and the death of the Fenwicks' cat. But little May is always in her mind, and suddenly, out come some thoughts about the baby's diet: 'Cow's milk & water seems too heavy for Baby just now & won't keep down … shall try arrowroot & sago'. With hindsight one may wonder, how pure was the water?

This letter is incomplete, partly because the top of one page is missing, but also because it stops in mid-sentence, as if Sophie had been temporarily distracted but in any case intended to finish the writing next day. However, the letter remained unfinished except for a hurried postscript on a separate scrap of paper:

> Saturday 28th Feb. This morning there is a change in our darling – great weakness from dhrea & sickness. Dr G. is giving Portwine every ½ hour. God grant it may give her strength – it seemed to come on all at once. I am grieved to send a bad account, don't be anxious. So far the wine has kept down so we may hope & pray that all will be well. Mrs Wood is here I'm thankful to say …

What happened next is told to her mother in a two-part letter begun on 3 March, a Tuesday, and continued on the 5th. In places, Sophie's usually neat handwriting becomes an untidy scrawl, and her punctuation, always erratic, almost deserts her. It has been edited here and there for ease of reading.

> My own dearest Mother – the P.S. to my last letter will have prepared you for very very sad news of our darling child – her little spirit fled away at ¼ past 4 this morning, & so great were her sufferings that we could almost thank God for it – bitterly as we feel our loss ...

Sophie goes back to relate the progress of the illness from the previous Friday up to the writing of the postscript the following day. She goes on,

> Mrs Wood came & remained all night, it was a sad time, diarhea [ *sic* ] continuing & occasional sickness pulling her down. The next morning early Mrs Wood laid her down in the cot thinking it would rest her little weary bones, she uttered a little cry & her eyes fixed wide open. I lifted her out & called to Dr G. who was just leaving. Convulsions followed, not very violent, after wh. she was delirious for a time. They called in another doctor, Dr Paul, a very clever man for children ... They hoped if there was no return of the convulsions she would do well, but about 4 she was very weak & another long attack followed (lying on Mrs Wood's lap, we holding her dear little hands), & after for more than an hour such piercing screams from pain in the head.
> Thursday morning. Darling Mother do not grieve too much for me, God is merciful – My own dear husband is very very ill but so happy in Christ his only grief is for me, & God who has supported me so far will do so to the end if it pleases him ... There is a hope & that is all, it is a privilege to see such patience & resignation to the Divine will. Bless all the circumstances wh. have brot. three souls to heaven, regret not one single thing.

Sophie signs herself off but then the letter continues, in part:

> I will not shrink from saying the truth, it is Cholera – but the sickness & diarrhea ( *sic* ) have ceased – I am well thank God – he never touched a thing while our Child was so ill & was made sick by finding our poor cat all but dead & smelling fearfully (it was sent at once down to the sea to be drowned & I did not smell it) – he had sickness at once & slight diarrhea but thought nothing of it till yesterday - about 6 after a happy afternoon together talking of our Child he fainted, & sank from that time ...

There is some ambiguity as to the point at which Percy's death occurred, but the ending is clear enough: 'My dear ones are happy in Christ's bosom – oh the joy & peace.'

The causes of cholera were little understood in Sophie's time. She evidently believed it to be an air-borne infection, rather than the product of contaminated water or food. Hence her insistence that she did not smell the diseased cat. In a condolence letter to Sophie's mother, Mrs Blood quoted Dr Gordon as saying that Percy's condition was 'principally caused by over-anxiety [for his child] & lack of nourishment & rest ... so that when the disease attacked him he had no strength to rally from it'. Sophie later retracted her disparaging remarks about Gordon, who apparently showed kindness to her after the event. In the circumstances, one might well consider this to be the least he could do.

Sophie's religious certainties and the joy she expresses at the snuffing out of the two lives most dear to her will undoubtedly cause some people to recoil. It must be said first of all that death in her day was an ever-present fear. It could strike suddenly and without warning. As in the case of her father, her refuge was an unshakeable belief in God's mercy and in the promise of eternal life. In heaven she would be with her loved ones again, and in the flesh. They meanwhile had been released from the dreadful suffering that had so torn at her heartstrings, and would never know pain or unhappiness again. How could she do anything but be thankful for them? 'It was such intense happiness when the little angel spirit took flight – so peacefully at last with her dear eyes fixed on me', she tells her mother. God, in his mercy, had taken them to himself.

This of course raises the question of why she was left behind, denied the bliss that May and Percy had been called to share. And the answer is, 'For my sins'. She is happy 'in the new feeling that Christ's blood has washed away my sins wh. are so many & great'. In her next sentence she voices the hope that God will continue to spare her the temptations of the world, 'for I know my terrible weakness'. To punish herself, poor Sophie has turned to self-flagellation.

Let us look at her record. In the past 17 months this 24-year-old girl has exchanged the comfortable security of her home in England for the difficulties and dangers of a foreign land. With no previous administrative experience she has taken on the management of a household of 17 servants, and of working parties of soldiers' wives. She has presided over Percy's dinner table, entertaining senior army officers and other dignitaries of the *Raj*. It has been a valiant effort and we can believe that Percy told her so.

In a postscript to the same letter she accuses herself of 'my old pride & reserve'. If indeed she possessed these qualities, they could have come from the Peel side of the family: Sir Robert Peel, a cousin of Sophie's mother Anne, was noted for his aloofness. But there is nowhere any evidence of this in Sophie, certainly not in the loving relationship that she and Percy shared, nor in her tender care for little May. Her letters home are anything but reserved. In fact the more one examines the case she tries to build against herself, the more the scales are weighted in her favour and the more admirable does she seem.

Sophie was by no means without friends. On hearing the news of Percy's death, General and Mrs McCleverty made her leave her house in the fort and welcomed her into their own home. 'She is now with me,' Mrs McCleverty wrote to Sarah in Belgaum, 'and all that sympathy and kindness can do for her shall be done.' She sent a similar message to Sophie's mother, adding, 'It is such a comfort to my husband and me in this sorrow that we can be of use to your dear Child, whom to know is to love.'

Exhausted at first, emotionally, but also physically from lack of food and sleep while nursing May and Percy, Sophie was encouraged to rest as much as possible. When Mrs McCleverty was called away for one reason or another, other friends like Constance Blood would come and stay with her. Each evening she would go for a drive 'in a close carriage … with Mrs McCleverty, Mrs Blood & Lady Grant, in turn'.

Sarah wrote to her from Belgaum, six letters in two weeks, the first two in close succession as she heard first of May's death and then of Percy's. It had been decided that Sophie should return to England accompanied by the good Mrs Porter. Willy Godfrey-Faussett, now a colonel, travelled across from Belgaum to make arrangements for the journey and for the shipment of Sophie's belongings. Mindful of their shared aversion, in one of her letters Sarah wrote, 'I wish you had the *dish cover* I made, of old net and cap wire to protect my head from the cockroaches, I found it such a comfort.'

And so, in early April, Sophie and Mrs Porter, the Scripture Reader's wife, boarded the steamer for Southampton and home. Behind her, in St Mary's churchyard, Sophie left the graves of her husband and child, each with a sprig of myrtle beside it, planted by herself.

# 13

# *Sophie's Story (almost) Concluded*

Sophie arrived at Southampton on 1 or 2 May 1863. Her mother and her sister Georgie were there to meet her and accompany her back to Remnantz. There she was to live for the next 20 years, supporting her mother at social events, doing her bit for charity, joining other family members on a surprising number of excursions abroad, and attending the weddings of her younger sisters. Bobby Fearnley-Whittingstall, who at first showed some impatience with Sophie and ended by admiring her greatly, regrets that 'she was content to drift with the tide' and 'let her gifts lie fallow for so long'.

> With her youth, good looks and experience of the married state, with her abilities and accomplishments … she cannot have lacked for suitors; nor, assuming she felt no desire to hold another baby in her arms, did she lack at least the opportunity of making a name for herself as artist, writer, or both.[1]

But for all her piety, and the assurance that her two darlings were 'not lost but gone before', and to a far more blessed state than this, Sophie, the one left behind, had had her own earthly happiness destroyed and her world turned upside down. It would take many months, if not years, for her to recover her equilibrium. Moreover, having given her heart once and had it cruelly pierced, she would not soon risk giving it again. Marriage was too dangerous an adventure. For safety and comfort she needed her childhood home. As for making the most of her gifts, there is no evidence to show that Sophie was ambitious. Clearly she enjoyed her painting and sketching, and as time went on she reached a high level of proficiency. But had it been suggested that she should turn professional, I think she would have smiled and shaken her head. She took pleasure in doing it, and that was enough.

Meanwhile, one by one, her sisters were leaving home. Georgie, her favourite, was married in 1866 and Ellen Anne in 1869. When Emma followed in 1874, only Sophie, her youngest sister Mary-Louisa and their mother Anne were left at Remnantz, for the sadly disabled Eddy had died of 'hysterical atrophy' in 1868, aged 26. 'My props are falling from me,' wrote 66-year-old Anne at the end of 1873, when love was blooming between Emma and the Rev. Robert Trefusis, vicar of Chittlehampton in Devon.

Sophie was by nature a carer, the sort who would be there for anyone who needed her, whether it was her mother or a soldier's wife or, as in the present case, her unfortunate cousin Grace. A cousin by marriage only, 'Gracie' was the wife of the Rev. Florence Thomas Wethered, whose father, Florence James, was the vicar of Hurley when Mrs Goodman was writing her story of the Pears family. In fact he held the benefice for 30 years and, since he was also the patron, was able to appoint his son to succeed him for another thirty.

In the late summer of 1864, in a letter bubbling with enthusiasm and with many underlinings, Gracie asked Sophie to join her and 'Flo' for a short holiday at Sandown, the seaside resort in the Isle of Wight. Gracie was suffering from what had been diagnosed as an abscess in her chest and it was thought the sea air would do her good. The three of them and Gracie's little maid Anne travelled down by train. As they neared the coast Sophie's attention was caught by what seemed at first to be 'a bit of a beautiful dream'.

> We past [*sic*] close by the Gosport Barracks & directly we stopped at the Station I heard the well known Bugle sound, the dear old Band struck up & the Regt. marched past not 50 yards away – I was glad that the buildings soon hid them & I did not see the Colonel – it seemed almost too much. I had no idea that we shd. go up to the Station or wd. certainly have let them know … however I shall make a point of it on my way back.

The lodgings at two guineas a week were comfortable and had a good view of the sea. Sophie found herself acting as 'Housekeeper & Paymaster', adding, 'Happily we lost no luggage, Mr Flo being an advocate for letting it take its own chance' (in contrast to Percy, who always 'saw to the luggage' very effectively). The weather, though, was 'wild – we are nearly blown out of our beds at night'. And, alarmingly, when attempting to sketch from the cliff top, 'I was taken off my feet & rolled into a ditch (dry) my parasol disappearing over the Cliff'. But she felt she was being of real help to Gracie, especially as 'Flo is a poor sort of nurse'.

While at Sandown she had written to Mrs Porter, the lay reader's wife who had accompanied Sophie on her homeward voyage and was now with the regiment at Gosport. The news that Sophie was in the area had been joyously received by all those who had known her, and she was begged to visit them on her way home. Meanwhile Gracie's condition had worsened and she was to be taken to see a specialist in London; since her parents were visiting nearby it was agreed that Sophie could be spared for one night at Gosport and would join Gracie's train the following day.

Her hosts were a Captain and Mrs Charleton. The latter's description of the visit as 'a little sun rising over the Regiment, gladdening all hearts' probably did not help to calm what Sophie called her 'quakes'. But she was greeted with such warmth and affection that she wrote to tell Georgie

> what a happy day I have spent in my married home, as the 69th will always seem … From breakfast time till two o'clock everyone was coming to see me – the 2 Officers' wives, then the Soldiers' wives in detachments, then some of the Officers.

That evening, eight of the men who had known her came to the Carletons' house, and

> with Captain and Mrs C. with me to help me with the talking, there the dear men stood round the room, bolt upright, looking so nice in brilliant new clothes put on for the occasion. I rather quaked, shook hands with them all & said I was glad to see them &c. Sergeant Fisher spoke up, said it was a great pleasure &c. &c. & then the others chimed in. I sat down & managed to ask a great many questions, & the dear men answered so nicely. I sent messages to the absent ones – & those who had taken to bad ways – & said I shd. depend on seeing them next time.

There was a poignant little interview with a soldier called Mills, clearly one of Sophie's admirers as he had presented her with a brooch on her leaving Madras. He evidently had an Indian girl friend because, in Sophie's words, on coming home, 'he had had to leave his lady love behind'. Now he had taken to drink, 'much to everyone's sorrow for he is such a good-hearted fellow'. He had asked to see her, and only her, in order to talk about it.

He had prayed, he said, but that had done no good and he felt like putting an end to his miserable life. Sophie urged him to take the pledge, which Percy had found was the only remedy for an habitual drunkard. Mills promised to do so the following day. 'No, I said, it must be today, but nothing wd. induce him to promise that, for he said he shd. only break it – tomorrow he wd. be on guard & wd. begin then. He asked if he might write & tell me in a fortnight if he had kept his promise – of course I said he might … I cannot but fear for him, but hope too. (Whether it was her fear or her hope that was justified we are never told.)

Sophie and Gracie were to stay at 38 Great Cumberland Place, the London home of Sophie's Aunt Young, where Owen had spent his last days two-and-a-half years before. They arrived there on Friday 6 October, and before the weekend was over Gracie had undergone emergency surgery. It was performed by the eminent Sir James Paget after whom two diseases have been named, one of them concerning breast cancers. It is not clear where the operation took place – Paget was a consultant at St Bartholomew's Hospital – but on Sunday night she was back in her room at Great Cumberland Place, with Sophie on the other side of an open door.

It was a restless night for all of them, including Flo who had arrived the previous day. Gracie was plagued by shivering fits and vomiting and was unable to keep down either the medicine or the brandy and water that Paget had prescribed for her. At about one a.m. Flo was sent to fetch Paget, who, however, refused to come until nine, sending Flo back with more medicine which Gracie immediately threw up. When he did examine her later, Paget seemed unsure of himself. As Sophie tells it,

> I went into another room with him & asked if there was cause for alarm – he said it certainly was an anxious case for she seemed in such an exhausted state & must be caused by something besides the abscess – he *hopes* it is occasioned

by the formation of a *second abscess* – but also feared it may be the beginning of
Erysipelas or Fever (not catching).

He sent for a nurse to come and sit by her. Flo telegraphed Gracie's parents,
Samuel and Emma Best, alerting them to their daughter's state; then Sophie
sat by him, to pray with him and 'keep him still'.

That night Paget returned at one, and again at five-thirty, bringing different
colleagues for advice. The first thought (improbably) that Gracie had scarletina,
the second, 'that the "matter" had got into the system and poisoned the blood'.
It was, said the first doctor, 'a most extraordinary case'.

Gracie died 'quietly & peacefully' that evening. A few days earlier she had
told Sophie that 'she had had from the first a feeling that she should not get
over this – that she thought it would turn to Cancer'. Behind her she left two
small children, a boy Edmund Peel and a girl Marion Grace. In another week
she would have been twenty-four.

Sophie was not with her at the death. She, Flo and Anne, the little maid,
had been warned of possible infection and lodgings had been found for them
nearby in Old Quebec Street. The nurse, whose job it was to face such risks
(although none was actually involved in this case), remained throughout at
Gracie's bedside.

So dependent on Sophie had Flo become that he begged her not to leave
him but to stay for a while with his parents and himself at Hurley vicarage.
This she was glad to do. Flo's mother, Esther-Ellen, was another Peel, a sister
of Owen's wife Anne, and was therefore Sophie's aunt. 'Darling Sophie,' she
wrote to Anne at this time, 'what should we *all* have done without her, what a
perfect creature she is … Flo can't bear to be without her.'

Did he ever propose marriage to his widowed cousin? If so, she was wise
to refuse him.

Gracie's body was brought down from London and buried in Hurley churchyard. Three years after her death Flo married Mary-Josephine Bonsor and by
her had seven more children. Gracie's son Edmund followed the family tradition
and attended Christ Church, Oxford, where his tutor was the Rev. Charles
Dodgson; after taking holy orders he went on to become vicar of Staverton
near Daventry. From his daughter Ursula we get a disturbing picture of the
'terrible' way her grandfather Flo treated his children. He was a tyrant, she told
Diana and me, like Mr Barrett of Wimpole Street. The children were never
allowed to speak at meals or to go out anywhere – all, according to Ursula,
had nervous breakdowns.

Flo succeeded his father as vicar of Hurley in 1868, and 10 years later
published a worthy if narrowly focused book about the parish: *St Mary's Hurley
in the Middle Ages, Charters and Deeds*. Oddly, for a man of his calling, he seems
to have gone out of his way to make enemies. Gracie's sister Mary was married
to the Rev. Sir James Phillips, Bart., for 38 years the vicar of Warminster in
Wiltshire. Together the two of them founded the Missionary College of St
Boniface, which, according to Phillips' obituary in *The Church Times*, 'carried
the name of Warminster into every part of the British Empire'. Politically,

**24** *Visit with Alice to the Altmarkt in Dresden, June 1869. From Sophie's Sketchbooks 'Travels in Europe'. Sophie's early drawings appear tentative and stylised compared with this later work. It seems likely that she took lessons after her return from India.*

Phillips was a Gladstonian; that and his high churchmanship would not have endeared him to the Rev. Florence T. Wethered. But there must have been some other slight, real or imagined, to account for the violence of Flo's feelings towards him.

'Do let me know when the Viper Philipps [*sic*] is excluded from Convocation', he begins a letter to an ordained Hickman cousin in 1885. And he goes on:

> Lady Philipps has lately written to my wife to stop me from congratulating the fool on his new Mitre, on post cards!!

If a rumour had got out that Phillips was in line for a bishopric, then it could have been no more than that. It seems that he had already declined the deanery of Winchester, and in 1889 'he took very unresentfully his defeat when standing again for Convocation'.[2]

Evidently the cousins, too, had had a falling out, for the rest of the letter is an attempt to build bridges – to 'let bygones be bygones', in Flo's words – and the Rev. William Hickman is invited to visit. Then, as if the emollient words have gone too much against the grain, he cannot resist a final swipe in the postscript: 'D— *all* the Radicals! Specially Gladstone & "Home Rule"!'

Between 1867 and 1873 Sophie made five excursions to the Continent or beyond with other members of the family. Two were simply for pleasure: a three-week tour of southern France and the Italian Lakes with OPW, his wife Alice, Sophie's 20-year-old sister Emma, and the lonely widower Flo; and another three-week trip, this time to Germany with the OPWs. It was in Dresden on 6 May 1869 that the couple's third son, Walter Percival, was born. The following month, while OPW was off seeing the sights of St Petersburg, Sophie and Alice were guests at

**25** *The decision to move on to Biarritz.*

a musical evening given by the poet Robert Bridges and a friend at their rooms at Dresden.[3] It is not known how the friendship between Bridges and the OPWs began, but they continued to keep in touch, and in 1900 he sent a volume of his poems to Alice, saying in a note, 'We enjoyed our visit immensely.'

But two of the journeys were for reasons of health. The Wethereds of those days were especially prone to lung disease, and Sophie's 18-year-old sister Mary-Louisa, one of the sufferers, had been told by her doctor to drink the waters at Eaux Bonnes in the Pyrenees. This required a major expedition of two months in the summer of 1868, and in addition to Sophie and Mary-Louisa included their brother Tom, 'Aunt Florence' (the recently widowed mother of Flo) and the much-loved family retainer Mrs Tyler.

At Eaux Bonnes, where they stayed for two weeks, Mary was given *les Douches*. As Sophie reports it, not very helpfully, 'She sits facing into what looks like a screened-off basin, a towel round her neck. Two female attendants do their knitting at the other end of the long room.' Sophie rendered a scornful verdict

**26** *Vieux Port, Biarritz.*

on the spa: 'Eaux Bonnes is where people with bad coughs are sent to be made worse.' During their stay there, a noisy party of early risers scared Aunt Florence into appearing in Sophie's hotel room at three a.m., convinced that 'a massacre of the Hugenots [*sic*] was about to take place'.

Next, Mary-Louisa was ordered by the local doctor 'to complete the cure', as he put it (three question marks inserted by Sophie) by taking the salt baths at Salies-de-Bearn. The journey started badly. 'We had not proceeded 20 yards [by carriage to the nearest station] when the leader, after much plunging, fell down – & we go on with only two horses.' And there is disappointment to follow. 'After 9 days at Salies, of intense heat, bad food, discomfort by day, & croaking frogs by night, Mary has become so weak & ill that we break to the good Doctor our determination to start the next day for Biarritz.'

These travels, and others at home in the UK, offered endless opportunities for Sophie to exercise her art. Her sketchbooks are full of her drawings and watercolours, some picked out in exquisite detail, others done in just a few lines and often with humour. Her 'Vieux Port' at Biarritz is a charming scene of parents bathing in the shallows with their children. She also drew the travellers' arrival home at Remnantz, a day early and very relieved to be back. Alas, beneath the caption Sophie has written, 'Mary worse, instead of better for the trip'.

Mary-Louisa was a fair artist herself, and we have a delightful painting of a train which she did as a little girl. But possibly due to her illness one senses an anger in her work, which tends towards the weird and the grotesque. A pencil drawing of her by Sophie shows a very pretty child propped up in bed, with Sophie and the doctor and a dog in attendance. Mary died on 26 January 1876 aged twenty-five. The cause was diagnosed as cirrhosis of the lung, or pulmonary fibrosis.

In common with other medical writers of pre-penicillin days, J. M'Gregor-Robertson prescribes 'removal to a warm and equable climate' for sufferers of lung disease. His *Household Physician* is an impressive volume, leather-bound, well-illustrated and running to more than 1,100 pages. There is no publication date but from the magnificence of the men's moustaches and the laciness of the ladies' clothing it would appear to have been issued about 1900.

Robert Wethered's doctor evidently believed in the M'Gregor-Robertson remedy, for in October 1871 Robert was packed off to Mentone on the Italian Riviera to spend the winter with

**27**  *Return to Remnantz,*
*6 August 1869.*

his wife Edith and his sister Sophie.[4] There were trips to Monaco and walks in the surrounding hills, but the climate was not uniformly warm and equitable. One of Sophie's pictures shows Robert huddled before a fireplace, a blanket over his shoulders, while she blows on the damp wood in an attempt to coax a flame out of it; cups and bowls are scattered on the floor to catch raindrops falling from the ceiling. Once Sophie came down in the morning to find a 'lively stream flowing through the passage' of the Hotel d'Italie.

On 8 November Edith gave birth to a baby girl, Katherine Sophie, who was baptised at the Anglican church in Mentone. According to the rites of the Church at the time, the mother of the newly born was expected to be 'Churched' – an act of self-abasement that has long since been dropped from the prayer book. Whether for this reason or not, Edith was not in church for the designated service, and as Sophie wryly notes, 'The Rev. W. Barber Churched the entire congregation of St John's under the impression that Mrs R.P. Wethered was present.'

On the way home they stayed at Hyères, near Toulon, where they were joined for some days by Georgie and her clergyman husband Charles Mackworth Drake. It was here that, for reasons not explained, baby Katherine died with a suddenness reminiscent of Sophie's little May. On 5 April she appears in a Sophie drawing, being held aloft by her father as he lies on his bed. By the 26th her life is over. After burying her in the cemetery at Hyères, the little party continued its journey home.

Robert and Edith had no more children, and he himself died in November of the following year. Phthisis (tuberculosis) is the cause given on his death certificate.

Shortly afterwards Edith and Sophie set out on a tour of North Africa, which lasted five-and-a-half months and provided them with some adventures. A broken carriage shaft at a remote spot in Algeria meant that they were 'forced

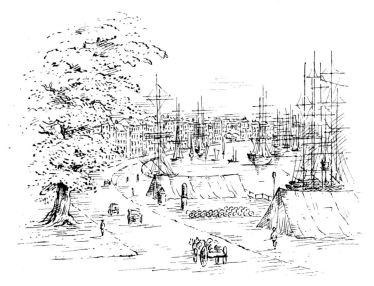

**28**  *Bordeaux from the hotel window.*

**29** *Robert expostulates at the sight of the oversize nurse sent to look after his and Edith's baby.*

to spend the night in the roughest & dirtiest little wayside restaurant & to have our meals with 15 barefooted Spanish fishermen'. Not the sort of thing these Marlow ladies were accustomed to. On their way home they stopped off at Hyères to visit the little grave.

One by one the people Sophie had helped care for had been taken from her in their youth. Surely such a string of heartbreaks must have tested even her faith to the limit. But in 1881 two things happened that were to change the direction of her life. In February her mother died, aged 73, leaving her the sole occupant of Remnantz. And in April the governors of Sir William Borlase's School appointed a new headmaster: the Rev. Michael Graves.

He arrived at a time when the 1624 charitable foundation was at a crossroads. The founder, in his will, had provided for 'a Schoolmaster to teach twenty-four poor children to write, read and cast accounts, such as their parents and friends are not able to maintain at school ...'. Under the Education Act of 1870, however, *all* children were to receive cheap or free education, which could be said to have made Sir William's charity redundant. The decision of the governors (still called 'feoffees' then), in consultation with the Charity Commissioners, was to expand the school and improve it:

> The School was to be a day school for boys, and, if the Governors thought fit, room was to be made for boarders. Immediate provision was to be made for fifty day boys, and the new buildings were to be so planned as to allow for convenient extensions ... The Headmaster was to live in the residence assigned to him, and to have no other employment.[5]

This was the situation when young Michael Graves was selected from a field of 'at least 56 applicants' to take over as headmaster. In an interview with the governors, of whom the vicar, the Rev. J.A. Cree, was chairman and Tom Wethered vice-chairman, he was asked what additional accommodation he thought the school would need. According to the minutes,

> He stated that first of all a new schoolroom was essential. He considered there
> ought to be a drawing room, a study, a dining room (to be both for himself and
> the boarders), a kitchen and scullery, all, if possible, downstairs, two bedrooms
> (for himself and his mother), bedrooms for six boarders at least, to begin with,
> and one for servants.

If the governors were surprised by this formidable list they put a brave face
on it. If all these conditions were met, they said, would Mr Graves accept the
post? Mr Graves agreed. His tenure would turn out to last nearly 15 years. From
school records and minutes of meetings, J.C. Davies has rated him 'a headmaster
with vision and enterprise, capable of quick decision and capable, too, of gently
leading reluctant governors along paths they often feared to tread'.[6]

Links between the school and the Wethered family have always been strong,
and with Borlase and Remnantz facing each other across the street, it was
natural that Michael Graves and Sophie should meet at an early stage. It says
much for Sophie's charm and her qualities generally that she should engage
the affections of this serious young man, so many years her junior. He was 25,
she was approaching 43 – a gap of 17 years, very like that between her age
and Percy's, only the other way round.

Of course propinquity played its part. At the end of the school day Michael
would cross the road and slip through a small door into the Remnantz garden
in order to pay her court. This habit did not go unnoticed by any of Sophie's
nephews and nieces who happened to be about, and the headmaster's means of
access is known to this day as 'Uncle Michael's door'. It would be interesting to
know by what paths these two from such very different backgrounds discovered
an identity of thought.

Michael proposed to Sophie as she was about to leave for a visit to her sister
Ellen Anne, and he did not get his answer straight away. Ellen Anne was married
to Robert Godfrey-Faussett. He was the third son of Godfrey and Sarah, and,
like his father, an academic. First-class honours in mathematics had led to a
distinguished career as a lecturer, and later as Steward and then Treasurer of
Christ Church. This was interrupted in 1855 when he took himself off to the
Crimean War, working briefly in the army's commissariat department. While
in the Crimea (so the story goes), he unexpectedly ran into his brother Willy,
then a captain in the 44th, who told him off for risking his life. Robert adored
his Ellen Anne – his 'little mouse', as he called her: there survives an amusing
poem, illustrated by himself, about how she made him leave the house when
their little son developed chicken pox.

The couple's home was Cassington in Oxfordshire, where Robert had the
living, and it was from there, on 3 August 1883, that what Sophie described
as her 'momentous letter' was sent. Wasting no more time, she and Michael
were married on 8 September in the village of Binfield. Many years later one
of Sophie's nieces received a proposal of marriage from a man twenty years
older than herself, and came to Sophie for advice. 'A husband,' she was told,
'is no problem if you are sure you love him and he loves you. I was blissfully

**30** *Sophie and her mother 'gambling'.*

happy with Percy and now I'm blissfully happy with Michael. It's what he is that counts – not how old he is.'

As a headmaster's wife Sophie appears to have been in her element, caring for the boys as if they were the family she never had, and fondly remembered by them as a result. The Rev. G.E. Davis joined the school as a new boy in 1881, the year Michael took over, and left in 1891, by which time the numbers had risen from 33 to about 160.[7] 'In every sense of the word,' he writes, 'Mrs Graves was a gracious lady, a cultured person who devoted herself to the boys' interests, and did much, through her many relations and connections, to add to their number.'

When Sophie's health began to show signs of stress, Michael, although not yet forty, resigned from his post to become vicar of Turville, a charmingly picturesque village in the Chilterns. As recently as 1984 the King James Bible she presented to the church was still there on the lectern. Another legacy of their tenure is the renamed Church Cottage. This is the once-famous 'Sleeping Girl's Cottage', where 11-year-old Ellen Saddler apparently fell into a coma as a result of a brain abscess and slept uninterruptedly for nine years, from 1871 to 1880, when she woke little the worse for her ordeal. Whether the story was genuine, or an unscrupulous money-making scheme on the part of her mother, nobody knows. But if the village was still being troubled by curiosity seekers in Michael's and Sophie's time, it seems a good enough reason for changing the name.

By 1915 Sophie had had 18 years of performing the tasks of a conscientious vicar's wife, and at 78 had more than earned her retirement. She and Michael moved back to Marlow and into an attractive Georgian style house called Tilecotes, just a few hundred yards from Remnantz in Oxford Road. It had an acre of garden and had apparently been built on land acquired by Sophie's father Owen from Sir William Clayton. There we must leave them while other bits of the story are brought up to date.

# 14

# *Uncle Tom and the Commission of the Peace*

'Certainly he is a Brewer, but the House of Commons is full of Brewers, and
they are all, without exception, Magistrates'.

> The Prime Minister, Lord Beaconsfield, in a
> letter to Lord Cottesloe, 13 September 1877.

In the general election of 1874 Tom Wethered was returned unopposed,
although there had been controversy over his selection. The protest came
from Colonel T.P. Williams, a grandson of the Copper King and a Member for
Marlow from 1820 to 1868. According to Williams, Tom had been a stop-gap
candidate who had agreed to give way to Williams's son Owen at the end of
the Parliament. Tom denied making any such promise and was supported in
his candidacy by Higginson, Scott-Murray of Danesfield, and other influential
Tories. Owen Williams apologised for his father, who, he said, 'could never
quite realise that Marlow had long ceased to be a pocket borough'. He was
elected in 1880, after Tom had retired from politics.

Tom's two terms in the House were divided more or less evenly between
the premierships of Gladstone and Disraeli. It was a time when each of the
two great statesmen was attempting to out-Reform the other. In 1867 Disraeli
had pushed through a Second Reform Bill – the 'great leap in the dark', in
Lord Derby's phrase – which added a million new voters to the electorate. The
Gladstone government of 1868-74 passed a series of further reforms, among
them the Education Act of 1870, which aimed to make elementary education
available to every child in the land, the introduction of the secret ballot in
1872, and the Cardwell reforms of 1871 which finally abolished the purchase
of commissions in the Army.

The year 1872 also saw the passage of the 'clumsy and unpopular Licensing
Act', regulating the opening hours of public houses.[1] This brought about the
so-called 'brewers revolt', and was exaggeratedly claimed in some quarters to
have caused the defeat of the Liberals in 1874. In May 1871, while the Bill
was still under debate, Tom published a letter in *The Times* offering his own
10-point plan for the licensed victuallers' industry.

During his 12 years in Parliament, Tom took up little of the Members'
time with his own speeches. A search through Hansard for the period shows
his taking the floor on only three occasions: once in connection with the

Licensing Bill, once with a question about child deaths from erysipelas, and finally, on 11 August 1879, to ask the Chancellor of the Exchequer, Sir Stafford Northcote,

> whether instances have not lately occurred of Lords Lieutenants of Counties refusing to place in the Commission of the Peace gentlemen who ... are in every way qualified for the office, on the ground that they are connected with the brewing business ... ?

To become a justice of the peace, or magistrate, was what Tom desired above all else. His sense of self-worth would not be satisfied until this well merited distinction, as he saw it, was his. So far he had been frustrated, on the grounds that it was a magistrate's duty to rule on licensing and other matters affecting public houses. Tom's pride was deeply hurt. His father had been appointed to the Bench, as had his uncle Lawrence William, and *they* were brewers. He went on to ask the Chancellor: would the Government be prepared to instruct Lord Lieutenants 'that being engaged in the brewing business shall not be a disqualification for appointment as a justice of the peace'?

Sir Stafford, a kindly but seemingly ineffectual man (Lord Randolph Churchill dubbed him 'The Grand Old Woman'), was measured in his reply. Recommendations for the position of county magistrate, he told the House, were made by the Lord Lieutenant to the Lord Chancellor, who would normally concur in the appointment. The Government had no knowledge of the grounds on which recommendations were made or not made. However – and here he threw Tom a bone – many brewers were on the Commission of the Peace, and in the Government's opinion, 'the fact that a gentleman was engaged in the brewing business was no disqualification for his appointment as a justice'.

So the Government had added its weight to Tom's side of an argument that had already gone on for more than three years. But would it be enough to sway the Acting Lord Lieutenant? In the absence of the Duke of Buckingham, currently overseas as governor of the state of Madras, his duties as Lord Lieutenant had fallen to his deputy Lord Cottesloe, of Swanbourne House near Winslow, a former M.P. for the county. It was the duke's opinion that being in the brewing trade *did* constitute a disqualification, and he had more than once refused to recommend Tom for the Bench. Hence Cottesloe's reluctance to act independently on Tom's behalf. But none of this had weakened Tom's resolve, as his correspondence shows. Here is a flavour of the fifty and more letters that went back and forth to various dignitaries in the course of his campaign. It is hard to imagine, today, anyone's taking a personal grievance all the way to the Prime Minister, but Tom Wethered was not one to do things by halves.

> October 21st 1876, TOW to the Prime Minister, Lord Beaconsfield: '... It has been galling to me to find myself repeatedly passed over ... and to see young men of my acquaintance, whom I have known as boys, placed over my head ...'
> As for the conflict-of-interest issue: 'I need not remind your Lordship that the law disqualifies brewers from acting in cases in which they can be in any way interested ...'
> October 24th, Prime Minister to Lord Cottesloe, forwarding TOW's letter: 'It seems to me to be a case wh. deserves your attention.'

September 8th 1877, TOW to Prime Minister (a polite reminder): '... you were good enough to reply through your secretary that you would at once give my letter your best attention ... but not having heard from you ...'

September 13th, Prime Minister to Cottesloe: 'It is a year since I addressed you ... & I regret to say nothing has been done. What answer can I make him? He is a Member of Parliament for a County Borough and comes from a truly respectable family. Certainly he is a Brewer, but ...'

September 15th, Cottesloe to Prime Minister: 'Your letter has placed me in a great difficulty ... If you feel so strongly on the subject as to require that it shall be done, I must yield to your authority. But I would ask you as a favour to myself to allow the matter to stand over, until the return of the Lord Lieut. The Duke has been absent now for nearly two years, & he has always assured me that he did not intend to retain the Government of Madras above three years, so there is only one more year for Mr Wethered to wait – when it is not impossible that the Duke may revise his decision.'

Cottesloe, in his twisting and turning, had tried to argue that the Marlow Bench was well supplied with magistrates. But the chairman, G.H. Vansittart of Bisham Abbey, a strong supporter of Tom's case, pointed out that for reasons of age or living at a distance, several of them never attended. There had been times when it was difficult to muster as many as two. Another ally was J.C. Cobbold, M.P. for Ipswich and well known to Tom as president of the Society of Country Brewers. Cobbold had written directly to the Lord Chancellor, and received a reply that repeated exactly the words of Tom's petition to the Chancellor of the Exchequer:

March 9th 1878, W.M. Cairns, Secretary of the Commission of the Peace, to J.C. Cobbold: 'I am directed by the Lord Chancellor to inform you that after giving the matter his fullest consideration, he is of the opinion that the fact of a gentleman being engaged in the Brewing business shall not be regarded as a disqualification for appointment as justice of the Peace.'

By the end of the decade Tom felt it was time to call in some political debts.

March 22nd 1879, TOW to the Prime Minister: 'In advancing my claims to Lord Cottesloe's consideration, I did not care to mention any political services I have rendered to my party, for it occurred to me that no good Conservative can claim much credit for promoting the cause he has at heart ...'

There follows a rather fulsome recital of all he has done for the party: how, in 1868 for example, 'I came forward myself at considerable personal sacrifice to rescue the seat which would otherwise have been lost to our party; and in 1874, in spite of bad health and against the wishes of my family, I consented again to hold the seat ...' But while he would never ask any favours of Lord Cottesloe in return for all this, he would expect fair treatment ... The letter ends on a note of appreciation:

I have to thank your Lordship sincerely for all that you have already done on my behalf. I have in my possession letters addressed by your Lordship to my grandfather in the years 1833 & 34,[2] which I value as evidence of the friendly feeling which existed between yourself and my family, and I appreciate all the more on this account the kindly interest you have taken in a matter personally affecting his grandson.

The following year Tom at last achieved his magistracy, perhaps because the duke, on his return from Madras, decided to relent. But there was another letter that I like to think was instrumental. It was dated 29 May 1879 and was addressed to Lord Cottesloe by his son Charles Freemantle:

> My dear Pappy ... I wish you could see your way to put the man into the Commission and have done with it! I am sure the Duke would have yielded long ago, and I think the Prime Minister and the Lord Chancellor are showing great forbearance! ... Your affc Son, C.W. Freemantle.

Charles' elder brother Thomas was the Member for Buckingham, the seat held by Disraeli before his elevation to the peerage. On the day Tom Wethered asked his question of the Chancellor, Freemantle arrived late in the House and could only pass on to his father what he had been told of

**31**   *Thomas Owen Wethered.*

the exchange. Lord Cottesloe was then about eighty-six. It says something about the depth of his concern, and about the level to which Tom had managed to raise the issue, that he had wanted an immediate and verbatim report.

In his day Tom's grandfather Thomas had been an important local figure, who, for a hundred years and more, turned Marlow into a company town. He was also by a clear margin the head of the Wethered family. Owen, Tom's father, had enjoyed a similar, if less patriarchal position, for Lawrence William, his brewery partner, was more than 12 years younger and never as prominent in the town. With Tom and OPW, only four-and-a-half years apart, it was a different story. Both were blessed with the energy, ambition and leadership qualities that one associates with men of substance in the Victorian heyday. Both took leading roles in local activities and were generous (as indeed they could afford to be) with their donations to schools, sports clubs, the church and other bodies. Both were closely involved in the founding of new enterprises such as the Rifle Volunteers and the Marlow Railway, and both, of course, were hands-on partners in the brewery as well.

In all of this they seem to have supported one another's efforts; if there was any rivalry or petty jealousy it remains unproven. Each was secure in his position in the world and grateful to the Providence that had placed him there. Status was important to both of them, in Tom's case obsessively so, as we have seen. One of OPW's little vanities was to decorate as many of his possessions as possible with his monogram and family crest. But if their egos were large, so was their liberality and community spirit.

Certainly Tom had the shorter fuse and took less trouble to avoid making enemies. But if OPW's was the more equable temperament he could nevertheless be moved to anger, as when he fulminated against Sir Stafford Northcote. As leader of the Conservative Opposition in the Commons it had fallen to Sir Stafford to mount an attack on, among other things, Gladstone's handling of the Sudan crisis of 1885 in which General Gordon met his death at the hands of the Mahdists. Infuriated by his inept performance, OPW wrote a stinging letter of complaint to W.H. Smith, former Leader of the House and a neighbour in nearby Hambleden village. Describing Northcote's vote of censure as 'a milk and watery Resolution', OPW concluded, 'I would rather see any man of average common sense – taken haphazard out of the street – become our leader than retain Sir S. Northcote in that position.' Strong words for a patient man.

On the death of the Duke of Buckingham in 1889, OPW wrote again to W.H. Smith, suggesting that he 'put in a good word with Lord Salisbury [the Prime Minister] in favour of T.F Fremantle' as the new lord lieutenant. 'He *must* be a peer very soon,' OPW wrote, 'for even Lord Cottesloe can't live for ever [by now his lordship was 91], and his appointment would be very popular in the County.' However, the duke's immediate successor was to be Sir Nathaniel Rothschild.

In the late 1860s the brothers' extra-curricular paths had divided as OPW remained committed to his soldiering and Tom turned to politics, moving into local government after his 12 years in Parliament. He served on both the County Council and on the Board of Surveyors, a ramshackle collection of guardians and overseers that looked after Marlow's affairs until replaced by a Parish Council in 1891. This was succeeded by the Urban District Council, which Tom 'agitated for' but did not serve on.[3] However, it was through 'his generous gift of a considerable amount of money',[4] among other donations, that the Council was able to rid Marlow of the infamous fair which had clogged the High Street with its stalls and caravans and acted as a magnet for thieves and pickpockets each year for many years. The money went to compensate the Williams family, who had long ago bought market rights to the street and had been receiving tolls from the fair.

It was perhaps on one of Tom's journeys down to Marlow from Westminster that the often-related episode of the hatbox occurred. As the train slowed and seemed about to stop, Tom leaned out of the window to discover the reason, at which point the train gathered speed and Tom's top hat flew off his head and away into the countryside. On the luggage rack was his leather hatbox, which he now reached for and hurled through the window after the hat.

Witnessing this curious behaviour, a fellow-passenger is alleged to have said, 'Excuse me, sir, I don't like to seem inquisitive, but can you tell me why, after losing your hat, you throw a perfectly good hatbox after it?'

'Yes', said Tom. 'Because I want my hat back.' The box contained a label with Tom's name and address. In due course, a bit muddy perhaps but otherwise undamaged, both hat and box were delivered to him at Seymour Court.

In 1902 the Rev. John Light succeeded Herbert Fearnley-Whittingstall as vicar of Marlow. On hearing of the appointment a friend of his told him, 'You know they say the prayers differently there.'

'Oh?'

'Yes, they say, "For thine is the kingdom, the power and the *brewery*".'

What Mr Light cannot have been prepared for was the brewery, in the shape of Uncle Tom, storming down the hill one October morning and hammering on the vicarage door. 'I'll soon have you out of there, you Jesuit!' he is reputed to have growled when the door was opened.

It was the hated ritualism again. Mr Light had led a procession to celebrate the harvest festival. Doubtless it was more restrained than the one at Haydock in the 1860s, nor did the vicar lose his job, but the story illustrates the depth of feeling that a symbol of 'popery' (as it was seen) could arouse in an evangelical like Tom. As late as the 1960s the then vicar of Marlow and his churchwarden went head to head over as seemingly innocuous a practice as the reservation of the Sacrament, and that time the vicar did leave the parish.

Tom lived on at Seymour Court until his death in 1921. Although, as the eldest son of his father, he was the owner of Remnantz, he could not pass the property on to his children because it was entailed down the male line and he and Edith had only daughters. It was rumoured that she once miscarried with a boy and failed to tell him, but the truth about that will never be known. Instead, he leased Remnantz to OPW's eldest son, Francis Owen, or Frank, who was my grandfather, and by that time a widower with a pair of twins.

It is part of family lore that Tom was in the habit of walking about Marlow, hands behind his back and a half-crown in his open palm. He would never turn round when he felt the coin being removed because he knew, so he said, that it would only be taken by someone who really needed it. Although Tom was known for his generosity, there will be those who find that particular story too good to be true. The best we can do in the absence of proof is point to Tom's memorial stained glass window in the south wall of All Saints' church. There, in the lower left-hand corner, is a picture of St Nicholas secretly putting money through the window of a poor man's house. Readers must draw their own conclusions.

# 15

# *Brewers and Others*

For a summary of how the family business had been faring we must return briefly to 1836. That was a landmark year for the brewery. The sad unseeing mill horses walking their endless rounds, providing power to grind the malt and work the hoist and pump and yeast press, had at last been replaced by a brisk Boulton & Watt steam engine.[1] Big London breweries like Whitbread's had been using steam for more than fifty years, but, like everything else, it was a matter of cost-effectiveness. Thomas had been producing not much more than 20,000 barrels a year, which was roughly the point below which it was not economical to invest in steam. Whitbread's annual production at the time was something like 130,000 barrels.

It was also in 1836 that Thomas had brought two of his sons, Owen and Lawrence William, into the partnership with him. Accounts for 1837 show the share capital of each of the two junior partners to have been £ 8,000, together representing half the total share capital of the company. After Thomas's retirement in 1839, his half share was divided between them.

In contrast to the worthy but sober-sided Owen (as we imagine him), Lawrence William, 12 years younger, shows signs of having been more high-spirited. In a portrait painted in early middle age he wears the half-smile of a man who knows how to have a good time. He was a good horseman and fond of sports, like his friend Tom Smith. Of his love life we know only that he married late, but in circumstances that are quite startling. Bobby Fearnley-Whittingstall tells the story:

> For many years he had enjoyed a reputation as Marlow's most confirmed bachelor, although in 1851, when he was 41, he created something of a stir in the family circle. With others of the Wethered clan, he had gone to Swinton [Manchester] to attend the wedding of Anne Wethered's brother, Edmund Yates Peel, to Catherine Anne Hurt. Lawrence William, seeing her for the first time, was bowled over, and as she paced slowly up the aisle on her father's arm, he turned to his astonished neighbour and said in a fierce undertone, 'That, sir, is the woman I shall marry, and none other.' He was never more serious in his life. Heaven would have to help him by eliminating Edmund Yates Peel, but heaven did, and Edmund died in 1861. And in January 1867, three weeks after Lawrence William's 57th birthday, Catherine Anne made him 'the happiest of men'.

A daughter, Catherine-Mary, was born to them in 1870.[2] Previously, Lawrence William had enjoyed being the bachelor uncle to his many nieces and nephews.

**32**  *Brewery workers, c.1880.*

Uncle LW, as they called him, now lived at Stubbings House near Maidenhead; it was his custom to give a wedding dinner for each niece when she became a bride.

The brewery was now justified in calling itself Thomas Wethered & Sons. For some time it had been the main industry and biggest employer of labour in the town. It not only controlled the retail end of the brewing trade with its public houses, but also provided much of the raw materials from farms it owned or leased in the neighbourhood. Given good harvests and not too swingeing taxes, it was pretty well self-sufficient.

But the Owen/Lawrence William years appear to have been a time of consolidation rather than expansion. According to a brewery source,

> At the beginning of the 1840s the number of the Brewery's tied houses was 70, and 30 were bought during that decade. However, only 12 were added during the 'fifties, so that by 1860 the Brewery's performance seems to have reached a plateau. The very even production levels and the lower average profits suggest that Thomas's two sons ... were following their father's practice of not seeking actively for new markets.

With Owen's death in 1862 the partnership devolved on to Tom and OPW, his two eldest sons, his share of the business being divided between them. Their uncle Lawrence William withdrew from the partnership but retained his half-share of the business. One gets a flavour of the brewery in the late

19th century from a group photograph, probably taken in the 1880s. It could have been earlier but the two figures in top hats look very like a head brewer and under-brewer, and the first head brewer – Mr J.S. Kirkpatrick – was not appointed until 1880; before that the partners did the job themselves. On the left of the picture is a drayman with his horse, and there is a fellow in a woolly cap, probably a maltster; they wore red caps and were known as 'canaries'. Above is the old 1832 fermenting room with its slatted windows. When the brewery tower was built beside it in 1903, it was to house a new fermenting room with a water reservoir and a refrigeration plant.

Wages in the 1880s averaged 14 shillings a week for lower paid workers, plus various bonuses such as 'harvest money' and 'harvest home' money. That the industry was still firmly tied to agriculture is shown by the fact that brewery workers' wages were pegged to those of farm workers, the former not to exceed two shillings a week more than the farm labourers were paid. A more skilled worker such as a cooper could earn £21 a week.

The links to the local farms lasted until 1889 when it was decided to close down the maltings. There were five of them altogether, all in different parts of the High Street. By this time, to quote our anonymous brewery employee, 'a wider selection of grain could be obtained, prepared under up-to-date methods by specialists in the art of malting'. So once again, malting and brewing were becoming separate industries.

Tom Wethered and his brother OPW were men of many interests besides brewing. OPW, as we have seen, was wedded to his Rifle Volunteers and spent much time and energy on their affairs. Tom, having decided to leave soldiering to his brother, had made politics his avocation, presumably with similar demands on his time. A third brother, Robert, had joined the partnership, but he was not a well man and died in 1873. How deeply were Tom and OPW committed to the family business, and what effect were their outside interests having on the company's performance?

The third generation is often the one where ties to the family firm start to fray, usually in the cause of social advancement. Both Tom and OPW were products of Eton and Oxford; both were wealthy (due to the efforts of their forebears) and, in their own small sphere, men of influence. It was natural that they should seek to move in higher social circles, the one at Westminster, the other at county level. But they were not so stupid as to let the golden goose die of neglect, and the goose did quite nicely under their management. What drove them was an enviable self-confidence and apparently inexhaustible energy – in short, they were true Victorians.

For the first few years after Owen's death, production levels remained on the same plateau, at about 20,000 barrels a year. Twenty years later, by 1882, they had risen gradually to 25,644 barrels. The next ten years saw a decline, but never sinking below the 20,000 level, after which came a big rise until, by 1899, the year the partnership ended, output had reached 42,000 barrels a year.

The profit-and-loss picture is harder to read because we are missing the raw figures for this period. All we have are the dividends on profits, which are subject to many influences and show considerable fluctuations, although with a slight overall upward trend.

There was hardly an aspect of Marlow life in which these two brothers were not involved. In their younger days they were active in sports, especially cricket, where some interesting scratch sides took the field. There were matches between married men and single men, between the sunny side of the street and the shady side, and even between the cantoris and decani sides of the church. (Where would you find 22 young men attending Sunday worship today?) On 25 August 1865, to its shame, the Marlow Cricket Club lost by 88 runs to a side from the Marlow Choral Society; as secretary of the one and treasurer of the other,

**33**  *Frances Alice Wethered, known as Alice.*

OPW could be an impartial observer. He evidently had a fine bass voice for he performed as a soloist such pieces as *O Ruddier than the Cherry* and *Why do the Nations … ?*

In November 1867, a meeting was held to assess public support for a railway linking Marlow to the neighbouring small town of Bourne End, and so to the main GWR line to Paddington. OPW was in the chair. As with the Rifle Volunteers, there was some foot dragging, among others by Colonel Brownlow Knox who felt the railway had been overpriced. But strong support from the Marlow tradesmen, with the brewery (meaning the Wethereds) subsequently taking up a number of shares, carried the day. The Great Marlow Railway Bill passed through Parliament and on 13 July 1868 became an Act.

OPW now became chairman of the Great Marlow Railway Company, with Peter Borgnis, of Highfields in Marlow, as vice-chairman.[3] Other directors included Tom Wethered, James Carson of Spinfields, and Thomas Rolls of Palmer House. The eminent civil engineer Edwin Clark, also a resident of Marlow, agreed to serve as consulting engineer to the project. There were many challenges facing the new Board: the raising of capital, land acquisitions, and negotiations – not always amicable – with the mighty Great Western Railway whose rolling stock the Marlow line would be using. The workload must have been formidable. It would be five more years before the Marlow Donkey, as it is familiarly known, could make the two-and-a-half-mile journey across the green fields and along the riverside to Bourne End.

OPW became personally embattled with the GWR when that company objected to his riding on their engine's footplate in order to inspect the line. There was a sharp exchange of letters and one of the drivers, J. Saunders, was fined two shillings for allowing it to happen. OPW refused to back down, maintaining his right to inspect *his* line in this way, but whether or not he continued the practice or reimbursed Mr Turner his two shillings is not known.

In 1874 OPW handed over the chairmanship to his friend Peter Borgnis, while retaining a seat on the Board. When Borgnis resigned in 1887 due to failing health, OPW again took up the reins until his own poor health forced his retirement two years later. At a gathering at his home at the White House a group of the shareholders presented him with a grand silver salver, 'as a token of their sincere appreciation of his successful management and direction of the Company since its formation in 1868'.

One of the joys of my research for this book was to find that the partners' personal expenses were entered in the same ledgers as their brewery accounts. Thus, in OPW's case, we are allowed glimpses of his wife Alice's passion for birds and animals:

> 29th April 1864 – Board for birdcage, etc., 2/10
> 6th July 1864 – Dove house, £3.18.10
> 31st May 1866 – Repairing squirrel cage, 2/10ha.
> 10th December 1886, Painting Monkey house, 3/7

The story goes that when asked what she gave her pet lizards to eat, this wonderfully eccentric lady said airily, 'Oh, bread and milk, their natural food'. In fact she fed them on bluebottles, kept alive in what she called her bluebottle farm. Down in the cellars at Remnantz were two mouldering butterfly nets on long bamboo canes (ideal for drawing back the kitchen curtains) with which I like to think Alice chased her bluebottle prey. Another discovery at Remnantz was an ancient walking stick with a tiny electric bulb in the handle; if such early miniaturisation were possible, perhaps Alice *did*, as history relates, adorn her hair with electric lights when giving a dinner party.

Alice also enjoyed pistol shooting, and it was said that after her death her pistols were found jumbled up in the same drawer as some toffee along with some exquisite pieces of lace. (My sister Caroline finds nothing strange in that at all.)

Alice's *Dogs' Medical Dictionary*, published in 1907, is still on its shelf in the Remnantz library. The author, A.J. Sewell, MRCVS, was a man of impressive credentials, being 'Canine Surgeon to H.M. the King, also to H.M. the Queen, and to the Kennel Club, the Dogs' Home, the Dumb Friends' League, the Bulldog Club, etc., etc.' His book offers many curative measures for dog owners, and when all else fails there is an entry under 'Destroy Dogs, How to'. 'There is no doubt that the quickest and most painless way of killing a dog is by shooting,' Mr Sewell states confidently, before adding as an afterthought, 'providing the man is a good shot.'

**34** *Francis Owen Wethered.*   **35** *John Danvers Power.*

Alice's headstone in Marlow churchyard bears the fitting inscription 'He prayeth best who loveth best ...' The next line of the poem readers may supply for themselves.

OPW was a tireless traveller. In his red leather pocket diaries, among pages of personal information – expenses, birthdays, dates of family wills and probates, all listed in his tiny, neat handwriting – are the many journeys he made in Britain and abroad. In April 1881 he travelled to the United States. When his ship put in at Baltimore, he was surprised to be greeted at the gangway by an elderly gentleman who introduced himself as George Yeates Wethered. He had spotted Mr Owen Wethered's name in the local paper, where first-class passenger lists were published in those days. George and Congressman John, mentioned earlier, were both descended from a Samuel Wethered who had died in 1719 after being ruined in the South Sea Bubble, and whose widow Dolly (née Lewin) had emigrated to the United States the following year. George's own father, another Samuel, had spent time in the American Southwest; he was a friend of the lawman Kit Carson and (believe it or not) became known as Santa Fe Sam Wethered.

That meeting at the gangway was the start of a lasting friendship between the two families. L. Wethered Barroll, a cousin once removed of George Yeates and author of *The Wethered Book*, also came to know OPW and visited the family at Remnantz. He writes,

Owen Peel Wethered was tall, wore a beard and mustache, had blue eyes, and a gentleness of manner that came from a warm heart, a kindness which keeps him alive in the memory fifty years later.

The brothers' partnership ended in 1890 with Tom's retirement at the relatively early age of fifty-eight. Tom had no sons to succeed him in the business; his place was taken by his son-in-law John Danvers Power, husband of the eldest of Tom's three daughters, named Edith after her mother. OPW's and Alice's eldest son Francis Owen – or Frank – and his younger brother Walter joined their father as partners in the firm. In 1899 the partnership was dissolved, the partners becoming directors of a new limited company.

For continuity's sake, presumably, OPW stayed on as chairman, although already suffering from the TB that eventually killed him. Among all his other activities, in about 1887, when he was 50 he had bought a piece of high ground with magnificent views above Puerto Oratava[4] in Tenerife. There he

**36** *El Robado, the family seat in the Canaries.*

built a large stone mansion, roofed in slate which he imported from England. To install the pipe work he also imported a plumber, the curiously named Mr Ernest Uren. For the amusement of his guests he laid out a croquet lawn, a bowling green and concrete tennis court. The road leading up to the house had acquired the name El Robado (literally 'robbed'), and for reasons that are hard to guess at, OPW used it for his grand new property.

There, he and Alice began to spend not only the winter months but the whole year except for two months in the summer, becoming part of Orotava's small British community. Noted for his generosity, OPW also managed to ruffle his neighbours' feathers with his preference for having his own way. The English library was part of a building programme that included an Anglican church (All Saints') and a British club. A library committee had been set up and had identified a suitable site, which it proposed to purchase for the community. But at this late date the Colonel, as they called him, stepped in with a plan of his own.

It seems he wanted the library on his doorstep, for he offered to donate a piece of his property and backed this up with a large cash pledge. Ultimately it was too good an opportunity to miss, but the committee was divided. The vicar, the Rev. Arthur Humphreys, who was in the chair, felt obliged to stand down. In the minute book is a pencilled note: 'The original site was much the best.'

The rift was healed of course, and the episode ends on a surprisingly romantic note. Staying at El Robado at the time – evidently on an extended visit – was Edith Drake, Georgie's daughter and OPW's niece. She was drafted on to the library committee, where Arthur Humphreys was again in the chair, and subsequently appointed librarian. The unmarried vicar was clearly taken with her – one can imagine his finding all sorts of reasons for visiting the library – for the following year he made her his wife.[5]

OPW's absence from the board left Frank and Walter Wethered and John Power as the working directors. It was an awkward situation. Frank, as the eldest son, was the acknowledged chairman-in-waiting. But he was only 25, not long down from Oxford – where he distinguished himself as an oarsman if not scholastically – and with little business or brewing experience. John Power, six years and eight months his senior, was already a man of affairs. As a young man he had worked for his father's shipping business in Swansea, but in his own words, 'struggled to get out of the place'. He said, 'I have never recovered from my horror of a provincial manufacturing town and its inhabitants.' In 1884 he took a job as secretary to the Country Brewers Association, of which his future father-in-law Tom Wethered was chairman. While doing this he studied law and became a barrister at the Inner Temple, taking on licensing cases. He had parliamentary ambitions but these were unfulfilled. Instead, in the new reign, he worked for important national charities such as King Edward's Hospital Fund for London and – at the Queen's request – the Council of the Red Cross Society. It is not hard to see that his second-among-equals relationship with Frank could be a source of trouble, and so in time it was to prove.

One of the first acts of the new Board was to advertise for a general manager, and Power was delegated to screen the applications. His wife was convalescing after a minor accident, and to amuse herself she started leafing through the letters in the reject pile. One in particular caught her eye and she persuaded her husband to reconsider it. The letter was from a Colonel Frank Stevens. Not only did he get the job, he was a tower of strength to the brewery for more than 25 years. In fairness to Mr Power, it must be said that he told the story against himself at Stevens' retirement party in 1926.

Colonel and Mrs Stevens lived in the White House, where OPW and his family had lived and where managing directors continued to live right up to the 1950s. The Old House had become the living quarters of the head brewer, Mr J.L. Holland, and his under brewer. Each of them had a bedroom and sitting room with cooking and other 'attendance' laid on, plus coals and gas and the washing of table and bed linen. Their housekeeper was a Mrs Rainbow.

Employees showed a commendable degree of loyalty to the firm. Holland was there for 29 years, from 1891 until his death in 1920; he was appointed a director in 1917. And the minutes for 1925 record the death of C.H. Newman who was an office employee for 42 years after his father had served 34 years before him.

By 1905 the brewery's delivery radius was about 25 miles and for the longer journeys the railways were being used. Now the brewery began to mechanise its own transport, the horse-drawn drays being replaced, not yet by lorries but by steam traction engines, or 'road locomotives'. These strange-looking vehicles with their drivers perched on top were probably no faster than the old dray horses, and they had the added disadvantage that the combined weight of engine and trailer exceeded the five-ton limit for Marlow bridge. So for south-bound deliveries horses were needed to pull the trailers across. For return journeys the horses were summoned via a telephone link set up between the brewery and the village of Bisham on the other side of the bridge. With the coming of these engines the number of horses was reduced from 52 to three. The draymen were trained to drive the engines, and later the lorries, and became very good at it.

These cumbersome arrangements were fairly short-lived. Lorries started appearing in 1911 and by 1919 the famous Thorneycroft lorries that were such a potent symbol of the brewery for so many years were coming into service. Their names alone – *Perseverance, Victor, Onward, Progress* – spoke of confidence and prosperity. They cost £855 each for the chassis (with engine presumably), plus £188 for the body and accessories. If you wanted an electric horn or an illuminated sign you had to pay extra. The drivers took immense pride in them, keeping their paint fresh and their brasswork gleaming, and they won numerous prizes at the Commercial Road Users Association's annual parade in London.

Between 1902 and 1905 there was a downturn in the company's gross profits of about 11 per cent. Several things were blamed for this: bad harvests, a rise in

**37** *Saved for Posterity: the lorry* Perseverance *in 1987.*

the price of hops and in the tax on beer, and also a growing demand for bottled beer which was more expensive to produce. A hand-operated bottling plant had been installed in 1901, which gave way to successive stages of conveyor-belt automation. It was in the bottlery in 1913 that women were first employed in the brewery. They worked a 12-hour day, from six a.m. to six p.m., and were paid 10 shillings a week – 12 shillings for the forewoman. These were probably standard hours and standard rates for the time.

The company secretary's salary at the time was £175 a year. Charles Henry Yates was one of the brewery's most intriguing characters. He had joined the firm in 1876 as a boy of 14 and worked his way up to his present position, which he held until his death in 1935 – a total of 59 years. Even more remarkable than his corporate longevity was his innovative way with Board meetings. Somewhat in the manner of the White Queen in *Through the Looking Glass*, he would write the minutes *before* each meeting. He himself would not attend the meeting; he would simply expect the proceedings to conform to his version of them.[6] No doubt he took the view that he knew more about the workings of the brewery than did the directors, and he may well have been right.

Along with the dip in profits in 1905 came a comment in *The Investors Guardian* that the company was not soundly financed. On the one hand, said the paper, the brewery had no reserve fund, and on the other, the dividends paid out to the 17 shareholders (mostly family) were much larger than the company could sustain. But while profits continued generally unexciting up to 1915, the product itself was winning high honours. In 1914 Wethered's were awarded the coveted Championship Gold Medal at the Brewers Exhibition, along with silver medals and a bronze. There were further medals and diplomas in 1923 and 1925.

Following OPW's death in 1908, the chairmanship passed to Frank as expected and the vice-chairmanship to John Power. It can never have been an easy relationship and in 1916 things came to a head. The year's results had shown another dip in profits. At a directors' meeting Frank proposed a distribution to shareholders of about one third. John Power thought otherwise: he moved an amendment to say that all profits should be carried forward for at least the next two years. The alternative, he believed, would be 'the mortgaging or selling of properties on which the Company depends for its output'.

When it came to the vote it was one against one. The only other director present was Colonel Stevens, who wisely abstained. As chairman Frank had the casting vote so the amendment was defeated and Frank's motion carried. It was not the first disagreement the two men had had over policy, and shortly afterwards John Power resigned from the Board.

Ironically, he went just as things were about to get better. Since the 1890s, a small part of the brewery's revenue had been derived from wines and spirits which it bottled and sold. Now, in 1916, a mineral water plant was installed and went into production. Not that it made much difference to overall profitability, but one may ask whether, given the firm's low reserves, the year's poor performance figures were to do with outlay on the new plant. More interesting, though, is the question, What produced the handspring jump in net profits from £19,482 in 1916 to £35,453 in 1917, and the generally better results to come?

# 16

# *Love Story*

They met in the summer of 1895 when Frank was 30 and Adeline twenty-four. Adeline Harris MacTier was the daughter of Dr and Mrs William MacTier of Kinnessburn, St Andrew's, Fife. A portrait of her by a Marlow artist, Percy Wild, has been part of the household landscape ever since I can remember. She had glorious red-gold hair, and if her face was a little full for true beauty, she was nonetheless a very lovely girl. Her face in repose had a rather wistful look, but there was a merry side to her and one longs to see those blue eyes lit up with laughter. Deeply affectionate towards her own family, she was apparently distrustful of romantic love and 'scornful when other people rather lost their heads' – this according to her sister Minnie.

Frank, for his part, though so like his father in many ways, had not inherited OPW's degree of self-assurance, and where Adeline was concerned he admitted to feelings of inadequacy. Whether due to this or to her reserve, or both, their occasional meetings after the first did not come to anything for three-and-a-half years. By that time Frank was well along a career path influenced by his father. While at Eton he had joined the college's Volunteer Rifle Corps, and had subsequently been commissioned as a subaltern in OPW's Bucks RV. At Eton, reportedly on his doctor's advice, he had been a 'dry bob', playing cricket rather than becoming an oarsman; but on going up to Christ Church in 1882 he was persuaded by his cousin Edmund, a contemporary at the college, to ignore the doctor and to take up rowing.

Frank's oars, though long consigned to the cellars here, still remind us of his prowess on the river. He and Edmund rowed together for Christ Church, with Frank being made captain of the Boat Club in 1885. That year, for the first time, he rowed No. 6 in the Oxford boat, which beat Cambridge by two-and-a-half lengths. The following year and the year after, as President of the OUBC, he retained his place at No.6, but Cambridge won both races, the second time assisted by No. 7 in the Oxford boat breaking his oar.

Frank finally proposed to Adeline, and was accepted, on 18 December 1898, and it was as if their families had been holding their breaths. Frank telegraphed her father in Scotland, and was immediately rewarded with his consent although the two men had not yet met. Perhaps Adeline, too, had been holding her breath, for when she did fall in love there was no shilly-shallying,

**38**   *A Vertical Eight – Oxford 1887. Frank Wethered is fourth from the bottom.*

it was total surrender. From the house in Bourne End where she had been staying with a friend Nina Lehmann, and where Frank had proposed to her, she scrawled a pencilled note to her parents:

> The wires this a.m. will tell you the news – I simply can't believe it – I am walking on air … I am *longing* for you to know him, he is just the best and most beautiful character you ever new [*sic*] … How he can care for me I can't think, but he says he does and I believe anything he says!

She wrote a similar scrawl to her brother Willie. Their sister Minnie wrote to Willie with expressions of happiness, describing Adeline as 'crazily in love'. Towards the end of a long letter she says, 'It's rather a pity he's an Englishman, but dear me they are next best to Scotsmen, & he's not one of the horrid men who know nothing but business.' Frank's first letter to Dr MacTier is highly revealing. In showing his future father-in-law that he is well able to provide for Adeline, he tells us much about the state of the brewery and his own expectations:

> My income depends upon the Brewery here, in which I am a partner, having a twelfth share; but my Father has for some years past given up to me another twelfth share of the profits in consideration of the fact that he lives practically entirely in Teneriffe [*sic*] and has therefore to leave to me in some measure the management of his affairs … My income last year was about £2,200, and I hope that our Stock Accounts for the year ending last Oct. 10th … may show an increase of some hundreds as my share.
>
> I believe that my Father is prepared to settle some £8,000 on my wife, and in his will to make up this sum to about £20,000, and possibly, in as much as I believe I am his residuary legatee, this sum may be exceeded on his death. When this occurs I shall come into ⅓rd share of the profits of our business, and as these profits have for some years past been steadily increasing I hope that this may mean that I shall have from this source some £5,000 a year instead of what I now have …

Thus Frank is a man of means, with good prospects, and the business at present is doing well. The brewery, he tells Dr MacTier in confidence, is soon to become a private limited company, and to that end his cousin John Power is in Tenerife going over the relevant papers with Frank's father. He includes the Tenerife address but cautions that 'it is sometimes impossible to get a reply under nearly a month, on account of the ships calling there being but few in number'. One may guess that if, this being so, John Power's return to Marlow is delayed, it will not cause too much distress to either cousin.

It may seem perverse to nickname a red-haired baby Snowy, but Adeline was born in December and no doubt, in the months that followed, some fond relative hoisted her up and called her 'my little snowdrop'. In any case, the name stuck, though for family use only.

She was christened Adeline after her godmother, who married the 10th Duke of Bedford and became his duchess. In his family history A *Silverplated Spoon*, the 13th Duke notes that Adeline's husband, who was his great-uncle, 'was one of the shy Bedfords. He had no time for women but got himself compromised into marriage.'[1] There was talk of an indiscretion on a sofa, but as to what actually happened history is silent.

We know quite a lot about our Adeline's short life because, like Sophie, who was her aunt by marriage, she was a tireless letter-writer, and some of her letters – mostly those to her mother – have been lovingly preserved by the daughter who never knew her. We meet her first when she is 15 and boarding at Belstead School in Suffolk, where her mother also went. The principal, who was also the founder, was a strong-minded woman named Mrs Umphelby, known to the girls as Mamie. The widow of a failed businessman, she had founded the school in about 1837, along lines described by the *East Anglian Daily Times* in her obituary:

> Punishment was a thing unknown, and rebuke a thing of rarity ... For scholastic success, as it is commonly understood, she cared but little. But for fifty years she strove to replace the conventional, stereotypical pedantry which had for so long borne the name of a 'lady's education' with a higher and broader development, and drawing forth of all that was best in her pupils. She considered a simple, noble woman a somewhat higher being than one who had spent her best years in one continuous struggle to obtain an University degree.

This may suggest to us the sort of place to retard the cause of women's education by 20 years. But for the majority of middle-class women then, for whom a 'blue stocking' was someone bookish and dull, Mrs Umphelby's championing of Christian virtues and womanly graces would have touched deep chords. At least Belstead provided the caring environment essential for someone away from home for the first time, and there is no evidence in Adeline's letters to show that she was homesick or unhappy. She did obtain permission to write a second letter home each a week, but that may have been because she enjoyed committing her experiences to paper and, besides, we do not know how long she kept it up.

She mentions lessons in French, German, and English History. Also, 'Mamie gives us spelling in our class, & there is much need for it as a worse set I never saw.' Her own spelling derives from what the author Claire Tomalin calls 'the picturesque school', *viz* 'We are going tomorrow to the Bently woods to have our jubilee paper chace ... Griselda & I are to be hairs.' It was June 1887 and there was to be a 'Gala' that evening to celebrate the queen's Golden Jubilee.

Adeline had a lovely singing voice, according to her music teacher Madame Christie, but her piano playing was less successful. Forced against her wishes to give a performance, 'I played the first few lines an octave too low but changed to the right one to make a little variation & with a good suply of wrong chords stumpled to the final run and chords which hapily I got out right.' Poor Adeline! She left Belstead at sixteen-and-a-half, having spent just a year there. That December Mrs Umphelby died aged eighty-two.

Whatever the shortcomings of Adeline's education – and we don't know what happened to her after she left Belstead – by the time she was 22 and launched on to the London scene of carefully chaperoned parties and dances, she had developed a remarkable eye for detail. In June 1894 she was staying at Palace Gate, Kensington, with some cousins, Sir Guy and Lady Campbell, after paying an overnight visit to her godmother, the dowager Duchess of Bedford. Following the death of her husband the previous year, the duchess had left the ducal residence of Woburn Abbey in Bedfordshire for another Russell property, the very much smaller but still substantial Chenies Place in Bucks. It was there that the younger Adeline visited the elder one. Her account of her stay, written to her mother from Palace Gate, gives a perfect vignette of the widowed duchess's surroundings and her way of life.[2]

> I did so enjoy my little visit to Cousin Adeline. She was *so* nice to me, she's a very sweet woman, & I like her awfully, & her absolute loneliness goes to my heart.
>
> Well, she returned from her class & we went up to change, I into my pink & she into a black tea gown. I'd never seen her without her bonnet, & she came down looking so graceful & beautiful with a little white lace cap with strings under her chin. The gong rang & we walked arm in arm into the dining room. There was a tiny round table just on the edge of the bow window with 4 lighted candles & a chipendale [*sic*] chair at each end, the Butler standing at the back of hers & the footman behind mine. We sat down & dinner began, a delicious little dinner & the men went away between each course, which was such a blessing, & she rang a tiny silver bell when we finished, everything beautifully served & very nice. We talked all the time & then went into the drawing room & sat in two arm chairs, with a high lamp burning & a delicious wood fire crackling in the grate … We talked till past 11! Tea was brought in abt. 10 & we had that together. Then we rose to go to bed & Cousin A. touched a bell & the Butler appeared with two lighted candles in his hand, particularly nice ones with little round glass globes on them. We went up the little white staircase to bed …
>
> I went to bed & was woken by the birds singing outside my window in the morning, so nice it was, not a cab, not a car, only these delicious country sounds, you'd never imagine it was only 50 min. from London for it is absolutely in the country, no villas at all, just a funny little straggling English village with 'the Bedford Arms' in the middle, & the little church & school. At 8 the house maid brought me a delicious cup of tea & my water & I got up. Cousin Adeline said that the prayer gong went at 9.15, but she'd knock at my door for me on her way down, & so she did, & we went down to prayers held in the house keepers room, about 4 girls, 2 men, a boy & the maid & our two selves made up the party. After that came breakfast during which we talked of different mutual relations, of Andrew Lang, the Campbells, Pro. Jowett, whom she knew well & others. Then she said she had some letters she must write & would I amuse myself in the drawing room. She writes in her little boudoir, which has a delightful conservatory off it. Soon the pony carriage came round & she came in for me & we went up

together to get ready. Cousin A. drove, I sat beside her & the man up behind.
She took a large key of the church, and a bunch of flowers.

Adeline breaks off here to say, in parenthesis, 'Sir Guy has just come in &
taken two photographs of me writing, with a Kodak. I caught him in the act,
just looked up in time to find I was being shot at!' Having described Sir Guy's
roguish behaviour she resumes:

> The little church is quite near & we drove slowly up there in the lovely soft warm
> air and sunshine. We went through the church into the sort of chapel adjoining,
> where all the Dukes & Duchesses of Bedford are buried & where Cousin A.'s
> husband lies.[3] She has put up a v. handsome but simple sort of monument in
> the wall, of marble & grey granet [*sic*]. Hers is the only one with a text on it,
> the others are very handsome in their way & very large, with carved figures of
> the Dukes on top of a block of marble. She goes there every morning before
> breakfast, and every week she puts new flowers on a cross on the ground in the
> centre. To those who are buried there & have no stone or monument she is just
> going to put in beautiful stained glass windows. It is a v. interesting place & she
> tries to make it as little like (as she says) a museum as she can.
>     Then we drove round a bit to see a beautiful old Elizabethan manor house
> there is beside the church. Then we went into the village & walked slowly home
> & left the carriage for the coach man to bring, talking. We walked all over the
> garden & she shewed me all her alterations & improvements. She's v. fond of
> her garden & has this spring taken in a large piece of meadow & is making a
> water garden, rose beds, a spring garden, thick with blue hyacinths, daffodils
> & primroses.

The garden had been laid out for her by a young and little known designer named
Edwin Lutyens, then in his mid-20s and hardly older than Adeline MacTier.
According to an article in *Country Life*, 'Chenies Place was his first important
garden for an existing house ... and contains features that were to reappear in
slightly different forms in many of his later works.'[4] Adeline concludes:

> Then we strolled back to lunch, after which I put on my things & then the pony
> carriage came round, my box was strapped on behind & Cousin A. admired my
> neat little box. We said goodbye, & she said she'd enjoyed having me and asked
> me to write to her sometimes. I got in beside the man & we drove off, leaving
> Cousin A. standing there in the doorway, holding her big St Bernard by the
> collar, & looking so pretty, but so sad.

Whatever the circumstances that precipitated her marriage, it seems clear
that the duchess loved her husband. They were the same age, about 41, when
he died, the year before young Adeline's visit. Perhaps it is the white lace cap
that leaves an impression of the duchess as a little old lady. In fact, from a
snapshot we have of her it appears that she was tall and angular. She died in
1920 aged about sixty-eight.

Adeline would have made a good courtroom witness, for it seems that those
lovely eyes missed nothing. Such details as walking arm in arm into the dining
room, and the tiny silver bell, make her letter a visual experience for the reader.
But there is a curious omission. Although the little dinner was delicious, and
she also took breakfast and lunch with the duchess, there is no hint at all as
to what they had to eat.

**39** *Detail from the wedding photograph of Frank and Adeline. Top left, William MacTier, the bride's father; below him, from the left, the Duchess of Bedford, Mrs MacTier, the Rev. Herbert Oakes Fearnley-Whittingstall and, far right, the Rev. Owen Henry Wethered. In the front row next to the bridegroom is Adeline's sister Minnie.*

Frank and Adeline were married on 11 April 1899 at St Andrew's church, St Andrew's. It had been deemed unwise for OPW to attempt the journey to Scotland, so after a honeymoon among the Italian Lakes and the foothills of the Alps, the couple took ship for Tenerife so that Adeline might receive the blessing of Frank's parents. Fortunately for his descendants, Frank was a dedicated amateur photographer and his faded sepia pictures tell the story of his travels. After El Robado in May, it was back to England and a rented house called The Orchard, in Pinkneys Green near Maidenhead, which was to be the couple's home.

Another of Frank's hobbies – shared by many Englishmen of his generation – was hill and mountain climbing. He was an alpinist, and books of his such as *Alpine Notes* by George Wherry (1896) and *Among the Selkirk Glaciers* by W.S. Green (1890) stand side by side in the library with his mother's medical dictionary for dogs and collected poems of Robert Bridges. In August 1899 he took Adeline back to the Alps, where she can be seen in a snapshot manfully climbing a snow-covered glacier in a wide-brimmed hat and ankle-length skirt. In another picture she stands perilously close to a deep crevasse.

Frank was a meticulously tidy man. In the drawers of his tool chest are neatly labelled tins of everything from screws, cup-hooks and paperclips to penknives and ballroom pencils, often with ink drawings of the items within. Similarly, his photos – half a dozen hefty albums of them – are each carefully captioned and dated. Group shots are what he liked best, and those for the year after his marriage naturally include his new bride. People were stone-faced in photos then, and only in one, where a cat has jumped on to Adeline's shoulder, is there a flicker of her smile. It was taken at The Orchard in February 1900 and it is almost the last we see of her. The photos march steadily on through the album with much the same cast of characters as before – a sequence in Tenerife with OPW and Alice with friends and relatives – but now Adeline is missing. She died on 4 May, two weeks after giving birth to twins, a boy and a girl. The boy was my father.

Pyaemia, or blood poisoning, due to an adherent placenta, is what Adeline's death certificate tells us. Family tradition has it that the infection was brought by the monthly nurse who acted as midwife, but of course we shall never know for certain. What is certain is that poor Adeline died an untimely and probably very painful death, leaving Frank to mourn his wife of only a year, and the MacTiers their beloved Snowy.

OPW received the news in Tenerife with other family members. He immediately wired Dr MacTier that he was sending an unmarried daughter Evelyn Annie, known as Ivy, home to supervise the care of the twins. For her, aged 26, it was in effect a life sentence; for little Owen and Adeline it was the beginning of a strictly ordered childhood. Adeline's death hit Frank very hard. Two months later he tried to make sense of it in a broken-hearted letter to her mother.

> Every day only seems to tell me more how I loved her and what she had become to me … I suppose I am too selfish, for I am too apt to think of myself & my life here without her, & too little of her nearer God … It is of some comfort to me to think that perhaps it is God's will that I should go soon, and that He took her first because she wd. have felt my death more than I feel hers even – for she loved me in so marvellous a way …

He addresses her as 'Dearest Mother', and it is only on reading the letter that one realises that he is writing to his mother-in-law. Such a letter written to his own mother would have been the reverse of comforting.

Frank's eldest sister Alice Mary, known as Ailsie, had married – over some competition from other Marlow girls – the handsome young vicar of Marlow, Herbert Fearnley-Whittingstall. Herbert held the incumbency from 1890 to 1902, when his place was taken by the Rev. John Light. He and Frank enjoyed each other's company enough for the two of them to take a month-long tour of Europe together, setting off in July of that same year. It was a well-timed trip: two-plus years since Frank's bereavement, a time when people are beginning to think that the wound must have healed, but of course it seldom has.

Their travels took them through northern Italy, with its memories of happier days, and they were in Venice on 14 July, the day the St Mark's campanile fell. It was known that the collapse was imminent for a large crack had appeared on one side. Legend has it that the two men were out on the lagoon, that Frank had turned to say something to Herbert, and by the time he looked back the great belltower had been reduced to a pile of rubble.[5] Before-and-after pictures and others taken by Herbert were presented to Frank in an album at the end of their tour.

**40** *Adeline MacTier Wethered.*

With the brewery and the Volunteers, and many other voluntary undertakings, Frank had plenty to occupy his time. A Justice of the Peace since 1897, he was appointed a Deputy Lord Lieutenant of Buckinghamshire, and in 1910 was elected unopposed to the County Council. These were in addition to the various school boards and other committees on which he served in the town. In 1904 he bought his first car, a canvas-roofed Napier, almost as high as it was long, and said to be the first privately owned car in Marlow.

In 1914, with the rank of lieutenant-colonel, he took command of the First Bucks Battalion of what was now the Territorial Force. Together they underwent intensive training, but, by the time the battalion sailed for France in March the following year, Frank had been declared medically unfit. His trouble was likely to have been tuberculosis, as it had been with his father, OPW, who had died from it in 1908.[6] Persistence on Frank's part got him to France with the 1st/6th Battalion of the Royal Warwickshires, which he commanded for a year before being invalided home in May 1916. He was back in July, this time commanding the 1st/8th Battalion, and in August was in action at the Somme. On the 25th he wrote a pencilled letter to his children, now 16, Owen attending the Dartmouth Naval College, Adeline at boarding school.

> My darlings, We moved yest. aft. & slept alongside a largish pond. Had some shells in the aft. Those into the water made jolly splashes. I slept in my valise on boards and tops of boxes, with a few boxes above me, & under a small bank. No shells during the night. We had to find 440 men on working parties during the night, & I fear that some caught it, tho' I haven't heard from any officer yet.
>
> I counted 20 French & British balloons up at the same time just along our front near us, & 3 Boche's only. The Boche are having a rotten time of it with our guns. We are getting some of the balance against us during the 1st 1½ years put right now. I am v. well.
>
> Best love to you all,
> Your v. loving father, F.O. Wethered

There are no records of the 'gallant and distinguished service in the field' that brought Frank a mention in despatches, nor of why he was awarded the CMG.[7] But this glimpse of him in the front line with shells making 'jolly splashes' in a nearby pond does help to set the scene for us. The envelope is addressed to Miss A.A.M. Wethered at the current family home of Meadside, Marlow, these being the summer holidays from school. In a whimsical moment Frank has drawn every 'M' as a goalpost, each with a goalkeeper and a ball at his feet. Two days later, according to a contemporary account,

> Two companies had moved out in splendid style; but in 'D' Company all the officers were shot down early in the advance, and the men being without leadership overshot their objective and went too far to the left, with the result that the other company – 'C' – found the enemy resistance too strong.

'But,' the writer adds encouragingly, 'whether immediately successful or not, such incidents were all steps in the steady progress which paved the way for a more general attack.' World War One in a nutshell, perhaps.

In a family photo taken about 1906 (overleaf), Ivy is the one off to one side and holding the cat. Her face, while not unattractive, wears a disappointed look, as well it might. Life can have held no more charms for her than it did for the children in her care. She died unmarried, probably of intestinal cancer, in 1915. The regime she imposed on the twins for their own good was a strict one, so that Dorothy and Evelyn Light, the daughters of the vicar, were much in awe of her and reluctant to come and play. To develop the children's linguistic skills Ivy employed a Swiss governess, and at mealtimes they spoke French and German on alternate days, English being permitted only on Sundays. After lunch they were each allowed a piece of chocolate, but not to ask for it. Since the treat was frequently forgotten, and since prompting could not be construed as asking, at least in Owen's and Adeline's minds, they took to muttering substitute words like 'chocoladdles' in an effort to trigger Ivy's memory. If Frank had preferred a less prescriptive upbringing for them, he would certainly not have wanted to step on Ivy's toes. On her death, with Frank away in the army, his cousin Edith Humphreys, recently widowed, came to look after the children's welfare, but only on condition that Adeline, then aged 15, was sent to boarding school.

The war had not improved Frank's health and in June 1917 he was placed on the Territorial Reserve. That year he married for the second time: Margaret Dyer of Farnham Common, Bucks; he was 52, she twenty-nine. Pretty, with fair red hair, Margaret was entertaining and fun to be with. She was also a talented water-colourist. For Frank it was a happy second marriage despite worsening health problems. Like his father, he eventually retired to Tenerife, where he died on 23 August 1922. His grave is in the cemetery in Puerto Oratava near OPW's.

Frank and Margaret had one child, a son Francis John born in 1918. Prevented by a TB shoulder from serving in the Second World War, he was nevertheless killed by enemy action in 1940, when the ship in which he was travelling to the Middle East for the British Council was torpedoed and sunk by a U-boat off the Cape of Good Hope.

**41**    *The older generations and the new, 1906.*

1   *Evelyn Annie ('Ivy') Wethered 1873-1915*
2   *Sophia Graves (née Wethered) 1838-1920*
3   *Rev. Michael Graves 1855?-1934*
4   *Rev. Robert Godfrey-Faussett (widower of Ellen Anne Wethered 1846-1900) 1827-1908*
5   *Col. William Godfrey-Faussett (widower of Sarah Elizabeth Wethered 1834-1894) 1825-1913*
6   *Emma Mary Trefusis (née Wethered) 1848-1927*
7   *Frances Alice Wethered (née Ellison) 1844-1918*
8   *Alice Mary ('Ailsie') Fearnley-Whitting-stall (née Wethered) 1866-1946*

9   *Sarah Godfrey-Faussett (unmarried daughter of Godfrey Faussett and Sarah Wethered, daughter of Thomas) 1831-1928*
10  *Thomas Owen Wethered 1832-1921*
11  *Owen Peel Wethered 1837-1908*
12  *Henrietta Aldridge (unmarried daughter of J. Aldridge and Georgina Wethered, daughter of Thomas) 1843-1932*
13  *Francis Owen Wethered 1864-1922*
14  *Adeline Alice MacTier Wethered 1900-1974*
15  *Owen Francis MacTier Wethered 1900-1981*
16  *Hugh Ellison Wethered 1889-1938*

# 17

# *Closing Down*

For a few years after Frank's death in 1922 there were no Wethered directors on the Board. His brother and co-director Walter, a captain and honorary major in the Suffolk Regiment, whose home had been Blounts at the top of Chalkpit Lane, had died in 1917 aged forty-seven. With Frank gone, John Danvers Power agreed to rejoin the company and he was elected chairman in Frank's place. His son Piers had joined the Board the previous year. (Frank's widow Margaret was made a director in 1924 but died two years later.)

Meanwhile it appeared that a large block of OPW's holdings in the company had never been taken up. In 1926 it was valued at £82,000 and there were signs of a move towards a hostile take-over by interests in the City. In what was seen as a rescue package the bulk of the shares were bought by the sugar magnate Sir Richard Garton and his brother Charles. It was of course the largest share acquisition ever made outside the family.

The Gartons' company, Manbre & Garton, were suppliers of sugar to the brewery and Sir Richard was already a shareholder and member of the Board. Now he was joined on the Board by Charles Garton, who was described as 'one of the most experienced men in the brewing world'. The Garton influence remained strong, with Sir Richard's son Stanley replacing him after his death, and a nephew Kenneth Durrant also joining the Board.

The minutes recording the bail-out by the Garton brothers also noted the Board's gratitude to the Rev. Owen Henry Wethered 'for his successful efforts to preserve [the business] on its present lines, both by his management of the general negotiations involved and his own purchase of very nearly £20,000 worth of shares'.

It is interesting that Owen Henry should have been entrusted with the negotiations over the share dealings, pointing as it does to a rapprochement between the Wethereds and the Powers. (John Danvers was by then in his late 60s and would die the following year.) The eldest of OPW's sons after Frank, he was one of the survivors of this depleted family, four of whom had died in infancy, and another son, Thomas Arthur, in 1903 at the age of thirty-one. In a family photograph taken in about 1890 Owen Henry appears as a lanky, amiable young man of about 23 with fair thinning hair – a characteristic of later Wethereds. Another product of Eton and Christ Church, he went into the Church and was known to his nieces and nephews as 'Uncle Bish' in the expectation that he would become a bishop. He never did, nor did he marry, but for 19 years was a popular vicar of Boldmere, near Birmingham. On his retirement due to ill health he was presented with an illuminated testimonial and a 'telescopic and adjustable table' which his parishioners hoped would be 'useful under existing conditions' – presumably a bedside table.

Thomas Arthur, or Tomar as the family called him, had been a consulting engineer with (for a Wethered) a rather unorthodox private life. In March 1897 he had become married to a girl of no social pretensions named Annie Laura White. Annie Laura had earlier had an affair with a London-based Italian, Giulio Del-Rivo, resulting in the birth of a baby girl. Tomar and Del-Rivo were of a similar age and Del-Rivo, like Tomar, was an engineer. The rest is speculation, but it is certainly possible that the two men knew each other, and if Giulio, a Catholic, was constrained from marrying outside his faith, then Tomar – himself attracted to Annie Laura – might well have decided to make an honest woman of her, her baby daughter having been put out for adoption.[1] The woman Giulio subsequently married was not only a co-religionist but a granddaughter of the great fighter for Catholic emancipation, Daniel O'Connell.

Beside Tomar's name in *Burke's Landed Gentry*, that sop to upper-middle-class vanity, is the single letter *m* for 'married'. His wife's name is missing, as is the date of their wedding at the register office in Islington, Laura's home district at the time. One might think that the family had refused to dignify her with an entry in *Burke*, but that is not necessarily the case. A snapshot taken by Frank at El Robado in February 1903 shows 'Lola' (the twins' name for Laura) in the midst of a group that includes both OPW and Alice – a sure sign that Tomar's pretty wife had been accepted by the family, whether or not the family was aware of her past.

Following Tomar's death, about eight months later, Annie Laura married a Canadian poet Edward Vernon Nott, and took to calling herself Leila, so she may have become untraceable by the time of the entry in Burke. The story handed down to us was that Tomar had married his nurse on his deathbed, a fiction devised, perhaps, to cover the missing information. Tomar was the first Wethered to die and be buried in Tenerife, suggesting that, like his father and his brother Frank, he was a victim of TB.

Ivy (Evelyn Annie), the stern guardian of Frank's twins, had died unmarried in 1915, her dreams of happiness unfulfilled. So now, in 1926, of the original 12 children of OPW and Alice there remained just two married daughters – Alice Mary Fearnley-Whittingstall (known as Ailsie) and Cisely Edith Esbell Laurence – along with Owen Henry and the baby of the family, the angelic-looking Hugh Ellison Wethered.

Seventeen years younger than Tomar, the nearest brother to him in age, Hugh has acquired a black-sheep reputation, whether because he was the first member of the family to be divorced, or for related or other reasons, is not known. After Eton and Trinity, Cambridge, he was commissioned in the Welsh Guards, attaining the rank of major. Personal information is lacking, except that he was twice married and, according to his daughter Bettine, left no money when he died in 1938. His first wife Joan (they were married in 1914, divorced in 1933) is remembered for being given refuge from the Blitz on London by Frank's daughter Adeline – Joan's cousin by marriage – at Adeline's family's house in Pangbourne, but soon having to leave because she was 'teaching the children bad language'.

But it was Hugh's and Joan's daughter Bettine who spectacularly went off the rails, and was ostracised by the family as a result. Hers is a sad story of estrangement from her mother (whom she accused of purloining money intended for herself), of drug abuse, marriage, divorce and remarriage, then widowhood, destitution and begging letters. She seems to have been fond of her second husband, one Alan Turner with an address in Paris, but he died while they were living in Majorca, leaving her almost penniless. Shortly afterwards, while shopping in the market in Palma, she apparently trod on some rotten boards and fell eight feet into the cellar, breaking her femur.

A woman named Baroness Von Ripper, for whom Bettine had been doing some secretarial work and who was with her at the time of the accident, wrote on Bettine's behalf to my father Owen, asking for financial help. The British consul in Palma added his support. Owen had been appealed to by Bettine three months earlier; he had responded with a cheque for £50 and received an effusive letter of thanks. Now he sent her a further £25, saying that he could do no more. If these amounts seem niggardly, one must remember that all this took place in 1963, when money was many times its present value, and that Owen, although head of the family, was no more to Bettine than her second cousin and did not want to be considered her golden goose.

I recall two family occasions at which Bettine was present. One was the funeral of Blanche Ellison, one of Alice's sisters, when she arrived late and to whispers of 'It's Bettine' from those in the pews. She was a striking looking woman in her 40s with long platinum tresses and, one need hardly add, was the cynosure of all eyes. This was before the accident in Majorca.

Somehow, this turn-of-the-century generation shows signs of fraying at the edges. They lack the sparkle and warmth and solidarity of the Victorians who preceded them. To be fair, they are not nearly so well documented, and perhaps the intervention of the 'Great War' contributed to an aura of melancholy that seems to hang over them. But that is not to say that they never had any fun. As part of their contribution to the building fund for the new Institute, the family devised evenings of 'Theatrical Entertainment'. Short plays with such titles as *The Loan of a Lover* and *A Husband in Clover* were performed in the music room of the town hall, with Wethereds ranging from Frank down to Ivy taking all the parts.

Still living in 1926 was Emma, the youngest but one of Owen's and Anne's children, now the widow of the late Bishop of Crediton, Robert Trefusis. There is a charming story of the couple's courting days when Robert was a young curate at the parish church in Buckingham. When walking home together after an evening out it was considered unseemly for them to hold hands; instead, they held a short stick between them in order not to lose each other in the dark. On a windowpane in what was once Emma's bedroom at Remnantz are her initials – EMW – with the date – 1st May 1874 – neatly engraved with her engagement ring a week before her wedding.

Like so many of the Wethered daughters, Emma was a woman of determination and resourcefulness. By the time of the First World War, after Robert had been elevated from vicar of Chittlehampton, in North Devon, to Bishop of Crediton, he and Emma were living in the chantry of Exeter Cathedral. One of the vergers, a man named Palmer, had returned from the front having had his nose blown off in the fighting, and too disfigured, he told Emma, to resume a job that exposed him to the public gaze. Emma refused to listen to his protestations. Clever with her hands, she constructed a new nose cut from a biscuit tin, painted flesh colour and soldered to a steel spectacle frame. According to her grandson, Robert J.R. ('Jack') Trefusis, 'it was a splendid success and Palmer continued as verger for many years. I well remember him wearing his metal nose.'[2]

Like her sister Sophie, Emma was a devoted carer. As the bishop grew older and his health began to fail, she would take it upon herself to hide his shoes rather than have him go out to early service on cold winter mornings.

In June 1920 Emma travelled up from Devonshire to be at Sophie's bedside as she lay dying. Sophie's thoughts were taking her back over her remarkable life, to her marriage to Percy and later to Michael, and to all that had happened in between. Looking up at her sister, she uttered the never-to-be-forgotten words, 'Don't tell Michael ... but I can't wait to see Percy again.'

In naming a successor to John Danvers Power the directors made an interesting choice. Colonel J.R. (Joe) Wethered was the son of Florence Thomas Wethered by his second wife Josephine Bonsor. He was thus a great-grandson of the founder Thomas and brought a welcome return to the Board of the family name. Unlike his father and grandfather, both of whom had been vicars of Hurley, he chose a military career, passing through Sandhurst and being gazetted an ensign in the Gloucestershire Regiment in 1893. He fought in both the Boer and Great Wars and was six times mentioned in despatches as well as being awarded the DSO and CMG. He had a desk job at the War Office when he was invited, in 1927 at the age of 53, to come to Marlow.

A professional soldier may seem an odd choice for chairman and managing director of a brewery, but there were many such appointments in industry at the time. Colonel Joe would have been thought 'good with men', and besides there was the precedent of Colonel Stevens. The brewery prospered under his leadership, which lasted for some 15 years and saw the beginning of the Second World War.

With the war came the need for fuel conservation, and industries were told by Government to combine deliveries to cut down on road journeys. Under an arrangement with Simonds brewery of Reading, therefore, Simonds houses

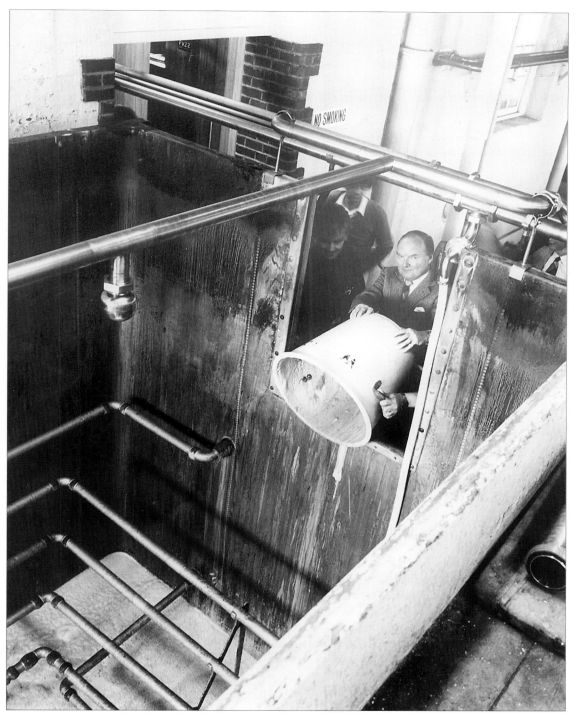

**42**   *A last bucket of yeast being tipped in by the author, 1987.*

**43** *Front view of Remnantz today.*

in the Marlow area started serving Wethered beer, while Wethered houses in and around Reading served Simonds. We are not told how the former Simonds customers felt about this, but from some of those used to Wethered's beer there was an outcry. On two separate occasions towards the end of 1941 – one before and one after the scheme was in place – Mr H.S. Smith of the *Borough Arms* public house in Reading led a deputation of fellow-publicans to the brewery to complain. They were 'all very alarmed by the drop in trade and the unhappiness of their customers', Smith told the Board the second time they met; to make his point, he produced a petition signed by 3,929 drinkers who preferred Wethered's beer.

Colonel Joe congratulated Smith on his presentation and expressed sympathy with the publicans' position. But he went on to explain that unless the breweries did 'play up', as he put it, to the Government's directive, then the Government could take control of the whole industry. By way of a clincher he noted that in the year 1940-1, trade in the Wethered houses in Reading had increased by 14.5 per cent over the previous year. What the colonel perhaps forgot to mention was that beer consumption had gone up across the whole of Britain as a result of the war.

Joe Wethered was followed as chairman in 1942 by Piers Power, the son of John Danvers and a grandson on his mother's side of Uncle Tom. Kenneth Durrant and Stanley Garton became joint managing directors. They were joined on the Board by young John Wethered, the son of Frank and Margaret, who was to die by enemy action the following year. Once again the family name disappeared, until Frank's elder son, Owen Francis MacTier Wethered, was elected to the Board in 1945.

The rest of the story is quickly told. In 1945 Strong's brewery of Romsey began putting out feelers towards a take-over of Wethered's. Their initial overtures were declined, but in 1949 the directors accepted an offer of £1.25 million for the company.[3] What prompted the decision to sell? Of course it was financial pressure. Much of the plant needed replacing. At the beginning of the Second World War there was a question as to whether it would last for the duration, and the decision apparently was to chance it. But by 1947 the head brewer was reporting that the plant was 'critically worn out'. Moreover, the country was going through what my father referred to as 'a storm of prices'. It seemed to the Board that the time had come to get out.

**44**  *Rear view of Remnantz today.*

My father Owen was a career naval officer, recently returned to Britain from service overseas. He was new to the business, and indeed to the business world – the world in which his co-directors dwelt. His was in large part a sentimental attachment; theirs, with the exception of Piers Power, a purely financial one. It was really no contest.

As my father explained it to me, it came down to a choice between selling the brewery or selling Remnantz. Whether or not he *could* have saved the brewery on his own is questionable, but in any case it was Remnantz that he chose to save, and that would certainly have been my mother's wish. The house had come to him via his great-uncle Tom, who had lived there following his mother Anne's death in 1881, until about 1912 when he took Edith to live at Seymour Court having leased Remnantz to his nephew Frank. For a man of his temperament it must have been galling to have inherited the family home from his father but be unable to leave it to his own heirs. 'Alas,' he wrote in one of his little poems, 'Alas, that I must go/Far from the home so well I love and know.' He died in 1921 aged eighty-eight.

Frank survived him by only 18 months, so my father came into the property as a sub-lieutenant in the navy at the age of twenty-two. For 15 years Remnantz was let while he followed his career and, so far as possible, his wife and later his children went with him. But in 1937 a letter with a Marlow postmark arrived at the house we had leased in Plymouth. It was from Mr Shone, the local solicitor, advising my father of his fear that the current tenant, a lady who had been running Remnantz as a boarding establishment, might be about to abscond leaving unpaid rent. He advised my father to come to Marlow and deal with the matter. This he did, bringing my mother with him.

It was my mother's first sight of the house, and the beginning of a love affair that would last for 56 years.

'Why don't we live here ourselves?' she asked him.

'Would you?' he said, surprised and very pleased that she should want to take it on.

The following year it became our home.

# Notes

Chapter 1

1 The letter had come into the hands of Mrs Eileen Younghusband, a connection of the Wethereds through marriage, who kindly passed it on to me.
2 Of course it was tetanus.
3 The children of three of Thomas's and Sarah's daughters, Sarah, Anne and Georgina.
4 Anne Wethered's diary.

Chapter 2

1 *History of Hertfordshire* by J.E. Cussans 1879. Cussans gives 12 May as the date of the wedding.
2 Ann's signing of the register with her 'mark' seems curious in view of her father's apparent position in society. Was she really illiterate or was there some other explanation such as an injury to her right hand? A sight of her will might have cleared up the mystery, but no will nor even a baptismal certificate has come to light.
3 Both names survive in the family to this day.
4 Not the present building of that name, which appears to be of Georgian origin.
5 The alliteratively named picture – 'Huntsman, Hounds and Hare on a Hill above Berkhamsted' – was sold at Sotheby's in 1986 for £319,000.
6 *The Wethered Book*, privately printed in the United States in 1967.
7 A barrel was 36 gallons by volume, whether in a barrel or not.
8 Peter Mathias, *The Brewing Industry in England 1700-1831*, Cambridge University Press 1959.
9 Williams, a former solicitor, had amassed a fortune through copper mining interests in Anglesey. He established smelting and milling operations in several parts of England and Wales, and in 1788 bought the copper mills at Temple, just upriver from Marlow. By then, according to his biographer, J.R. Harris, 'he was dictator of the national copper trade'.
10 *Posse Comitatus* 1798.
11 Peter Mathias, *op. cit.*
12 Saccharometer, an instrument for measuring the amount of sugar in a liquid.
13 Perhaps Charles senior should have done the same. He showed an interest in education by serving on the committee of the National School in Marlow.

*Chapter 3*

1  R.H. Thoumine, *Scientific Soldier, A Life of General Le Marchant 1766-1812*, Oxford University Press 1968.

2  Hugh Thomas, *The Story of Sandhurst*, Hutchinson & Co. 1961.

3  *The Staff and the Staff College*, Constable & Co. Ltd 1927.

4  *Sandhurst, the Royal Military Academy*, Country Life Books 1980. Colonel Shepperd's attitude is understandable. His own active service led to the loss of both legs in the Normandy campaign of 1944.

5  The minutes of the meeting are held at Sandhurst, ref. WO99/5.

6  *His Majesty's Warrant. Containing the Rules, Orders and Regulations Necessary in the First Instance for the Formation, Conduct and Good Government of the Junior Department of the Royal Military College. Also the Regulations of the Formation of the Collegiate Board with the Authorities Vested in the Same* (The Centre for Buckinghamshire Studies, Aylesbury.)

7  In the Thames, presumably.

8  Hugh Thomas, *op. cit.*

9  R.H. Thoumine, *op. cit.*

10  A son of Mr Pears later converted the house to a preparatory school, Woodcote House, which flourishes to this day. Two sons and three grandsons of this writer were educated there, as (it turned out) was his own grandfather, of whom more later.

11  Dates here are uncertain. Mervé's service record (from the *Musée de la Legion d'Honneur* in Paris) gives 1797 as the date of his arrival in England. However, British forces had been withdrawn from northern Europe by 1795.

12  Hugh Thomas, *op. cit.*

13  The purchase of commissions and promotions was only abolished in 1871.

*Chapter 4*

1  The Rev. — Knollis, formerly vicar of Penn, and partner of the Rev. James Pears at the preparatory school for cadets at Maidenhead Thicket.

2  After a state visit to celebrate the signing of the first Treaty of Paris in May.

3  Brother of Dr Thomas Arnold, of Rugby, and uncle of the poet.

4  Wellington's popularity was short-lived. It was not helped by the tactlessness of the British Government in appointing him, the conqueror of the French, as Ambassador to France. In October 1814 he was withdrawn amid fears for his personal safety.

*Chapter 5*

1  The National Society for Promoting the Education of the Poor in the Principles of the Established Church. In today's language, a system of C. of E. primary schools where children were taught the three R's, albeit with a heavy emphasis on religious studies.

2  Gunwharf, where the Remnants had their foundry, is today a leisure centre by the river.

3  'John Stradley 1757-1825', an unpublished paper by V. Moore.

4  *The Royal Arsenal*, Oxford University Press 1963.

5  A diary entry for 21 May: 'I walked to the Docke where I met Mrs Ackworth alone at home, and God forgive me! what thoughts I had, but I had not the courage to stay …'

6   It was not unusual for a ring to be left to a friend or acquaintance as something by which to remember the giver.

7   Not to be confused with the 2nd Earl who was Wellington's cavalry commander at Waterloo. His earldom was a second creation after his namesake had failed to produce an heir. Although both of the Paget family, they were only distantly related.

8   Sir Arthur Bryant, *The Age of Elegance*, Collins 1950.

9   Spotted by my sharp-eyed wife while resting her legs in the church.

*Chapter 6*

1   Pronounced 'Shawlden' by the locals.

2   Harriet Foote, shortly to become Mrs Edward Bridges. Bridges' sister Elizabeth was the wife of Jane's brother Edward; she died following childbirth the day after the above letter was written.

3   There had been some leasehold land as well. Until 1813 rent was being paid to a 'Mr Austen', i.e. Edward Austen or, more properly, Edward Knight. See footnote 5 below.

4   Erected in 1863, a successor to the church where Thomas and Sarah were married, though of the same plain medieval design.

5   Formerly Edward Austen. Jane's brother Edward had been adopted by the wealthy and distantly related Thomas Knight and his wife Catherine, who had no children of their own. He had subsequently inherited much landed property including Godmersham Park in Kent and Chawton House in Hampshire, along with the cottage at Chawton where his mother and sisters came to live. It may well have been through him and the Chawton/Shalden connection that Sarah Wethered came to know Cassandra and Jane.

6   Why he is unable to speak, whether from embarrassment or lack of opportunity, is not explained. Elsewhere he is referred to as saying things, so this cannot be his disability.

7   It is unclear who is meant by 'Mr Wethered' here. Thomas's half-brother George had died the year before.

8   Tom Cribb, a well-known prize-fighter of the 18th century.

*Chapter 7*

1   Anne Wethered's diary. This Anne is Owen's new wife (*née* Peel), not his and Edward's sister who is the one referred to above.

2   There is no address or salutation but it seems safe to assume that Elizabeth-Ellen was writing to her mother.

3   Possibly James Ward, the husband of Martha Smith's daughter Elizabeth, and therefore a cousin of Elizabeth-Ellen's by marriage.

4   Entries in Thomas's account book show transport and funeral expenses totalling £367. Edward's 'young horse' sold for £17 10s. od.

5   *Disraeli*, Methuen 1966.

6   Col. Thomas Peers Williams (C) and Sir William Robert Clayton, Bt (L).

7   The Marquess of Chandos (C) and Charles Scott Murray (C) of Danesfield House, Marlow.

8   Another highly placed friend of Disraeli was the Lord Chancellor, Lord Lyndhurst. A notorious womaniser, he is said to have been the model for W.S. Gilbert's 'highly susceptible chancellor' in *Iolanthe*. Once asked if he believed in platonic friendship, he is reported to have said, 'Yes, but after. Not before.'

9   *Political Change and Continuity, 1760-1885: A Buckinghamshire Study*. David & Charles 1972.

10  *Borlase, 1624-1957* (third edition).

Chapter 8

1   From *Records of Bucks*, Volume 6, by A.H. Cocks.

2   In 1876, 1889 and 1899 respectively. The chancel with its lovely reredos was designed by J.O. Scott.

3   A.H. Cocks, *op. cit.*

4   Although detached from the diocese of Lincoln in 1837, Marlow was not transferred to Oxford until 1855. In the meantime – such are the mysterious workings of the Church of England – it was in the gift of the Dean and Chapter of Gloucester.

5   Details from *Pigot's Directory*, 1842, cross-checked with the Poor Rates for 1838.

6   Now trendily renamed *The Lion* and *The Clayton*.

7   Actually it was Taplow. Maidenhead's main line station did not open until 1871.

8   Quoted by Frank Booker, *The Great Western Railway* (second edition), David & Charles 1985.

Chapter 9

1   A collection of them was published in 1909 under the title *Verses Grave and Gay*.

2   Anne Wethered's diary.

3   Francis Peel was vicar of Burghwallis in Yorkshire. The couple had nine children, eight of whom were girls.

4   Richard W. Davis, *Political Change and Continuity 1760-1885, A Buckinghamshire Study*, David & Charles 1972.

5   *The Bucks Herald.*

6   Colmer's articles, *Memories of Marlow*, appeared in *The Bucks Free Press* in the 1930s.

Chapter 10

1   The epaulettes he wore are still in the family's possession.

2   We do not know what sources James used for his family tree, which is somewhat at variance with that of J.E. Cussans.

3   It existed only in typescript until 1998 when it was published by the Buckinghamshire Record Society with a foreword and notes by Professor Ian F.W. Beckett.

4   Mr Gilbey's son Alfred joined the Volunteers that same year. He later recalled: 'It was all arranged without my being consulted by Col. Wethered and my father when I was 17 years of age.' In 1900, as a lieutenant-colonel, he assumed command of the 1st Battalion.

Chapter 11

1   Quoted by the late R.E. Fearnley-Whittingstall (a grandson of OPW and 'Cousin Bobby' to me) in his book about Sophie, *I Can't Wait to See Percy Again*. He points out that if the date is correct, Sophie was 17, not 16 at the time of the Shoe Dance. I am indebted to him for the facts of Percy's early career and other information gathered by him.

2   The widowed Sarah had returned to her family in Marlow and moved into the house then known as The Cottage. The house was later given the name of Quoitings, until it was demolished in the year 2000 and replaced by a block of flats.

3   But actually erected to honour the emperor Diocletian in the fourth century.

4   *Heaven's Command* by James Morris, 1973.

5   A word still used by my parents' generation – usually 'too killing' meaning hilarious.

6   *Pax Britannica, The Climax of an Empire*, 1968.

7   i.e. needlework, as elsewhere.

8   The Rev. Francis Peel, AM's husband.

9   And by some for being 'managing'.

10  Old Nico was her Marlow dressmaker.


*Chapter 12*

1   Pat Jalland, *Women, Marriage and Politics 1860-1914*, Clarendon Press 1986.

2   Pat Jalland, *op. cit.*

3   Sir Hope Grant, the Commander-in-Chief.


*Chapter 13*

1   R.E. Fearnley-Whittingstall, *op. cit.*

2   *The Church Times*, 23 February 1912.

3   In 1913 Bridges was appointed Poet Laureate. During the First World War he published *The Spirit of Man*, an anthology of poetry and prose chosen for its spiritual content, which I found helpful during the second war. Today he is probably best remembered for hymns such as *All My Hope on God Is Founded* and *When Morning Gilds the Skies* (tr. from the German).

4   Menton is now on the French side of the border.

5   *A History of Borlase School* by J.C. Davies, Aylesbury, G.T. de Fraine & Co. Ltd, 1932.

6   J.C. Davies, *op. cit.*

7   Today's number of both boys and girls is not far short of a thousand.


*Chapter 14*

1   *Gladstone, Disraeli & Later Victorian Politics* by Paul Adelman, Addison Wesley Longman Ltd, 1970, 1997. Under the Act, closing times would vary according to the size of the locality: in 'metropolitan districts' at 12.30 a.m., in 'towns and populous places' at 11 p.m., and all other places at 10 p.m.

2   Now in the possession of his great x2 nephew, myself.

3   In 1974 Marlow came under the jurisdiction of the Wycombe District Council.

4   *The South Bucks Free Press.*


*Chapter 15*

1   The face-plate is on view in the old brewery site, now a residential development.

2   I was unaware of Catherine-Mary's existence until after her death in 1961, when I realised I had missed a chance to meet one of Thomas's grandchildren.

3   The complete story of the line is expertly told in *The Marlow Branch* by Paul Karau and Chris Turner, Wild Swan Publications Ltd, Didcot.

4   Since renamed Puerto de la Cruz.

5   Edie Humphreys is a memory from my youth. She lived in Tenerife but returned
    to England periodically – and for the war years – to visit family and collect cast-off
    clothing for 'my poor Spaniards'. Widowed and childless, she loved children and
    they loved her.

6   I have had confirmation of this story from my cousin John Power (a grandson of
    John Danvers), who managed the brewery from 1951 to 1956, and from Gordon
    Palmer, an employee whose father, Horace Palmer, succeeded Yates as company
    secretary.

*Chapter 16*

1   *A Silver Plated Spoon* by John, Duke of Bedford, Cassell & Co. 1960. According to
    the caption beneath her picture in the book, 'She and her sister, who was coerced
    into marriage with a homosexual, did good works and doted on children. This
    was a pity since they never had any.'

2   This is a slightly shortened version with minor editing of punctuation.

3   Dating from the time when Chenies Manor was the estate of the dukes of Bed-
    ford.

4   'A Lutyens Garden Restored' by Arthur Hellyer, *Country Life* 22 November
    1984.

5   Funds were raised to rebuild it and the replica stands there today.

6   The cause of death is not given on either of the certificates issued by the British
    consulate in Tenerife. We have Alice's testimony that OPW had his disease as a
    young man, and we assume it to have been TB. Could the doctor's warning to
    Frank about going on the river have meant that he had the chest infection as a
    boy, or did he acquire it later as a result of his being a smoker? The reused tins
    in his tool chest once contained cigarettes or, in some cases, throat lozenges – a
    grim warning to those who followed.

7   Companion of the Order of St Michael and St George.

*Chapter 17*

1   This intriguing theory was put forward by Keith Sherwood, a great-grandson of
    Giulio and Annie Laura, to whom I am grateful for his kindness in introducing
    me to them.

2   The late Jack Trefusis was himself an exemplar of resourcefulness as well as cour-
    age. In the final phases of the Second World War, Major Trefusis single-handedly
    brought about the surrender of 60 German soldiers who were about to set fire to
    the historic Hotel de Ville in Brussels. In his excellent German, he pointed out
    the wickedness of what they were doing and invited them to give themselves up,
    which they did.

3   In 1968 Strong's in its turn was bought out by Whitbread's which has since
    disposed of the brewing side of its business. Wethered's was closed down in 1987,
    supposedly because of a shift in public taste towards canned lager and away from
    the cask beers for which our brewery was justly famous.

# *Index*

Compiled by Auriol Griffith-Jones

Page numbers in **bold** refer to illustrations